Grade 5

Making Meaning®

SECOND EDITION

DEVELOPMENTAL
STUDIES CENTER

Strategies That Build
Comprehension and Community

Developmental Studies Center wishes to thank the following authors, agents, and publishers for their permission to reprint materials included in this program. Many people went out of their way to help us secure these rights and we are very grateful for their support. Every effort has been made to trace the ownership of copyrighted material and to make full acknowledgment of its use. If errors or omissions have occurred, they will be corrected in subsequent editions, provided that notification is submitted in writing to the publisher.

"Zoo" by Edward D. Hoch, originally published in *Fantastic Universe*. Copyright ©1958 by Edward D. Hoch. Reprinted by permission of the Sternig & Byrne Literary Agency. "Is Dodge Ball Too Dangerous?" from TimeForKids.com Sports News, May 15, 2001. Copyright © *TIME For Kids*. Used with permission from *TIME For Kids* Magazine. "Turn It Off!" from *TIME For Kids* World Report Edition, April 12, 2002. Copyright © *TIME For Kids*. Used with permission from *TIME For Kids* Magazine. "Review of *The Legend of Sleepy Hollow*," by Jennifer B. Reprinted with permission from Spaghetti® Book Club (www.spaghettibookclub.org). Copyright © 2000 Happy Medium Productions, Inc. Excerpt from *Richard Wright and the Library Card*, by William Miller. Copyright © 1997 William Miller. Used by permission of Lee & Low Books. Excerpt from *Wildfires* by Seymour Simon. Copyright © 1996 Seymour Simon. Used by permission of HarperCollins Publishers. Excerpts from *Earthquakes* by Seymour Simon. Copyright © 1991 Seymour Simon. Used by permission of HarperCollins Publishers. Excerpt from *Life in the Rain Forests* by Lucy Baker. Copyright © 2000 by Lucy Baker. Used by permission of T&N Children's Publishing. Excerpts from *Letting Swift River Go*, by Jane Yolen. Copyright © 1992 Jane Yolen. First appeared in *Letting Swift River Go*, published by Little, Brown and Co. Reprinted by permission of Curtis Brown, Ltd. Excerpt from *A River Ran Wild*, by Lynne Cherry. Copyright ©1992 Lynne Cherry. Reprinted by permission of Houghton Mifflin Harcourt Publishing Company. All rights reserved. "Mrs. Buell" from *Hey World, Here I Am!* by Jean Little. Text copyright ©1986 Jean Little. Illustrations copyright © 1989 by Susan G. Truesdell. Used by permission of HarperCollins Publishers.

All articles and texts reproduced in this manual and not referenced with a credit line above were created by Developmental Studies Center.

Developmental Studies Center
2000 Embarcadero, Suite 305
Oakland, CA 94606-5300
(800) 666-7270, fax: (510) 464-3670
www.devstu.org

ISBN-13: 978-1-59892-745-0
ISBN-10: 1-59892-745-0

Printed in the United States of America

1 2 3 4 5 6 7 8 9 10 MLY 12 11 10 09 08

Table of Contents

Unit 6

Making Inferences

FICTION AND EXPOSITORY NONFICTION

During this unit, the students make inferences to understand causes and effects in narrative and expository text. They continue to use text structure to explore narrative text. They also use schema to articulate all they think they know about a topic before they read. During IDR, the students think about the inferences they make as they read independently. Socially, they develop the group skills of including one another, contributing to group work, and using prompts to extend a conversation. They also have a check-in class meeting to discuss a problem.

Week 1 *Richard Wright and the Library Card*
by William Miller

Week 2 *Wildfires* by Seymour Simon

Week 3 *Earthquakes* by Seymour Simon
Life in the Rain Forests by Lucy Baker

Week 1

Overview

UNIT 6: MAKING INFERENCES
Fiction and Expository Nonfiction

Richard Wright and the Library Card
by William Miller, illustrated by Gregory Christie
(Lee & Low, 1997)

In this fictionalized account, writer Richard Wright gains access to a library card and a new world of books and ideas.

ALTERNATIVE BOOKS

Only Passing Through: The Story of Sojourner Truth
by Anne Rockwell

Frida by Jonah Winter

Comprehension Focus

• Students *make inferences* to understand causes and effects in narrative text.

• Students continue to *use text structure* to explore narrative text.

• Students read independently.

Social Development Focus

• Students analyze the effect of their behavior on others and on the group work.

• Students develop the group skill of using prompts to extend a conversation.

DO AHEAD

• Prior to Day 1, decide how you will randomly assign partners to work together during the unit.

• Prepare the "Clues to Inferences in *Richard Wright and the Library Card*" chart (see Day 2, Step 2 on page 247).

• Make transparencies of the "Excerpt from *Richard Wright and the Library Card*" (BLM20–BLM21).

• Prepare directions chart for Guided Strategy Practice (see Day 3, Step 3 on page 252).

• Prepare to model asking *why* questions in independent reading (see Day 4, Step 3 on page 255).

Making Meaning Vocabulary Teacher

If you are teaching Developmental Studies Center's *Making Meaning Vocabulary* program, teach Vocabulary Week 12 this week. For more information, see the *Making Meaning Vocabulary Teacher's Manual*.

Day 1

Materials

- *Richard Wright and the Library Card*
- Chart paper and a marker

Being a Writer™ **Teacher**

You can either have the students work with their *Being a Writer* partner or assign them a different partner for the *Making Meaning* lesson.

Teacher Note

The prompts are:

- *I agree with you, because…*
- *I disagree with you, because…*
- *In addition to what you said, I think…*

Read-aloud

In this lesson, the students:

- *Make inferences* as they hear a story
- Discuss setting, plot, and character
- Explore social and ethical issues in the story
- Begin working with new partners
- Read independently for up to 30 minutes
- Use prompts to extend a conversation

1 ▶ **Pair Students/Brainstorm Prompts to Extend Conversations**

Randomly assign partners and have them sit together. Explain that during the next few weeks the students will work in these pairs.

Review that in previous lessons the students learned to ask clarifying questions, confirm their partners' thinking by repeating back what they heard, and use prompts to add to their partner conversations. Remind them that they should be using these skills as needed in their partner conversations.

Point out that sometimes partners finish what they are saying quickly, and then end up sitting without saying anything for the rest of the partner discussion time. Ask:

Q *What suggestions do you have to help partners keep their conversation going?*

Q *What might be some prompts partners can use to get them talking again?*

Students might say:

"Tell me more of your thinking about _____."

"Let's talk a little more about _____."

"Another way to think about it might be _____."

As the students make suggestions, write these on a sheet of chart paper entitled "Prompts to Extend a Conversation." If the students do not suggest ideas, offer some like those in the "Students might say" note.

State your expectation that during "Turn to Your Partner" or "Think, Pair, Share" partners will continue talking until you signal them to end their conversations. Encourage the students to use the prompts on the chart as well as the skills they learned previously as they work today.

 ## Introduce *Richard Wright and the Library Card*

Remind the students that they have been using the strategy of *making inferences* to help them make sense of stories and poems. Explain that this week they will continue to make inferences and review story elements, including character, setting, conflict, and plot.

◀ **Teacher Note**

You may want to remind the students that when they *make inferences* they use clues from a story or poem to figure out something that is not stated directly.

Tell the students that the story you will read aloud is *Richard Wright and the Library Card*. Show the cover of the book and read the names of the author and illustrator. Explain that the story is based on a true incident from the life of Richard Wright, a famous author. To provide background knowledge about Wright, read or paraphrase the "Author's Note" on the last page of the book.

Explain that the setting of the story is the 1920s in the South, when segregation was a way of life. During this time, many blacks moved north, seeking freedom and opportunity in states without segregation laws. Remind the students that earlier in the year they heard the story *Uncle Jed's Barbershop,* which is also set in the South during this time.

◀ **Teacher Note**

If necessary, remind the students that segregation is the practice of keeping people of different racial groups apart, and that segregation was practiced throughout the United States from the late 1800s through the mid-1900s.

You might preview the text and illustrations with your English Language Learners prior to reading the book aloud to the class. During the reading, you might stop periodically to have the students briefly discuss what is happening in the story. Possible stops are at the bottom of pages 12, 22, and 27.

3 ▶ **Read *Richard Wright and the Library Card* Aloud**

Read the book aloud, showing the accompanying illustrations.

Suggested Vocabulary

rebel army: the army of the South (Confederacy), which fought against the North during the Civil War (p. 5)

ash cans: trash cans (p. 9)

optician: person who makes and sells eyeglasses (p. 10)

spines: part of books where the pages are fastened together (p. 21)

Dickens: Charles Dickens, an English author from the 1800s (p. 25)

Tolstoy: Leo Tolstoy, a Russian author from the 1800s (p. 25)

Stephen Crane: American author from the late 1800s (p. 25)

ELL Vocabulary

English Language Learners may benefit from discussing additional vocabulary, including:

the war: the American Civil War (p. 5)

longed: wanted very much (p. 7)

funny papers: comic strip pages of the newspaper (p. 7)

4 ▶ **Discuss Plot, Setting, and Character in the Story**

 First in pairs, and then as a class, discuss the following questions. During the partner discussions, remind the students to continue talking until you signal them to end their conversations. Tell them to use the prompts on the "Prompts to Extend a Conversation" chart, as needed.

Ask:

Q *What happens in this story (what is the plot)?*

Q *What is the setting (time and place)? Why is it an important part of this story?*

Teacher Note

The purpose of these questions is to help the students explore the social and ethical themes in the book and make a personal connection to the text.

Q *What kind of person is Richard? What in the story makes you think that?*

Students might say:

"There was a lot of prejudice during the time of the story. That explains why the white people at the library are mean to Richard."

"He's smart. He reads all kinds of books and understands them, and he figures out how to get a library card."

"He lies to get the books. That shows he's determined to read."

"In addition to what [Michael] said, I think he's also brave. He goes to Memphis by himself when he's seventeen, and he asks the white man for his library card."

Q *What do you admire about Richard Wright? What can we learn from his life that might help us in our own?*

During the whole-class discussion, be ready to reread passages from the text and show illustrations again to help the students recall what they heard. Also, as the students make inferences about the plot, setting, and characters, point them out. (You might say, "The author does not say directly that Richard is smart, but you inferred that, or figured it out from clues in the story.")

Remind the students that as they talked about the setting, plot, and characters in the story, they made inferences. Explain that in the next lesson they will continue to explore making inferences as they read the story.

▶ **Teacher Note**

Facilitate interaction among the students during the whole-class discussion with questions such as:

Q *Who will confirm [Travis's] thinking by repeating back what you heard [him] say?*

Q *Turn to your partner and discuss whether you agree or disagree with what [Travis] just said.*

Q *Did you agree or disagree? Explain your thinking.*

▶ **5** **Reflect on Partner Conversations**

Facilitate a brief discussion about how the students did extending their partner conversations. Share your own observations, and ask:

Q *What prompt on the "Prompts to Extend a Conversation" chart did you try using today? How did that help to keep you and your partner talking?*

INDIVIDUALIZED DAILY READING

 Document IDR Conferences/Have the Students Discuss Setting, Characters, and Plot

Tell the students that at the end of IDR they will talk in pairs about the setting, characters, and plot in their books.

Have the students read books at appropriate reading levels independently for up to 30 minutes.

Use the "IDR Conference Notes" record sheet to conduct and document individual conferences.

 At the end of independent reading, have each student discuss the setting, characters, and plot of her book with her partner. As the pairs talk, circulate and check in with them. If a student is struggling, ask questions such as:

Q *Who is the main character of your story?*

Q *How would you describe the main character?*

Q *What is the setting of the story? Is the setting important? Why?*

Q *What is the plot so far?*

Q *What do you think will happen to the main character? Why?*

Day 2

Guided Strategy Practice

In this lesson, the students:

- *Make inferences* as they hear a story
- Discuss character change in a story
- Read independently for up to 30 minutes
- Use prompts to extend a conversation

1 Review Using Prompts to Extend Conversations

Remind the students today to focus on talking for the whole time during partner conversations, using the prompts on the "Prompts to Extend a Conversation" chart as needed. Tell the students that you will check in with them at the end of the lesson to see how they did.

2 Highlight Clues to Inferences in *Richard Wright and the Library Card*

Remind the students that they heard *Richard Wright and the Library Card* yesterday. Direct their attention to the "Clues to Inferences in *Richard Wright and the Library Card*" chart, on which you have written the following sentences from the book:

> "As long as he kept his head down, as long as he began every sentence with 'sir,' Richard was safe."

> "'I want to read books. I want to use the library, but I can't get a card,' Richard said, hoping Jim would not laugh in his face."

> "After work, Richard walked through the crowded streets to the library. He felt as if he were on a train to Chicago, as if he were traveling north already."

Explain that these are sentences in the story from which a reader can infer how Richard feels. Read the sentences aloud. Then explain that you will read the story aloud again, and that you will stop after each of the lines and have the students use "Think, Pair, Share" to talk about what they infer about Richard's feelings.

Materials

- *Richard Wright and the Library Card*
- "Prompts to Extend a Conversation" chart, from Day 1
- "Clues to Inferences in *Richard Wright and the Library Card*" chart, prepared ahead (see Step 2)
- "Reading Comprehension Strategies" chart

Prompts to Extend a Conversation

- Tell me more of your thinking about…
- Let's talk a little more about…

ELL Note

Remind the students that when they *infer*, or *make inferences*, they use clues from the story to figure out something that is not stated directly.

3 **Reread the Story**

Reread the story slowly and clearly. Stop after each of the charted sentences (on pages 10, 14, and 19). Reread each sentence; then have the students use "Think, Pair, Share" to think about and discuss:

Q *What can you infer about how Richard feels?*

Have one or two pairs report their inference at each stopping point; then reread the passage and continue reading to the next stopping point. Do not spend too long at any one stop.

> *Students might say:*
>
> "We inferred from these sentences that Richard probably feels afraid and intimidated. He has to be careful around white people or he will get into trouble."
>
> "Richard is afraid Jim will make fun of him, but he wants a library card more than anything, so he's determined to ask Jim for help."
>
> "We figured out that Richard is feeling happy and free. He thinks reading books will help him have a better life."

If the students disagree significantly on what inferences make sense for any of the three clues, discuss this before continuing with the lesson. Ask the students to refer to the text to support their opinions, and ask probing questions such as:

Q *What do you think Richard might be thinking at that moment? What in the book makes you think that?*

Q *Why do you think Richard is worried that Jim will laugh at him? Explain your thinking.*

4 **Discuss Character Change in the Story**

Review that characters often change over the course of a story. Facilitate a whole-class discussion by asking the following questions:

Q *The sentence "Richard knew he would never be the same again" is a dramatic clue that he has changed after staying up all night reading. How do you think Richard has changed? Explain your thinking.*

Reread the following passage on page 25: "He read about people who had suffered as he had, even though their skin was white. They longed for the same freedom Richard had spent his life trying to find." Ask:

Q *Why might reading about these things have changed Richard so dramatically?*

> *Students might say:*
>
> "Maybe the words he read made him feel like he wasn't the only one struggling for freedom."
>
> "I addition to what [Grady] said, maybe he understood that not all white people acted like the ones around him. In different times and places, they have suffered, too."

Point out that in most stories the author does not say directly how a character changes. In this case, the reader must infer how Richard changes.

Explain that many of the students naturally made inferences throughout the story and that one of the goals of studying inference is for them to become more aware of making inferences. Being aware of making inferences will help them think more about what they read.

▶5 Reflect on Partner Conversations

Facilitate a brief discussion of how partners worked together, and share examples you noticed of partners confirming and clarifying each other's thinking and using prompts to add to or extend the conversation.

INDIVIDUALIZED DAILY READING

▶6 Document IDR Conferences/Review the Reading Comprehension Statregies

Direct the students' attention to the "Reading Comprehension Strategies" chart and remind them that these are the strategies they have learned so far this year. Ask them to notice which strategies

Reading Comprehension Strategies

- recognizing text features

they use and where they use them during their reading today. At the end of IDR, they will share with the class.

Have the students read independently for up to 30 minutes.

Use the "IDR Conference Notes" record sheet to conduct and document individual conferences.

At the end of independent reading, have each student share his reading and a strategy he used—the name of the strategy and where he used it—with the class. Have students who cannot think of a comprehension strategy they used discuss what they read.

EXTENSION

Learn About Other African American Authors

Have the students work individually or in pairs to research and report on the lives of prominent African American writers. Some possible authors are: Maya Angelou, James Baldwin, Amiri Baraka, Frederick Douglass, Ralph Ellison, Alex Haley, Francis Harper, Zora Neale Hurston, Toni Morrison, Mildred D. Taylor, Alice Walker, Phillis Wheatley, and August Wilson.

Day 3

Guided Strategy Practice

In this lesson, the students:

- *Make inferences* to explore causes of events in a story
- Read independently for up to 30 minutes
- Use prompts to extend a conversation

1 ▶ Review Using Prompts to Extend Conversations

Explain that today partners will continue to focus on using prompts to extend conversations. Review the items on the "Prompts to Extend a Conversation" chart.

2 ▶ Introduce Exploring Causes

Remind the students that they have been making inferences to help them understand what is happening in stories such as *Richard Wright and the Library Card* and *The Van Gogh Cafe*. Point out that they can also use the strategy to help them figure out *why* something happens—what causes an event to happen as it does in the book.

Explain that today they will explore why some things happen as they do in *Richard Wright and the Library Card*.

3 ▶ Explore Causes in *Richard Wright and the Library Card*

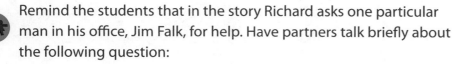

Remind the students that in the story Richard asks one particular man in his office, Jim Falk, for help. Have partners talk briefly about the following question:

Q *Why does Richard choose Jim Falk to help him?*

Materials

- *Richard Wright and the Library Card*
- "Prompts to Extend a Conversation" chart
- *Student Response Book* page 33
- Charted directions, prepared ahead (see Step 3)
- *Assessment Resource Book*
- Transparencies of the "Excerpt from *Richard Wright and the Library Card*" (BLM20–BLM21)
- *Student Response Book,* IDR Journal section

Teacher Note

Have students who are unable to read the excerpt on their own read it quietly aloud with a partner, or you might read it aloud yourself as the students follow along. Then have them go back and underline the clues in the passage. ▶

 Note

English Language Learners may benefit from extra support to make sense of the excerpt. Show and discuss the illustrations on pages 14–17 again; then read the excerpt aloud as they follow along, stopping intermittently to talk about what is happening. The students may benefit from explanation of the following words and passages:

- "ignored"
- "Richard had been sent to the library to check out books for him."
- "a suspicious look"
- "cautiously"
- "'I'll write a note,' Richard said, 'like the ones you wrote when I got books for you.'"

Without discussing the question as a class, direct the students' attention to the excerpt from *Richard Wright and the Library Card* on *Student Response Book* page 33 and explain that the excerpt is the part of the story in which Richard asks Jim Falk for help. Explain the following directions, which you have written on chart paper:

1. Read the excerpt quietly to yourself.

2. Reread the excerpt, and underline sentences that help to answer this question: Why does Richard select Jim to ask for help?

3. Talk with your partner about the sentences you underlined and the inferences you made about why Richard chooses Jim.

As the students work individually and in pairs, circulate and ask them the following questions to help them think about the inferences they are making and confirm and clarify each other's thinking:

Q *You underlined ["Only one man seemed different from the others."] What did you infer from that sentence about why Richard chooses Jim?*

Q *Can you confirm [Mary Ann's] thinking by repeating back what you heard [her] say?*

Q *Do you agree or disagree with [Mary Ann]? Why?*

Q *What question do you want to ask [Mary Ann] to better understand what [she's] thinking?*

CLASS COMPREHENSION ASSESSMENT

As you circulate among the students, notice which sentences they underline and ask yourself:

Q *Are the students identifying clues that explain why Richard selects Jim?*

Record your observations on page 16 of the *Assessment Resource Book*.

Discuss as a Whole Class

When most pairs have finished, place the transparencies of the excerpt from *Richard Wright and the Library Card* on the overhead projector. Repeat the question; then ask a few students to share the sentences they underlined and the inferences they made. Facilitate a discussion among the students, using questions such as:

Q *Do you agree or disagree with what [Jamil] and [his] partner shared? Why?*

Q *Does Jim Falk really think differently from the other white men? What in the excerpt supports the opinion that he [does/doesn't] think differently?*

Students might say:

"I underlined the sentence 'Jim Falk kept to himself, and the other men ignored him, as they ignored Richard.' I figured out that Richard thinks Jim is an outsider like he is. That's why he chooses Jim."

"In addition to what [Latisha] said, I think Richard chooses Jim because he's a reader and might understand another reader. The sentence I underlined about that is 'Several times, Richard had been sent to the library to check out books for him.'"

"I think Jim Falk does think differently from the others, because he gives Richard his library card."

"I disagree with [Mattie]. I think Jim Falk doesn't think differently from the other white men, because he was immediately suspicious of Richard, and he is also nervous about getting into trouble if anyone finds out he has helped Richard."

Point out that the author does not directly say *why* Richard chooses Jim, but that the students can infer this from the story. Explain that writers often don't explain why events happen in a story or why characters behave as they do. Instead, readers have to make inferences to figure out why.

Explain that in the next lesson the students will practice making inferences about why things happen as they do in their independent reading books.

INDIVIDUALIZED DAILY READING

5 ▶ Read Independently/Have the Students Write in Their IDR Journals About Strategies They Used

Have the students read independently for up to 30 minutes.

As the students read, circulate among them. Observe their reading behavior and engagement with the text. Ask individual students questions such as:

Q *What is your book about?*

Q *What made you decide to read this book?*

Q *(Nonfiction book) What do you already know about [planets]? How does knowing this information about planets help you understand this book?*

Q *(Fiction book) Who is the main character in your book? How would you describe him?*

Q *What comprehension strategies are you using to help you understand the character and what is happening?*

At the end of independent reading, have each student write in her IDR Journal about her reading and a strategy she used—the name of the strategy and where she used it. Have students who cannot think of a strategy write about their reading. Have a few students share their writing with the class.

ELL Note

Before the students begin to read independently, preview the questions you plan to ask them as they are reading.

ELL Note

If your English Language Learners are struggling to write, have them draw to express their thoughts about their reading.

Day 4

Independent Strategy Practice

In this lesson, the students:

- Explore causes of events as they read independently
- Use prompts to extend a conversation

1 Review the Week

Remind the students that this week they heard *Richard Wright and the Library Card* and explored characters, setting, and plot. Review that they also made inferences as they thought about why things happen the way they do. Explain that today they will explore causes in the books they are reading independently by asking *why* questions.

Remind the students that they also practiced using prompts to extend their conversations. Encourage them to continue to practice this skill today.

2 Read Independently Without Stopping

Ask the students to use self-stick notes to mark the place they begin reading today, and have them read independently for 10 minutes.

3 Model Asking *Why* Questions

After 10 minutes, explain that you would like them to reread and use "Stop and Ask Questions" to identify places where they can ask *why* questions about the book. They will use additional self-stick notes to mark the places where questions come to mind, and they will write the questions on the notes.

Model the procedure by briefly introducing the text you selected. Read several sentences aloud, and think aloud about a *why* question that comes to mind. Jot the question on a self-stick note, and place the note in the margin where you stopped reading.

Materials

- Narrative texts at appropriate levels for independent reading
- Small self-stick notes for each student
- Book for modeling *why* questions (see Step 3)
- "Prompts to Extend a Conversation" chart

Teacher Note

To prepare for the modeling, have the questions you will ask in mind ahead of time. (For example, using the book *Uncle Jed's Barbershop,* you might read page 11 and ask, "Why do most people think Uncle Jed will never open his own shop?")

ELL Note

Your English Language Learners
may need extra support
to generate questions.

4 ▶ Reread Independently and Ask *Why* Questions

Have the students reread independently for 10 minutes, stopping
to mark places where questions arise and recording the questions
on the notes. Circulate and look for evidence that the students are
able to write *why* questions. Some students may have difficulty
generating questions. To help these students, you might ask:

Q *What is happening in this part of the book? What question that
begins with* why *can you ask about this part of the book?*

Q *What is the main character doing, or how is the character
behaving? What question that begins with* why *can you ask about
the character?*

5 ▶ Have Partners Discuss Their Questions

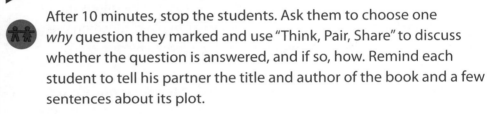

After 10 minutes, stop the students. Ask them to choose one
why question they marked and use "Think, Pair, Share" to discuss
whether the question is answered, and if so, how. Remind each
student to tell his partner the title and author of the book and a few
sentences about its plot.

6 ▶ Discuss Questions as a Class

Have a few volunteers share their questions with the class. Remind
each student to say the title and author of the book. Probe the
students' thinking by asking:

Q *What was happening in the text when your question came
to mind?*

Q *Is the question answered? If so, is it answered directly, or did
you figure out the answer by making an inference? Read us the
passage where it is answered.*

Q *What do you want to ask [Nathan] about [his] book or what
[he] shared?*

Reflect on This Week's Partner Work

Facilitate a brief discussion about how partners worked together. Ask:

Q *What did you enjoy about working with your partner this week?*

Q *What is one way your partner work is improving? What is one thing you want to keep working on as you continue to work together? Talk to your partner about your thinking.*

 Making Meaning
Vocabulary **Teacher**

Next week you will revisit this week's reading to teach Vocabulary Week 13.

Week 2

Overview

UNIT 6: MAKING INFERENCES
Fiction and Expository Nonfiction

Wildfires
by Seymour Simon
(HarperTrophy, 1996)

This book describes the destruction caused by major wildfires and their role in maintaining the balance of nature.

ALTERNATIVE BOOKS

The Truth About Great White Sharks by Mary M. Cerullo

The Universe by Seymour Simon

Comprehension Focus

- Students *make inferences* to understand causes and effects in expository text.

- Students *use schema* to articulate all they think they know about a topic before they read.

- Students read independently.

Social Development Focus

- Students analyze the effect of their behavior on others and on the group work.

- Students develop the group skills of including one another, contributing to group work, and using prompts to extend the conversation.

- Students have a problem-solving class meeting.

DO AHEAD

- Make a transparency of the "Excerpt from *Wildfires*" (BLM22).

- Prepare the directions chart for Guided Strategy Practice (see Day 3, Step 3 on page 271).

- Decide on a topic for the problem-solving class meeting (see "About Problem-solving Class Meetings" on page 274).

- Collect a variety of expository texts at appropriate reading levels for the students to read independently during IDR this week. (For information about Developmental Studies Center's Individualized Daily Reading Libraries, see page xxvii and visit Developmental Studies Center's website at www.devstu.org.)

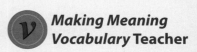

Making Meaning
Vocabulary Teacher

If you are teaching Developmental Studies Center's *Making Meaning Vocabulary* program, teach Vocabulary Week 13 this week. For more information, see the *Making Meaning Vocabulary Teacher's Manual.*

Read-aloud

In this lesson, the students:

- Explore causes and effects in an expository text
- Learn "Group Brainstorming"
- Read independently for up to 30 minutes
- Include one another
- Contribute to group work

About Causes and Effects

This week provides an informal introduction to exploring causes and effects in expository text. Identifying causes and effects can be challenging for students. In these lessons, the teacher asks specific questions (such as, "What caused the 1988 Yellowstone fire?" and "Why does the author say 'Not all fires are bad'?") to guide the students toward seeing and understanding these relationships. The students are not expected to master identifying cause and effect on their own. Rather, the lessons prepare the students to identify cause and effect relationships without support as they get older.

▶1 Introduce "Group Brainstorming"

Assign pairs to groups of four and have them sit together. Remind the students that in a previous lesson they learned "Heads Together" to talk in a group of four. Ask:

Q *What are some things you can do to help your work go smoothly in a group of four?*

Explain that today they will learn a cooperative structure called "Group Brainstorming," in which group members generate and record as many ideas as they can in a short period of time. Group members will state their ideas briefly, and these will be written down quickly by the group recorder, without discussion. Tell the students that all ideas should be recorded, and that the ideas do not have to be written as complete sentences.

Materials

- *Wildfires* (pages 10–16)
- Paper and a pencil for each group
- "Self-monitoring Questions" chart

Teacher Note ▶

The students learned "Heads Together" in Unit 5, Week 2.

Teacher Note

If your students are already familiar with "Group Brainstorming," you may not need to teach it. Briefly review the structure and continue with the rest of the lesson.

Choose a topic (for example, "fiction characters I like" or "topics I enjoy reading about") and model quickly jotting down a few of your own brainstormed ideas.

 Explain that the students will use "Group Brainstorming" to think about what they know about the topic of today's book before they hear it. Give the groups 30 seconds to determine who will be their group recorder today.

Teacher Note

The 30-second limit for choosing a group recorder encourages them to pick a recorder quickly without getting stuck in a selection process.

2 Introduce *Wildfires* and Brainstorm About Wildfires

Tell the students that the book you will read aloud over the next few days is called *Wildfires*. Show the cover of the book and read the author's name. Explain that the book is an expository text that gives information about wildfires.

ELL Note

You may want to explain that a *wildfire* is a *large fire that burns in an area such as a field, woods, or forest.*

 Have the students use "Group Brainstorming" to respond to this question:

Q *What do you think you know about wildfires?*

Give the groups 3–4 minutes to brainstorm and record their ideas; then stop them and have them review their list and select one idea to share with the whole class. Ask them to select a backup idea in case their first idea is shared by another group.

Have all the groups report their ideas; then ask if there are any other ideas the groups generated that were not reported.

Ask the students to keep their ideas in mind as they listen to the reading today.

◀ **Teacher Note**

Limiting the brainstorming time encourages the students to be brief and to get out many ideas without getting stuck on any particular idea.

Asking the groups to select a backup idea encourages them to listen to one another and to avoid repeating what others have said.

3 Introduce the Reading

Briefly explain that you will read only parts of the book and that today you will read pages 10–16, which describe a gigantic (very large) wildfire that took place in 1988 in Yellowstone National Park. You might want to point out Yellowstone National Park on a map.

ELL Note

Consider previewing each chapter of *Wildfires* with your English Language Learners prior to the class read-aloud. For example, you might show them the pictures and read or summarize the text.

Explain that you will stop periodically during the reading and have groups put their heads together to discuss what they have learned from the book up to that point.

 4 **Read *Wildfires* Aloud with Brief Section Introductions**

Suggested Vocabulary

abandoned: left behind (p. 10)

launched: started (p. 10)

lodgepole pines and spruce firs: two kinds of trees found in Yellowstone (p. 12)

embers: hot, glowing pieces of wood or coal from a fire (p. 12)

geyser: spring from which hot water and steam shoot up in bursts (p. 14)

tinderbox: (metaphor) something that can easily catch fire (p. 14)

ELL Vocabulary

English Language Learners may benefit from discussing additional vocabulary, including:

threatened structures: were dangerous to buildings (p. 10)

flammable: likely to catch fire (p. 14)

Teacher Note ▶

This week's read-aloud contains a lot of factual information that the students might have difficulty following. To support them, you will briefly introduce each section before you read it. This will help to focus the students' listening on the main ideas discussed in that section.

Tell the students that the first section you will read explains how the Yellowstone fire started. Ask the class to listen for what caused the fires. Read page 10, showing the illustration. Stop after:

p. 10 "Finally the officials abandoned their policy of letting lightning fires burn naturally, and they launched what was to become the greatest fire-fighting effort in the history of the United States."

 Have the students use "Heads Together" to discuss:

Q *What did you learn about the cause of the Yellowstone fire?*

After a minute or two, explain that the next part you will read tells how the wildfire spread out of control. Ask the class to listen to find out what caused the fire to spread. Reread the last sentence on page 10 and continue reading to the next stopping point:

p. 14 "It seemed as if the inn would soon be consumed by flames."

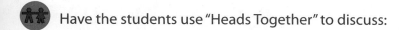 Have the students use "Heads Together" to discuss:

Q *What did you learn about what caused the wildfire to spread?*

After a minute or two, explain that the last part you will read today tells how the fires were stopped. Ask the students to listen for what stopped the fires. Reread the last sentence on page 14 and continue reading to the next stopping point:

> **p. 16** "Nearly two-thirds of the park had not been touched by fire, and even the one-third that had burned was starting to recover."

Have the students use "Heads Together" to discuss:

Q *What did you learn about how the Yellowstone fire was stopped?*

5▶ Discuss the Reading as a Class

Facilitate a discussion about the reading, using the following questions. Be ready to reread passages from the text to help the students recall what they heard.

Q *What started the wildfire in Yellowstone?*

> ***Students might say:***
>
> "The fire was started by lightning, but it got bad because it was so hot and dry in the park."
>
> "I agree with [Maya]. It said it hadn't rained in a hundred years."
>
> "I think I disagree with [Simon]. The book said that it rained less in 1988 than in any year for the previous hundred years."
>
> "In addition to what people have said, the book says that they let some of the fires burn for a while. Maybe that's why they got so big."

Q *What caused the fire to spread out of control?*

Q *What stopped the fire?*

> **Teacher Note**
>
> During the stops, listen for evidence that the students are discussing the book and understanding it. If necessary, reread parts of the text to help the students recall what they heard. Also, look for examples of groups working together well and groups having difficulty, and be ready to share your observations at the end of the lesson.

> **Teacher Note**
>
> These questions focus the students on the causes of the wildfire.

> **Teacher Note**
>
> Facilitate interaction among the students during the discussion by:
>
> • Probing their thinking by asking follow-up questions such as: *Can you say more about that? What in the book makes you think that? Why does that make sense?*
>
> • Using "Turn to Your Partner" or "Heads Together" to engage everyone in thinking about the important questions.
>
> • Asking them to agree or disagree with their classmates and explain their thinking.

Reflect on "Group Brainstorming"

Facilitate a brief discussion about how the students did with "Group Brainstorming." Ask:

Q *How did you take responsibility in your group today?*

Q *What went well in your brainstorming? What do you want to try next time to help your brainstorming?*

INDIVIDUALIZED DAILY READING

7 ▶ **Review and Practice Self-monitoring**

Refer to the "Self-monitoring Questions" chart and review the questions. Remind the students that it is important to stop to think about what they are reading and use the questions to help them track whether they are understanding their reading. When they are not understanding, they may need to reread, use a comprehension strategy, or get a different book.

Have the students read books at their appropriate reading levels independently for up to 30 minutes. Stop them at 10-minute intervals and have them monitor their comprehension by thinking about the charted questions.

Circulate among the students and ask individuals to read a passage to you and tell you what it is about.

At the end of the reading time, have a brief whole-class discussion about using the self-monitoring questions to track their reading comprehension. Ask and briefly discuss questions such as:

Q *How does noticing if you don't understand what you are reading help you when you read?*

Q *Why does rereading help you make sense of text?*

Q *Which comprehension strategy do you find the most helpful? Why?*

Self-monitoring Questions

- *What is happening in my story right now?*
- *Does the reading make sense?*

Day 2

Guided Strategy Practice

In this lesson, the students:

- Explore causes and effects in an expository text
- Read independently for up to 30 minutes
- Include one another
- Contribute to group work
- Use prompts to extend a conversation

1 Review Using Prompts to Extend Conversations

Tell the students that they will be using "Heads Together" again today to talk about their thinking. Remind them that a couple of weeks ago they practiced using prompts to extend the conversation as they talked in pairs. Refer to the "Prompts to Extend a Conversation" chart, and encourage them to use the prompts in their groups today and to continue to include one another and contribute responsibly to the group work.

State your expectation that during "Heads Together," group members will continue talking until you signal them to end their conversations.

2 Review the Previous Reading from *Wildfires* and Introduce Today's Reading

Show the cover of *Wildfires,* and review that in the previous lesson the students heard about the 1988 wildfire in Yellowstone National Park. Ask:

Q *What did you learn about the fire?*

Materials

- *Wildfires* (pages 18–24)
- "Prompts to Extend a Conversation" chart (from Week 1)

Prompts to Extend a Conversation

- Tell me more of your thinking about...
- Let's talk a little more about...

FACILITATION TIP

This week continue to **avoid repeating or paraphrasing** the students' responses. Help them to learn to participate responsibly in class discussions by asking one another to speak up or by asking a question if they don't understand what a classmate has said.

Explain that today you will read about how life returned to Yellowstone after the fire. Explain that you will stop periodically and have groups put their heads together to discuss their thinking up to that point.

 ### 3 Read *Wildfires* Aloud with Brief Section Introductions

Suggested Vocabulary

mosaic: (metaphor) picture made up of small pieces of colored tile, stone, or glass (p. 18)

smoke inhalation: breathing in smoke (p. 20)

fledglings: baby birds (p. 20)

in advance of: ahead of; before (p. 20)

reproduce: produce offspring; have babies (p. 22)

deprive: take away (p. 24)

 ELL Vocabulary

English Language Learners may benefit from discussing additional vocabulary, including:

millipedes, centipedes: two kinds of bugs (p. 18)

feast on: eat (p. 20)

Explain that the first part you will read tells about the first forms of life that appeared after the Yellowstone wildfire ended. Ask the class to listen for what they learn about these life forms. Read page 18, showing the illustration. Stop after:

> **p. 18** "The fields of new grasses and wildflowers attract grazing animals, and birds come from all over to catch insects in the meadows."

 Have the students use "Heads Together" to discuss:

Q *What did you learn about the forms of life that appeared after the wildfire?*

After a minute or two, explain that the next part you will read focuses on how animals are affected by wildfires like those in Yellowstone. Ask the students to listen for the effects of wildfires on animals. Reread the last sentence on page 18 and continue reading to the next stopping point:

> **p. 20** "Nature quickly adjusts to changes and finds new life even in death."

 ELL Note

You might prompt your English Language Learners to begin their response by saying, "I learned…."

Have the students use "Heads Together" to discuss:

Q *What did you learn about the effects of wildfires on animals?*

After a minute or two, explain that the last part you will read discusses how lodgepole pine trees, a type of tree in Yellowstone, were affected by the fire. Ask the students to listen for the effects of the fire on the trees. Reread the last sentence on page 20 and continue reading to the next stopping point:

p. 24 "Then the fires are likely to return, and the cycle of burning and rebirth will continue."

 Have the students use "Heads Together" to discuss:

Q *What did you learn about the effects of wildfires on lodgepole pine trees?*

4 ▸ Discuss Effects as a Class

Facilitate a discussion about the reading using the following questions. Be ready to reread passages from the text to help the students recall what they heard.

Q *What happened to the plants and animals in Yellowstone in the years following the 1988 fire? What examples did you hear of that?*

Students might say:

"The book says that birds built nests in the dead trees."

"I also heard the book say that fire helped a certain kind of tree to reproduce."

"I agree with [Josh]. It said the fire melted something and let the seeds out."

"In addition to that, the seeds got eaten by lots of little animals, so the fire made food for them."

During this discussion, point out that yesterday they identified the causes of the Yellowstone wildfire, while today they identified the effects of the wildfire on the natural environment. Explain that sometimes causes and effects are directly stated in texts. At other times, readers must use clues in the text to make inferences about causes and effects. Explain that recognizing causes and effects helps readers understand what they are reading at a deeper level.

◀ Teacher Note

During the stops, listen for evidence that the students are discussing the book and understanding it. If necessary, reread parts of the text to help them recall what they heard. Also, look for examples of groups working together well and groups having difficulty, and be ready to share your observations at the end of the lesson.

◀ Teacher Note

These questions focus on the effects of fire on the natural environment.

Explain that you will not read the rest of *Wildfires* aloud but that you will make the book available for students to read independently.

 Reflect on "Heads Together"

Share some of your observations of the groups during "Heads Together." Without giving names, describe what you saw in groups in which all the members were engaged and contributing and any examples of groups in which some members were not participating. For example, you might say:

Q *I noticed a group in which all four members were leaning into the center of the table and looking at each other. I also heard one group member ask another what she thought. How might these actions help a group work well together?*

Q *I noticed a group in which it looked like the students were working in pairs, rather than one group of four. Why might that happen? What can a group do to make sure they are working as a group during "Heads Together"?*

INDIVIDUALIZED DAILY READING

 Review Previewing a Text Before Reading/Read Independently

Remind the students that readers often look over a book before reading it. A reader will look at the cover, read the information on the back of the book, and preview the book by looking through the pages. Previewing a book is particularly helpful when reading expository text. Ask the students to take the time to do this today before reading their books, even if they have already started reading.

Have the students read independently for up to 30 minutes.

As the students read, circulate and stop and ask individuals questions such as:

Q *What did you notice about your book from looking it over before reading? How is this helpful to you?*

 ELL Note

Consider modeling this process for your English Language Learners.

Q (Expository text) *What are some features in your book? How might these features help you understand the text?*

Q *Do you think you will enjoy this book? Why do you think that?*

 At the end of independent reading, have the students share what they read with their groups.

EXTENSION

Research Wildfires

Interested students may want to do further research on wildfires and their impact on the natural environment. Other major fires over the past several years include the Cerro Grande (New Mexico) fire in 2000 and the San Diego (California) area fires in 2007. The students may also be interested in researching the use of controlled fires to prevent larger, more disastrous fires. The students can search the Internet for information using the keyword "wildfires."

Day 3

Materials

- *Wildfires*
- *Student Response Book* page 34
- Charted directions, prepared ahead (see Step 3)
- *Assessment Resource Book*
- Transparency of the "Excerpt from *Wildfires*" (BLM22)

Guided Strategy Practice

In this lesson, the students:

- Explore causes and effects in an expository text
- Read independently for up to 30 minutes
- Include one another
- Contribute to group work
- Use prompts to extend a conversation

1 ▶ Review the Social Skills Focus of Group Work

Explain that the students will work in small groups again today and that you would like them to continue to focus on using prompts to extend conversations, including one another, and contributing responsibly to the group work.

2 ▶ Review Exploring Causes and Effects

Remind the students that they heard parts of *Wildfires* and discussed the causes and the effects of wildfires. Review that a cause is the reason something happens and the effect is what happens as a result. Explain that today the students will talk more about the effects of wildfires.

Teacher Note ▶

If the students are having difficulty understanding cause and effect relationships, you might provide an example or two from everyday life. For example, if you strike a match (cause), the match flames (effect); if you drop a rubber ball (cause), the ball bounces (effect). Have the student use "Heads Together" to come up with other examples of cause and effect relationships.

3 ▶ Explore the Effects of Wildfires

Read page 4 of *Wildfires* aloud. Ask the students to consider this question individually:

Q *Why do you think the author says that not all fires are bad and that fires in nature can help as well as harm?*

Without discussing the question as a class, explain that there are many clues in the book to help them answer this question and that they will explore some of these clues today.

Direct the students' attention to the excerpt from *Wildfires* on *Student Response Book* page 34. Explain that the excerpt describes what happened in Yellowstone National Park after the 1988 fire. Explain the following directions, which you have written on chart paper:

1. Read the excerpt quietly to yourself.

2. Reread the excerpt, and underline sentences that help to answer this question: Why can fires in nature help as well as harm?

3. Use "Heads Together" to talk about the sentences you underlined, and why you chose those sentences.

As the students work individually and in groups, circulate and ask them the following questions to help them think about how they are making sense of the excerpt:

Q *You underlined ["Insects returned in great numbers and began to feast on the plants."] How does this sentence help to explain why fires in nature can help as well as harm?*

Q *Do you agree or disagree with [Jordan]? Why?*

Q *What question do you want to ask [Jordan] to better understand what [he's] thinking?*

> ## CLASS COMPREHENSION ASSESSMENT
>
> Circulate among the students and ask yourself:
>
> **Q** *Are the students identifying clues about why wildfires are not all bad?*
>
> Record your observations on page 17 of the *Assessment Resource Book*.

Teacher Note

Have students who are unable to read the excerpt on their own read it quietly aloud with a partner, or you might read it aloud yourself as the students follow along. Then have them go back and underline the clues in the passage.

ELL Note

English Language Learners may benefit from extra support to make sense of the excerpt. Show and discuss the illustration on page 25 again; then read the excerpt aloud as they follow along, stopping periodically to talk about what they are reading.

Discuss Effects as a Whole Class

When most groups have finished, place the transparency of the excerpt on the overhead projector, and ask the students to share the sentences they underlined and the inferences they made. Facilitate a discussion using questions such as:

Q *Do you agree or disagree with what [Olive] shared? Why?*

> **Students might say:**

> "I underlined the sentence 'Just two years after the 1988 fires, burned areas had sprouted new plants of all kinds.' Then it talks about bugs and other animals eating the new plants. Because of the fire there could be food for lots of creatures."

> "In addition to what [Nguyen] said, the fire burns down the tall trees so the light can reach the smaller plants. The sentence I underlined about that is 'Before the fire, the towering older trees blocked sunlight from the forest floor, allowing only a few other species of plants to flourish there.'"

Q *What effect will fire have on the continued survival of plants and animals in Yellowstone?*

Point out that there are many clues throughout the book to help the students understand what the author means by "…not all fires are bad. Fires in nature can help as well as harm." Remind the students that recognizing causes and effects helps readers understand what they are reading at a deeper level, and say that they will explore this more in the coming weeks.

INDIVIDUALIZED DAILY READING

 Read Independently/Discuss the Students' Reading

Have the students read independently for up to 30 minutes.

As they read, circulate among them and talk to individual students to find out whether they are understanding and enjoying their books.

Ask questions such as:

Q *What is your book about? What do you think will happen next?*

Q *Are you enjoying your book? Why do you enjoy it? Have you read other books by this author? If so, how are they similar? How are they different?*

Ask any student who is not enjoying her book why this is so, and explain that readers sometimes need to read a good portion of a book before they get into it. Other times, readers decide to get a new book. Ask the student whether she wants to choose a new book or read on.

Day 4

Materials

- Space for the class to sit in a circle
- "Class Meeting Ground Rules" chart
- Chart paper and a marker
- *Student Response Book,* IDR Journal section

> *Class Meeting Ground Rules*
>
> - *one person talks at a time*
> - *listen to one another*

Class Meeting

In this lesson, the students:

- Have a problem-solving class meeting
- Take responsibility for themselves
- Read independently for up to 30 minutes

About Problem-solving Class Meetings

Today's problem-solving class meeting can be used to discuss any problem the students are having as they work together. Think about problems you have noticed over the past several lessons, and choose one problem as the topic of today's class meeting. Common problems include students speaking unkindly to one another, excluding one another, not participating in partner or group work, dominating the work, disrespecting one another's ideas, not participating during the whole-class discussion, and not listening while others are speaking.

▶ 1 Gather for a Class Meeting

Make sure the "Class Meeting Ground Rules" chart is posted where everyone can see it. Review the procedure for coming to the meeting, and remind the students that they have been working together to create a caring and safe learning community.

Have partners sit together in a circle and ask them to make sure they can see all their classmates.

▶ 2 Introduce the Problem

Review the class meeting ground rules. Introduce the topic of the class meeting and describe the specific problem you have observed. Use a judgment-neutral tone and avoid identifying individual students. (For example, you might say, "Over the past couple of weeks, I've noticed that in some groups students have had trouble speaking to one another in a respectful way. I've heard put-downs and other words that are not kind. Because we've agreed to try to create a caring community in this class, this is a problem we need to talk about and solve.")

Discuss the Problem

Facilitate a discussion about the problem, using the following questions. These questions are designed to guide the students through a specific thinking process in which they (1) reflect on the problem, (2) consider the effects of the problem on their work and feelings, and (3) consider the importance of solving the problem and finding better ways to interact.

Q *What other examples of [speaking disrespectfully] have you noticed?*

Q *How does [speaking disrespectfully to one another] affect your work? How does it make you feel?*

Q *Why is it important that we [learn to speak in a more respectful way] in our class?*

 During the discussion, ask the students not to use names when giving examples and to avoid blaming or accusing others. Use "Turn to Your Partner" as needed during this discussion to increase participation, especially if you are hearing from only a few students. You can also use "Turn to Your Partner" if many students want to speak at the same time.

 Discuss Solutions

State your expectation that each student will be responsible for doing his part to solve this problem and to create a safe and caring community in the class.

Have the students use "Think, Pair, Share" to think about and discuss:

Q *What are some things we can try as a class to help us [speak more respectfully to one another]?*

Write the question at the top of a sheet of chart paper. Have a few pairs share with the whole class, and write their responses on the chart. If necessary, suggest some solutions yourself to stimulate the students' thinking (for example, avoid put-downs; say how you feel instead of shouting at someone; say "Excuse me" instead of "Move!"; apologize if you've hurt someone; and think, "How would I feel if someone said that to me?").

◀ **Teacher Note**

Many social problems in the class can be addressed by helping the students develop empathy for one another. Often students do not naturally develop or learn to act on a sense of empathy. Rather, they develop it through deliberate experiences hearing the feelings of others, particularly those whose feelings they have hurt. It is critical for the teacher to set a tone of safety and high expectations for how the students will treat one another in the class. In such a climate, sharing feelings can be very effective in helping the students learn to act in more caring ways.

Review the suggestions on the chart and ask:

Q   *Is there anything on this list that you can't agree to try in the coming days?*

Make adjustments to the list only if the students give reasonable explanations for why certain solutions are unfeasible. Explain that you would like the students to use the suggestions on the chart in the coming days, and that you will be checking in with them to see how they are doing.

▶5 Reflect on Ground Rules and Adjourn the Meeting

Briefly discuss how the students felt they did following the ground rules during the class meeting. Review the procedure for returning to their desks, and adjourn the meeting.

Display the chart where everyone can see it. Hold the students accountable by checking in periodically in the coming days to see how they are doing with the problem and what solutions they have tried.

The chart will be used again in Week 3.

INDIVIDUALIZED DAILY READING

▶6 Document IDR Conferences/Have the Students Write in Their IDR Journals

Have the students read independently for up to 30 minutes.

Use the "IDR Conference Notes" record sheet to conduct and document individual conferences.

At the end of independent reading, have the students write in their IDR Journals about their books. Ask each student to write whether or not she would recommend it to another fifth grader to read. Remind the students to give reasons for their thinking.

As a class, discuss questions such as:

Q   *What might you say to another fifth grader about your book?*

Q   *Would you recommend the book? Why or why not?*

Have several students share what they wrote. Remind the students that they can read another student's book when that person is finished with it.

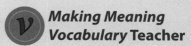

Making Meaning
Vocabulary Teacher

Next week you will revisit this week's reading to teach Vocabulary Week 14.

UNIT 6: MAKING INFERENCES
Fiction and Expository Nonfiction

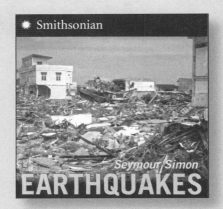

Earthquakes
by Seymour Simon
(Smithsonian/Collins, 1991)

Seymour Simon explores the mysteries surrounding earthquakes.

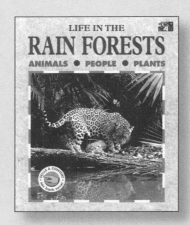

*Life in the Rain Forests**
by Lucy Baker
(Two-Can, 2000)

This book describes the animals, people, and plants of the world's rain forests and explains how rain forests are being destroyed.

*This book was also used in Unit 2, Week 1.

ALTERNATIVE BOOKS

Lightning by Seymour Simon

Icebergs and Glaciers by Seymour Simon

Comprehension Focus

- Students *make inferences* to understand causes and effects in expository text.

- Students *use schema* to articulate all they think they know about a topic before they read.

- Students read independently.

Social Development Focus

- Students take responsibility for their learning and behavior.

- Students develop the group skills of including one another, contributing to group work, and using prompts to extend a conversation.

- Students have a check-in class meeting to discuss a problem.

DO AHEAD

- Prepare the directions chart for Guided Strategy Practice (see Day 2, Step 3 on page 286).

- Make transparencies of the "Excerpt from *Earthquakes*" (BLM23–BLM24).

- Make transparencies of the "Excerpt from *Life in the Rain Forests*" (BLM25–BLM26).

- Prior to Day 4, collect the read-alouds from Units 5 and 6 to review making inferences.

- Review the topic of the problem-solving class meeting from Week 2.

- Make copies of the Unit 6 Parent Letter (BLM15) to send home with the students on the last day of the unit.

Making Meaning Vocabulary Teacher

If you are teaching Developmental Studies Center's *Making Meaning Vocabulary* program, teach Vocabulary Week 14 this week. For more information, see the *Making Meaning Vocabulary Teacher's Manual.*

Day 1

Materials

- *Earthquakes* (pages 5–13 and 24–29)
- Paper and a pencil for each group
- "Reading Comprehension Strategies" chart

FACILITATION TIP

Reflect on your experience during the past few weeks with **avoiding repeating or paraphrasing** students' responses. Is the practice beginning to feel natural? Are you integrating it into class discussions throughout the day? What effect is the use of this practice having on the students' learning and behavior? We encourage you to continue to use this practice and reflect on students' responses as you continue to facilitate class discussions.

 Note

You may want to explain that an *earthquake* is a *sudden shaking of the earth's surface.*

Read-aloud

In this lesson, the students:

- *Explore causes and effects* in an expository text
- Use "Group Brainstorming"
- Read independently for up to 30 minutes
- Include one another
- Contribute to group work

▶1 Review "Group Brainstorming"

Have the students sit in their groups of four. Remind them that last week they learned "Group Brainstorming," a technique in which group members generate and record as many ideas as they can in a short period of time. Explain that they will use "Group Brainstorming" again to think about what they know about the topic of today's reading. Ask:

Q *What are some things you want to keep in mind today to make "Group Brainstorming" go smoothly?*

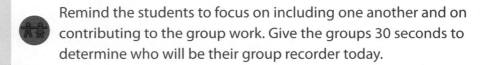 Remind the students to focus on including one another and on contributing to the group work. Give the groups 30 seconds to determine who will be their group recorder today.

▶2 Brainstorm About Earthquakes

Tell the students that today you will read from *Earthquakes*, another book by Seymour Simon. Show the cover of the book and explain that it is an expository text that gives information about earthquakes.

ELL Note

Consider previewing
Earthquakes with your English
Language Learners prior
to today's read-aloud.

Have the students use "Group Brainstorming" to respond to
this question:

Q *What do you think you know about earthquakes?*

Give the groups 3–4 minutes to brainstorm and record their ideas;
then stop them and have them review their list and select one idea
to share with the class. Ask them to select a backup idea in case
their first idea is shared by another group.

Have each group report its idea; then ask if there are any
other ideas the groups generated that were not reported. Ask
the students to keep their ideas in mind as they listen to the
reading today.

3 ▶ **Read Aloud with Brief Section Introductions**

Suggested Vocabulary

friction: rubbing of two objects, slowing their movement (p. 8)
colliding: crashing together (p. 13)
quicksand: loose, wet sand that heavy objects can sink into (p. 24)
tsunamis: huge, powerful waves (p. 29)

ELL Vocabulary

English Language Learners may benefit from discussing additional
vocabulary, including:

heavily populated area: place where many people live (p. 5)
are rare: do not happen often (p. 10)
sank: fell or dropped (p. 25)

Explain that you will read only parts of the book, and that you will
stop periodically and have groups put their heads together to
discuss what they are learning about earthquakes.

Tell the students that the first part of the book you will read explains
what causes an earthquake. Ask the students to listen for the causes.
Read pages 5–9, showing the illustrations. Stop after:

p. 9 "This kind of upward movement is called a thrust fault."

◀ **Teacher Note**

Because there is a lot of
geographic and geologic
information in the book, you may
want to have a world map and a
globe nearby to refer to during
the reading.

Teacher Note

During the stops, listen for evidence that the students are discussing and understanding the book. Also, look for examples of both groups working together well and groups having difficulty, and be ready to share these at the end of the lesson.

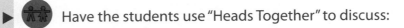 Have the students use "Heads Together" to discuss:

Q *What did you learn about what causes earthquakes?*

After a minute or two, explain that the next part you will read tells where most earthquakes occur. Ask the students to listen for where in the United States most earthquakes happen and why they happen there. Read pages 10–14. Stop after:

> **p. 14** "Scientists think that a huge, deadly earthquake will strike along the San Andreas Fault in the near future."

 Have the students use "Heads Together" to discuss:

Q *What did you learn about where most earthquakes occur in the United States and why?*

After a minute or two, explain that the last part you will read explains how earthquakes cause destruction. Ask them to listen for the different ways that earthquakes cause damage. Read pages 24–29. Stop after:

> **p. 29** "The tsunamis moved across the Pacific at speeds of hundreds of miles an hour, reaching as far as Hawaii and even Japan, four thousand miles away."

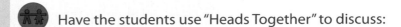 Have the students use "Heads Together" to discuss:

Q *What did you learn about how earthquakes cause damage?*

4 ▶ Discuss the Reading as a Class

Facilitate a whole-class discussion about the reading, using the following questions. Be ready to reread passages from the text to help the students recall what they heard.

Q *What did you learn about earthquakes that you didn't know before?*

Teacher Note

This question focuses the students on the effects of earthquakes. On Day 2, the students will focus on the causes of earthquakes.

Q *What did you hear about the different ways that earthquakes can be destructive?*

Students might say:

"The book talked about buildings falling down or sinking."

"In addition to what [Kyle] said, sometimes buildings fall into sand boils, and sometimes the ground along the fault drops."

"I also heard that earthquakes can cause giant waves that can wash away the coastline."

During this discussion, point out that the students are recognizing the effects of earthquakes on human life and on the natural world. Remind them that recognizing causes and effects helps readers better understand what they are reading.

Explain that other parts of *Earthquakes* tell how scientists measure earthquakes and earthquake damage, and that you will make the book available later for the students to read.

Tell the students that tomorrow they will continue to think about what they learn from *Earthquakes*.

5 Reflect on Group Work

Share some of your observations of the groups during "Group Brainstorming" and "Heads Together," and ask:

Q *How did your "Group Brainstorming" go today?*

Q *What do you want to do differently the next time you work in a group?*

INDIVIDUALIZED DAILY READING

6 Review Reading Comprehension Stategies

Direct the students' attention to the "Reading Comprehension Strategies" chart and ask them to notice which strategies they use and where they use them during their reading today. At the end of IDR, they will share with their groups.

Have the students read independently for up to 30 minutes.

Reading Comprehension Strategies

- recognizing text features

At the end of independent reading, have the students share their reading with their groups and ask one another questions about their books. Ask:

Q *What questions might you ask about a classmate's book?*

EXTENSION

Research Earthquakes

Interested students may want to do further research on earthquakes and their impact on life around the world. The U.S. Geological Survey has a website designed for young people: http://earthquake.usgs.gov/learning/kids. Other interesting websites can be found by searching using the keyword "earthquakes."

Day 2

Guided Strategy Practice

In this lesson, the students:

- Explore causes and effects in an expository text
- Read independently for up to 30 minutes
- Include one another
- Contribute to group work
- Use prompts to extend the conversation

▶1 Review Using Prompts to Extend Conversations

Tell the students that they will be using "Heads Together" again today, and remind them to talk until you signal them to end their conversations. Refer to the "Prompts to Extend a Conversation" chart, and encourage them to use the prompts and to continue to include one another and contribute responsibly to the group work.

▶2 Review Cause and Effect

Remind the students that over the past few weeks they have been making inferences to answer *why* questions, such as "Why does Richard Wright choose Jim Falk to help him in *Richard Wright and the Library Card*?" and "Why does Seymour Simon say that not all wildfires are bad in *Wildfires*?"

Remind them that when they answer questions like these, they are recognizing *causes* (the reasons something happens) and *effects* (what happens as a result of something). Remind them that understanding cause and effect relationships can help them make sense of what they are reading.

Show the cover of *Earthquakes* and review that yesterday the students learned about and discussed some of the destructive effects of earthquakes on human life and on the natural world. Remind them that the book also contains information about the causes of earthquakes.

Materials

- *Earthquakes*
- "Prompts to Extend a Conversation" chart
- *Student Response Book* page 35
- Charted directions, prepared ahead (see Step 3)
- *Assessment Resource Book*
- Transparencies of the "Excerpt from *Earthquakes*" (BLM23–BLM24)

Prompts to Extend a Conversation

- Tell me more of your thinking about...
- Let's talk a little more about...

Ask the students to consider this question quietly to themselves:

Q *What do you remember hearing about why earthquakes happen?*

Without discussing the question, explain that there are many clues in the book to help them answer this question, and that they will explore some of these clues today.

ELL Note

English Language Learners may benefit from extra support to make sense of the excerpt. Show and discuss the illustrations on pages 8 and 12 again; then read the excerpt aloud as they follow along, stopping intermittently to talk about what they are reading. They may benefit from a simple demonstration (using your hands) of how friction builds up between rocks until they "suddenly snap past each other." A globe may also be useful in helping the students visualize the plates that make up the crust of the earth.

3 Explore the Causes of Earthquakes

Direct the students' attention to the excerpt from *Earthquakes* on *Student Response Book* page 35. Explain that the excerpt describes what causes an earthquake. Explain the following directions, which you have written on chart paper:

1. Read the excerpt quietly to yourself.

2. Reread the excerpt, and underline sentences that help to answer this question: What causes an earthquake?

3. Use "Heads Together" to talk about the sentences you underlined, and why you chose those sentences.

Have students who are unable to read the excerpt on their own read it quietly aloud with a partner, or you might read it aloud yourself as the students follow along. Then have them go back and underline the clues in the passage.

As the students work, circulate and ask them the following questions individually and in their groups to help them think about how they are making sense of the excerpt:

Q *You underlined ["In one type of fault, called a strike-slip fault, the rocks on one side of the fault try to move past the rocks on the other side, causing energy to build up."] What does this sentence tell you about why an earthquake happens?*

CLASS COMPREHENSION ASSESSMENT

Circulate among the students and ask yourself:

Q *Are the students identifying clues about what causes an earthquake?*

Record your observations on page 18 of the *Assessment Resource Book*.

 4 ▶ Discuss Causes as a Class

When most groups have finished, place the transparencies of the excerpt on the overhead projector, and ask the students to share the sentences they underlined and the inferences they made. Facilitate a discussion among the students using questions such as:

Q *Do you agree or disagree with what [Terence] shared? Why?*

> **Students might say:**
>
> "I underlined the sentence 'The plates float slowly about on the mantle up to four inches a year.' When the plates start moving around, earthquakes happen."
>
> "I disagree with what [Cara] said. Earthquakes happen around the edges of the plates when they run into each other. See, I underlined 'The colliding plates cause most of the earthquakes along the West Coast.'"

Q *What question do you want to ask [Terence] about what [he] shared?*

Point out that the students are bringing together a lot of information in the excerpt to understand what causes an earthquake. Remind them that they have been discussing both the causes and the effects of earthquakes, and that they will look for cause and effect relationships to help them make sense of books in the next two days.

◀ **Teacher Note**

Other sentences the students might underline include:

- "For years, friction will hold the rocks in place. But finally, like a stretched rubber band, the rocks suddenly snap past each other."

- "From the focus, the energy of the quake speeds outward through the surrounding rocks in all directions."

- "As the plates move, they run into or pull away from each other, producing enormous strains in the rocks along their edges."

Discuss Group Work

Facilitate a brief discussion about how the students interacted by asking questions such as:

Q   *How did you take responsibility for yourself in your group today? How did you see someone else in your group take responsibility?*

Q   *How did your group do with talking for the whole time until I signaled you to come back together? Did you use any prompts on the "Prompts to Extend a Conversation" chart? If so, which ones? How did they work?*

INDIVIDUALIZED DAILY READING

 Read Independently/Think About Inferences

Ask the students to think about inferences they make as they read, and to try to be aware of when they are making inferences.

Have the students read independently for up to 30 minutes.

As the students read, circulate among them and talk to individuals to monitor whether they are making sense of their reading and are aware of making inferences. Ask questions such as:

Q   *What is your book about? What do you think will happen next? Why do you think that?*

Q   *What are you learning about the character(s) in your book? What parts of the text are revealing those things about that character?*

 At the end of independent reading, give the students time to share what they read and inferences they made with their groups and to ask one another questions about their books.

Day 3

Guided Strategy Practice

In this lesson, the students:

- Explore causes and effects in an expository text
- Read independently for up to 30 minutes
- Include one another
- Contribute to group work

1 ▶ Add to the "Reading Comprehension Strategies" Chart

Review that the students have been exploring causes and effects in both narrative texts (such as *Richard Wright and the Library Card*) and expository texts (such as *Wildfires* and *Earthquakes*). Remind them that cause and effect relationships are not always easy to see, but that recognizing these relationships can help readers understand what they are reading at a deeper level.

Direct the students' attention to the "Reading Comprehension Strategies" chart and add *recognizing cause and effect* to the chart. Explain that today they will continue to explore cause and effect in expository text.

2 ▶ Review *Life in the Rain Forests*

Show the cover of the book *Life in the Rain Forests* and remind the students that earlier in the year they heard the part of the book about the destruction of the rain forest. Explain that they will read an excerpt from *Life in the Rain Forests* today. To help them understand the passage, they will think and talk about the cause and effect relationships they notice.

Materials

- *Life in the Rain Forests* (from Unit 2, Week 1)
- "Reading Comprehension Strategies" chart and a marker
- *Student Response Book* page 36
- Transparencies of the "Excerpt from *Life in the Rain Forests*" (BLM25–BLM26)
- *Student Response Book*, IDR Journal section

Reading Comprehension
Strategies

- recognizing text
features

◀ **Teacher Note**

If necessary, review the book by reading some of the headings and showing some of the illustrations, reading or paraphrasing their captions.

▶3 Read the Excerpt as a Class and Individually

Direct the students' attention to the excerpt from pages 18–21 of *Life in the Rain Forests* on *Student Response Book* page 35. Explain that the excerpt describes how the rain forest is being destroyed. Ask the students to follow along as you read it aloud.

Suggested Vocabulary

timber companies: companies that cut down trees and sell wood

flees: runs away

felled: cut down

poor clay soils: soil that is not good for growing crops

nutritious topsoil: soil that is good for growing crops

anchored: held

slash-and-burn farmers: farmers who burn down areas of the rain forest to create space to farm

cultivate: farm

drenched: soaked

ELL Vocabulary

English Language Learners may benefit from discussing additional vocabulary, including:

bulldozers: machines used to move earth or push down trees

chainsaw gangs: groups of people with power saws

desert: dry area without many growing things

clear rain forest land to grow crops: remove trees to make space for farming

Ask the students to read the excerpt a second time on their own.

ELL Note

English Language Learners may benefit from extra support to make sense of the excerpt. Read the excerpt aloud again as they follow along, stopping intermittently to talk about what they are reading.

▶4 Discuss the Reading as a Class

At the end of the reading, facilitate a whole-class discussion using the following questions:

Q *What is this excerpt about?*

Q *How do trees protect the topsoil in a rain forest? What happens when trees are cleared (burned or cut down) from the land?*

Explore Causes and Effects in Groups and as a Class

Write the following information on the board:

> causes - the reasons things happen
>
> effects - what happens as a result of something

Review the meaning of *causes* and *effects,* and point out that there are several causes and effects in the excerpt. For example, the excerpt tells us that when trees are cleared from the land, the effect is that topsoil washes away in the rain.

 Ask groups to put their heads together to discuss:

Q   *What other causes or effects do you notice in the excerpt?*

As groups discuss this question, circulate among them and listen for evidence that they are making sense of the text. As you hear the students noticing causes or effects, point these out. (For example, you might say, "I heard Francisco say that when the topsoil washes away, the farmers can't grow crops on the land. So one effect of losing topsoil is that the farmers can't continue to farm the land.")

Place the transparencies of the excerpt from *Life in the Rain Forests* on the overhead projector. Have groups volunteer to share the causes and effects they noticed, and underline these on the transparencies as they share. Check for agreement, and use questions like those that follow to encourage the students to explain their thinking:

Q   *What in the excerpt makes you think that?*

Q   *Do you agree or disagree with [Carlos's] thinking? Why?*

> **Students might say:**
>
> "When all the topsoil washes away, the farmers can't grow crops on the land anymore. It says 'the land becomes too difficult to cultivate.'"
>
> "I agree with [Carlos]. In addition, I think another effect of getting rid of the trees is that the rain washes all the topsoil into the rivers and the rivers get clogged up."
>
> "If we continue to destroy the rain forest, the effect will be that thousands of different plants and animals will disappear forever."

Explain that tomorrow they will look for cause and effect relationships and inferences in their independent reading.

 Reflect on "Heads Together"

Facilitate a brief discussion about how the students interacted in their group during "Heads Together." Ask the students to think about how they personally contributed in a responsible way today, and have several volunteers share their thinking.

INDIVIDUALIZED DAILY READING

▶ **Document IDR Conferences/Have the Students Write in Their IDR Journals**

Encourage the students to continue to think about inferences they make as they read.

Have the students read independently for up to 30 minutes.

Use the "IDR Conference Notes" record sheet to conduct and document individual conferences.

At the end of independent reading, have the students write in their IDR Journals about what they read and any inferences they made as they read. Have a few volunteers share their writing with the class. Ask:

Q *What question do you have for [Kate] about [the main character of her book]?*

Q *What question do you have for [Nick] about the inferences [he] made?*

Day 4

Independent Strategy Practice

In this lesson, the students:

- *Make inferences* and explore causes and effects as they read independently
- Use a double-entry journal to record their thinking
- Include one another and contribute to group work
- Use prompts to extend a conversation
- Have a class meeting to check in about a problem

1 Review Making Inferences and Cause and Effect

Remind the students that over the past several weeks they have been exploring *inference,* including inferences about causes and effects, as a strategy to help them better understand their reading. Display the books and poems the students heard and read during Units 5 and 6, and review that they used inference to understand various aspects of these books, including the characters, what is happening, what something means, and why something happens. Explain that today they will practice being aware of inferences and cause and effect relationships as they read independently.

Remind the students that they also practiced contributing to group work, including one another in group work, and using prompts to extend their conversations. Encourage them to continue to practice these group skills today.

Explain that today the students will read poetry, narrative, or expository texts independently, then reread while paying attention to inferences they make and any cause and effect relationships they notice.

Materials

- Read-aloud books and poems from Units 5 and 6
- Texts at appropriate levels for independent reading
- Small self-stick notes for each student
- *Student Response Book* page 37
- "Class Meeting Ground Rules" chart
- Solutions chart from the class meeting on Week 2, Day 4
- *Assessment Resource Book*
- Unit 6 Parent Letter (BLM15)

2 **Read Independently Without Stopping**

Make sure that the students have a variety of texts at appropriate reading levels available to them. Ask the students to use self-stick notes to mark the place they begin reading, and have them read independently for 10 minutes.

3 **Prepare to Reread and Notice Inferences or Causes and Effects**

After 10 minutes, stop the students and ask them to reread, starting again at their self-stick notes. As they reread, they will use additional self-stick notes to mark places they make an inference or notice a cause or effect.

Explain that later they will use a double-entry journal to record their thinking.

4 **Reread Independently and Mark Clues**

Have the students reread independently for 10 minutes, marking as they read. Circulate and look for evidence that the students identify places where they make an inference or notice a cause or effect. Probe individual students' thinking by asking questions such as:

Q *What is this [book/story/poem] about?*

Q *What do you know about this [topic/character] based on what you just read?*

Q *Is that stated directly in the text? If not, what clue(s) tell you what you know?*

Q *What causes or effects are you noticing in your reading?*

Teacher Note

The students used a double-entry journal to record their thinking about inferences in texts they read independently in Unit 5, Week 3.

5 **Use a Double-entry Journal to Record Thinking**

Ask the students to turn to the double-entry journal on *Student Response Book* page 37 and write the title of the text they are reading on the blank line. Explain that they will choose one or two places they marked in their independent reading, write the words or sentences in the "What I Read" column, and write their thinking about the words or sentences in the "My Thoughts" column.

Have students who did not identify any inferences, causes, or effects as they read choose an interesting sentence from their reading to write about.

6 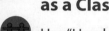 **Discuss the Double-entry Journals in Groups and as a Class**

Use "Heads Together" to have the students talk about what they wrote in their journals.

Then, have a few volunteers each share a journal entry with the class. Remind each student to say the title and author of his book and a few words about its topic. Facilitate a discussion by asking:

Q   *What was happening in the text when you made the inference?*

Q   *Why does the inference make sense based on what else you know about the book?*

Q   *How does that sentence describe the cause or effect of something?*

Q   *What questions do you want to ask [Leo] about what [he] shared?*

7 **Have a Brief Check-in Class Meeting About a Problem**

Tell the students they will have a brief check-in class meeting, and have them move into a circle. Review the class meeting ground rules.

Review the problem they discussed in last week's problem-solving class meeting, and direct the students' attention to the chart of solutions they generated. Ask:

Q   *How has our class been doing with the problem of [speaking disrespectfully to one another]?*

◀ **Teacher Note**

You might want to make note of students who did not mark their text at all. Interview them at another time to determine whether their books contain cause and effect relationships and opportunities to infer, and if so, whether they are able to recognize these.

Class Meeting
Ground Rules

- *one person talks*
  at a time

Teacher Note

This is the last week in Unit 6. In Unit 7, the students will explore expository text structures such as compare and contrast, chronological order, and cause and effect. If you feel your students need more experience with inference, including exploring causes and effects, you may want to repeat this week's lessons with an alternative book. Alternative books are listed on this week's Overview page.

You will reassign partners for Unit 7.

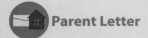
Parent Letter

Send home with each student the Parent Letter for this unit (see "Do Ahead," page 279). Periodically, have a few students share with the class what they are reading at home.

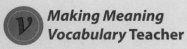
Making Meaning Vocabulary Teacher

Next week you will revisit this week's reading to teach Vocabulary Week 15.

Q *What ideas on the solutions chart have you tried? How did that work? If it didn't work well, what happened? What might you try instead?*

Q *What have you personally done to create a community in which we [speak respectfully] to one another?*

Solicit any new ideas for the solutions chart and add these. Tell the students that you will check in again to see how they are doing solving this problem. State your ongoing expectation that all the students will be responsible for doing their part to create a safe and caring community in the class.

Facilitate a brief discussion about how the students did following the ground rules during the class meeting. Review the procedure for returning to their desks, and adjourn the meeting.

INDIVIDUAL COMPREHENSION ASSESSMENT

Before continuing with Unit 7, take this opportunity to assess individual students' progress in inferring causes and effects to understand text. Please refer to pages 42–43 in the *Assessment Resource Book* for instructions.

Unit 7

Analyzing Text Structure

EXPOSITORY NONFICTION

During this unit, the students explore how articles can inform by highlighting pros and cons and by investigating one side of an issue. They examine how functional texts such as tables and directions are organized to inform readers. They also look at textbooks and think about how cause and effect, chronological, and compare and contrast relationships are used to organize the information. During IDR, the students use comprehension strategies. Socially, they take responsibility for their own learning during group work and develop the group skills of including one another and contributing to group work.

Week 1 "Copycats: Why Clone?"
"The Debate on Banning Junk Food Ads"

Week 2 "All-girls' and All-boys' Schools: Better for Kids"
"Do Kids Really Need Cell Phones?"

Week 3 "How to Make an Origami Cup"
"Ashton Hammerheads Schedule for July, 2008"
"Frontier Fun Park" Ticket Prices

Weeks 4 & 5
Survival and Loss: Native American Boarding Schools

Week 1

Overview

UNIT 7: ANALYZING TEXT STRUCTURE

Expository Nonfiction

"Copycats: Why Clone?"

This article discusses the pros and cons of cloning plants, animals, and humans.

"The Debate on Banning Junk Food Ads"

This article discusses the pros and cons of regulating television junk food advertising.

ALTERNATIVE RESOURCES

ASPCA Animaland, www.aspca.org/kids

Children's BBC News, news.bbc.co.uk/cbbcnews/

Comprehension Focus

• Students *use text structure* to explore nonfiction articles.

• Students explore how articles can inform by highlighting pros and cons.

• Students read independently.

Social Development Focus

• Students take responsibility for their own learning during group work.

• Students include one another and contribute to group work.

DO AHEAD

• Prior to Day 1, decide how you will randomly assign partners to work together during the unit.

• Collect magazine and newspaper articles for the students to examine and read independently throughout the unit. If possible, include examples of articles that inform by highlighting pros and cons.

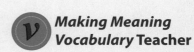

***Making Meaning Vocabulary* Teacher**

If you are teaching Developmental Studies Center's *Making Meaning Vocabulary* program, teach Vocabulary Week 15 this week. For more information, see the *Making Meaning Vocabulary Teacher's Manual*.

Day 1

Materials

- "Copycats"
  (see pages 310–311)
- *Student Response Book*
  pages 38–39
- "Self-monitoring
  Questions" chart

Read-aloud

In this lesson, the students:

- *Use text structure* to explore articles
- Identify what they learn from an article
- Read independently for up to 30 minutes
- Begin working with new partners and groups
- Practice "Heads Together"

About Expository Text Structures

The purpose of this unit is to help the students make sense of expository texts, including articles and functional texts, and to introduce the students to expository text structures found in many school textbooks, such as cause and effect and compare and contrast. In addition, the students explore different expository text structures used by authors when writing articles, such as highlighting pros and cons and informing from one side of an issue. The students have opportunities to examine such functional texts as directions, maps, schedules, and tables. The unit's primary goal is for the students to have an opportunity to explore these structures to help them make sense of what they are reading and to set the groundwork for exploration of these structures in later years. Mastery of these structures is not expected in this exploratory unit.

Being a Writer™ **Teacher**

You can either have the students work with their *Being a Writer* partner or assign them a different partner for the *Making Meaning* lessons.

 Get Ready to Work Together

Randomly assign partners and have pairs sit in groups of four. Explain that in the coming weeks, the students will work in pairs and small groups to read various kinds of expository texts and analyze how the texts are organized and written.

Ask and briefly discuss:

Q *What have you learned about working in groups that will help you as you work with your new group?*

Encourage the students to keep these things in mind as they work with their new groups today.

Review Expository Nonfiction

Remind the students that the purpose of expository texts is to inform the reader about a topic. Review that they have heard and read a variety of expository nonfiction already this year. Show and briefly review some of the expository texts they have heard, including *Chinese Americans* from Unit 2 and *Earthquakes* and *Wildfires* from Unit 6. Ask:

Q *What have you learned so far this year about expository nonfiction?*

Have one or two volunteers share.

> **Students might say:**
>
> "Expository texts give information about things like animals and history."
>
> "In addition to what [Gloria] said, they also have photographs, charts, maps, and things like that to help you understand what you are reading."
>
> "I look at the table of contents to get an idea about what I'm going to be reading."
>
> "We learned a lot about earthquakes and wildfires."

 ELL Note

To support your English Language Learners, summarize the article prior to reading it aloud. Then read the article aloud to your English Language Learners, stopping frequently to check for understanding. If necessary, reread sections of the article and discuss them with your students.

Introduce and Preview "Copycats"

Explain that today the students will hear a news article called "Copycats: Why Clone?" which gives information about cloning, or creating exact copies of people or other living things.

Remind the students that earlier in the year, the students skimmed articles by reading and thinking about the title, subtitle, and section headings before hearing the article. Have them turn to *Student Response Book* pages 38–39, where "Copycats" is reproduced, and quietly read the title and section headings. Ask:

Q *From reading the title and section headings, what information do you think might be in this article?*

Have a few students share.

Explain that you will read the article aloud, pausing during the reading to have the students use "Heads Together" to discuss what they are learning.

4 Read Aloud

Read the text of the article aloud, stopping as described below.

Suggested Vocabulary

techniques: special ways of doing something (p. 310)

genetic makeup: genes (p. 310)

the idea is controversial: people have different points of view about cloning (p. 310)

genetic disorder: disease that is passed from parent to child (p. 311)

ELL Vocabulary

English Language Learners may benefit from discussing additional vocabulary, including:

hi-tech: very advanced; scientific (p. 310)

identical: exactly the same (p. 310)

debate has raged: people have argued (p. 310)

ethical: right or wrong according to someone's beliefs (p. 310)

breed: type of plant or animal (p. 311)

desirable traits: things that make a plant or animal more valuable, such as bigger apples on an apple tree or thicker wool on a sheep (p. 311)

protect endangered species from extinction: make sure certain kinds of animals don't all die (p. 311)

ban: make a law against (p. 311)

Read the first two paragraphs of the article aloud, and then reread them, asking the students to listen for any information they might have missed during the first reading.

Teacher Note

If you notice the students having difficulty sustaining conversations in groups of four, consider having them talk in pairs instead.

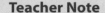

Have the students use "Heads Together" to discuss what they have heard. After a minute or two, signal for their attention and ask:

Q *What have you learned so far about cloning?*

Read aloud the text under the "Pro" heading. Stop after:

p. 311   "These discoveries might even save lives."

 Have the students use "Heads Together" to discuss what they have heard. After a minute or two, signal for their attention and ask:

Q   *What have you found out so far about cloning?*

Have a couple of volunteers share, and then read aloud the sections under the "Con" heading, continuing to the end of the article.

 Have the students use "Heads Together" to discuss what they heard in the second part of the article. After a minute or two, signal for their attention and ask:

Q   *According to the article, what are some problems with cloning?*

Have a couple of volunteers share.

 5 ▶ Discuss the Reading

Facilitate a whole-class discussion using the questions that follow. As the students respond, be ready to reread from the article to help them recall what they heard.

Q   *What are some of the ways cloning can be used?*

Q   *What did you find out about cloning that surprised you?*

Students might say:

"Cloning might help people who can't have children."

"I disagree with what [Emmett] said because the article says a cloned human being might not have a normal life."

"I was surprised that if we cloned people, we could give those clones special talents."

"In addition to what [Mya] said, I was surprised that farmers are already growing cloned plants."

FACILITATION TIP

During this unit, we invite you to practice **responding neutrally** with interest during class discussions. To respond neutrally means to refrain from overtly praising (e.g., "Great idea" or "Good job") or criticizing (e.g., "That's wrong") the students' responses. Although it may feel more natural to avoid criticism than to avoid praise, research shows that both kinds of response encourage students to look to you, rather than to themselves, for validation. To build the students' intrinsic motivation, try responding with genuine curiosity and interest (e.g., "Interesting—say more about that") while avoiding statements that communicate judgment, whether positive or negative.

6▶ Reflect on Working in Groups

Have the students use "Heads Together" to discuss:

Q *What went well working with your new group today? What can your group work on to make your work go more smoothly?*

Have several groups report what they discussed.

INDIVIDUALIZED DAILY READING

7▶ Review and Practice Self-monitoring with Articles and Other Expository Texts

Refer to the "Self-monitoring Questions" chart and review the questions. Remind the students that it is important to stop to think about what they are reading and to use the questions to help them track whether they are understanding their reading. When they do not understand, they may need to reread, use a comprehension strategy, or get a different text.

Have the students read articles and other expository texts at their appropriate reading levels independently for up to 30 minutes. Stop them at 10-minute intervals and have them monitor their comprehension by thinking about the questions on the chart.

Circulate among the students and ask individual students to read a passage to you and tell you what it is about.

At the end of the reading time, have a whole-class discussion about how the students used the self-monitoring questions to track their reading comprehension. Ask questions such as:

Q *Which self-monitoring question did you find the most helpful? Why?*

Q *What do you want to continue to be aware of when you read to make sure you understand what you are reading?*

Self-monitoring
Questions

- What is happening in my
story right now?

- Does the reading
make sense?

Day 2

Strategy Lesson

In this lesson, the students:

- *Use text structure* to explore articles
- Explore how articles can inform by highlighting pros and cons
- Read independently for up to 30 minutes
- Include one another and contribute to group work

1 Review "Copycats"

Have pairs sit in their groups of four. Remind students that yesterday they heard and discussed the article "Copycats: Why Clone?" Ask:

Q *What did you find out about cloning from the article?*

Have a few volunteers share what they remember.

2 Introduce Highlighting Pros and Cons

Remind the students that expository texts inform the reader; in this article the reader is informed about the reasons why people might or might not want to clone living things. Explain that authors organize articles and other kinds of expository nonfiction very deliberately to inform their readers in a particular way.

Explain that it is common for writers to inform the reader by highlighting the pros and cons of—or arguments for and against— something. This technique helps readers to consider both sides of an issue and deepen their understanding of the issue.

Explain that today the students will think and talk about how "Copycats: Why Clone?" is organized to highlight pros and cons.

Materials

- "Copycats" (see pages 310–311)
- *Student Response Book* pages 38–39
- "Self-monitoring Questions" chart

Teacher Note

As the students read, circulate and check in with individual students. Support struggling students by asking questions such as:

Q *What information did you read in this paragraph?*

Q *Why do you think the idea [that cloning might help save endangered species] is mentioned in the "pro" section of the article?*

If your students have difficulty reading the article independently, consider having them read in pairs or reread the article as a class before you have groups analyze it.

Teacher Note

Remind the students to connect their comments to comments made by others using the discussion prompts:

• *I agree with _____ because…*

• *I disagree with _____ because…*

• *In addition to what _____ said, I think…*

3 ▶ Reread "Copycats" and Discuss in Groups

Have the students turn to *Student Response Book* pages 38–39 and explain that they will read the article quietly to themselves and then use "Heads Together" to talk about what they noticed. As the students read, ask them to consider the following questions:

Q *What are some ways that cloning might help people?*

Q *What are some ways that cloning might be dangerous?*

 After the students have had a chance to reread, use "Heads Together" to have them discuss the pros and cons they noticed in the article. Circulate among the groups and notice whether group members are contributing to and including each other in the discussion. Note examples of what is working well in the groups to bring to the students' attention later.

4 ▶ Discuss Pros and Cons as a Class

When most of the students have had time to share in their groups, facilitate a whole-class discussion about the pros and cons in "Copycats: Why Clone?" by asking questions such as:

Q *According to the article, how might cloning help people? What did you read that makes you think that?*

Q *According to the article, what are some problems with cloning?*

Q *Are you more persuaded by the arguments for or against cloning? Explain your thinking.*

> **Students might say:**
>
> "I think cloning is good because it can help farmers breed better animals."
>
> "I disagree with what [Leah] said because the article says some cloned animals die when they're really young."
>
> "I agree with [Monica] that cloning people is dangerous because it might not work right."
>
> "In addition to what [Myron] said, the article says cloned vegetables can stay fresh longer."

Explain that tomorrow the students will hear and discuss another pro and con article, about junk food advertisements.

 5 ▶ Reflect on Working in Groups

Share any observations you made about how the students worked together during "Heads Together." Ask and briefly discuss:

Q *How did your group do with making sure everyone was included in the conversation? If everyone was not included, what can you do next time to make sure everyone is included?*

Q *How did you contribute to the group conversation during "Heads Together"?*

INDIVIDUALIZED DAILY READING

6 ▶ Practice Self-monitoring

Continue to have the students monitor their comprehension. Refer to the "Self-monitoring Questions" chart and review the questions. Ask and briefly discuss:

Q *Which of these questions have you found the most helpful when you are reading?*

Q *What do you want to continue to think about when you are reading independently today?*

Remind the students that it is important to stop to think about what they are reading and to use the questions to help them track whether they are making sense of it. When they do not understand what they are reading, they may need to reread, use a comprehension strategy, or get a different text.

Have the students read articles and other expository texts at their appropriate reading levels independently for up to 30 minutes. Stop them at 10-minute intervals and have them monitor their comprehension by thinking about the questions on the chart.

> ### Self-monitoring Questions
>
> - What is happening in my story right now?
> - Does the reading make sense?

Circulate among the students and ask individual students to read a passage to you, tell you what it is about, and which questions they are using to help them monitor their comprehension.

At the end of the reading time, have a whole-class discussion about how the students used the self-monitoring questions to track their reading comprehension.

EXTENSION

Read More About Cloning

You might have the students read and discuss other articles about cloning. You can find articles on such websites as www.sciencenewsforkids.org and www.askforkids.com; search these sites or elsewhere on the Internet using keywords such as "cloning humans."

COPYCATS

WHY CLONE?

Cloning is a hi-tech way to create a living thing that is an exact copy of another. Why would we want to create identical living things? For farmers, there are many reasons. Farmers already use cloning techniques to produce desired varieties of plants, such as apple trees that grow crisp, juicy fruit. One technique is to grow plants from cuttings taken from other plants. A plant that grows from a cutting is a clone because it has the same genetic makeup as the original plant.

In 1997, scientists succeeded in cloning the first mammal. Since then, debate has raged about whether it is ethical or necessary to clone animals—including humans. Although the idea is controversial, many scientists believe that cloned human beings will one day become a reality. Other technologies, such as organ transplants, once faced the same kinds of debate, and today they are widely used.

In 2006, the Food and Drug Administration approved the eating of meat from animals that have been cloned. In 2008, the FDA approved the sale of cloned animals in supermarkets without being labeled as such.

PRO

Building a Better Breed

Since the first mammal was cloned, scientists have cloned many other creatures, including cows, cats, and fruit flies. Today, farmers pair a male animal with a female and hope that they'll get offspring with desirable traits, such as animals that have thick wool or high-quality meat. In the future, they might use cloning as a quicker way to get that same result.

Protection from Extinction

Cloning might also be a way to protect endangered species from extinction. In 2005, scientists created clones of the gray wolf, a species once hunted to near extinction. Today, gray wolves are thriving in several states, including Minnesota and Wisconsin.

Human Health

There are many potential advantages of cloning human beings. It might give infertile couples a chance to have children of their own. Additionally, people who are likely to have a child with a genetic disorder might use cloning for the chance to produce a healthy child. Cloning could also be used to create healthy organs for people who are sick.

Cloning might help us to understand how human genes work. This could lead to the discovery of treatments for genetic disorders such as cystic fibrosis. Discoveries like these have the potential to make many people's lives easier. These discoveries might even save lives.

CON

Cloning for the Wrong Reasons

Where do we draw the line between the right reasons and the wrong reasons for using cloning? If human cloning is allowed in a few specific cases, people might begin to use it in other ways. For example, cloning might be used to create children who have specialized talents—such as amazing mathematical or athletic abilities—much like animals might be cloned for specific desirable traits. From there, cloning could lead to the creation of groups of people for specific purposes, such as fighting in war. Many people argue that it is wrong to experiment with human life in this way.

Health Risks

Studying human cloning has big complications. Real human cells must be used, so if a particular experiment did not work out, the result could be a flawed copy of a human being—and that person would never have a normal life.

So far, scientists have found it difficult to produce healthy clones of mammals. For example, studies done in Japan have shown that cloned mice have poor health and die early. About a third of the cloned calves born in the United States have died young, and many of them were too large. Many cloned animals appear healthy at a young age but die suddenly. We should expect the same problems in human clones.

Even if scientists were able to produce human clones that were physically healthy, other important parts of human development might be affected. For example, a person's mood, intelligence, and sense of individuality might not develop normally.

Legal Roadblocks

In most countries, it is against the law to clone a human being, because of the many ethical and safety concerns. The United States Congress is currently considering passing a law to ban human cloning.

Day 3

Materials

- "The Debate on Banning Junk Food Ads" (see pages 320–321)
- *Student Response Book* pages 40–41
- Several small self-stick notes for each student

 Note

Prior to reading the article aloud, summarize it for your English Language Learners. Then read the article aloud to them, stopping frequently to check for understanding. If necessary, reread sections of the article and discuss them with your students.

Read-aloud

In this lesson, the students:

- *Use text structure* to explore articles
- Identify what they learn from an article
- Read independently for up to 30 minutes
- Practice "Heads Together"

1 Review Highlighting Pros and Cons

Have pairs sit in their groups of four. Remind the students that they read the article "Copycats: Why Clone?" and noticed how the article gave readers information by highlighting the pros and cons of cloning living things. Ask:

Q *Which side of the issue did you find the most convincing, the pro or con side? Why was it the most convincing to you?*

Explain that today the students will hear and discuss another article.

2 Introduce and Preview "The Debate on Banning Junk Food Ads"

Introduce "The Debate on Banning Junk Food Ads" by explaining that it is another news article written for young people. The article discusses whether or not the government should control the messages children receive about food from television commercials.

Review that earlier in the week, the students skimmed "Copycats: Why Clone?" by reading the title and section headings before they heard the article read aloud. Explain that today they will skim "The Debate on Banning Junk Food Ads." Have them turn to *Student Response Book* pages 40–41, where the article is reproduced, and ask them to quietly read the title and section headings.

Ask:

Q *From reading the title and section headings, what information do you think might be in this article?*

Have a few students share. Remind the students to use this technique any time they read articles or other expository texts.

Explain that you will read the article aloud and stop during the reading to have the students use "Heads Together" to discuss what they are learning.

 Read Aloud

Read the text of the article aloud following the procedure described on the next page.

Suggested Vocabulary

obesity: unhealthfully high body weight (p. 321)
consumer: person who buys things (p. 321)

ELL Vocabulary

English Language Learners may benefit from discussing additional vocabulary, including:

advertising: messages, like television commercials, that tell people to buy things (p. 320)
devoted to: spent on (p. 320)
low in nutritional value: isn't made of things that are good for your body (p. 320)
bans: doesn't allow (p. 320)
influenced: made to do something (p. 320)
have the right: should be allowed (p. 321)
have access to: can find out (p. 321)

Read the first paragraph of the article aloud, and then reread it, asking the students to listen for any information they might have missed. Ask and briefly discuss:

Q *What have you learned so far about advertising?*

Have a few volunteers share, and then continue reading. Stop after:

> **p. 321** "Limiting junk food ads may be one way to help people make choices that will prevent obesity and other health problems."

 Have the students use "Heads Together" to discuss what they have learned so far. After a minute or two, signal for their attention and ask:

Q *What did you find out in the part you just heard?*

Have a couple of volunteers share, and then continue reading to the end of the article.

 Have the students use "Heads Together" to discuss what they heard in the second part of the article. After a minute or two, signal for their attention and ask:

Q *What did you find out in the second part of the article?*

Have a couple of volunteers share.

Teacher Note ▶

During the stops, listen for evidence that the students are discussing the article and understanding it. If necessary, reread parts of the article to help the students recall what they heard.

◢4 Discuss the Reading

 First in groups of four, and then as a class, have the students discuss questions such as:

Q *According to the article, why is there so much junk food advertising?*

Q *Why do some people think junk food advertising on TV should be banned?*

Q *What did you find out about junk food advertising that surprised you?*

Teacher Note ▶

If necessary, reread parts of the article to help the students remember what they heard.

Students might say:

"There is so much junk food advertising because kids watch so much TV."

"In addition to what [Jeremy] said, there is a lot of junk food advertising because when kids see it, they ask their parents to buy the food."

"The article said people think the ads should be banned because junk food is so unhealthy."

"I was surprised that 90 percent of the ads kids see are about junk food."

Explain that the students will reread the article tomorrow and discuss how it is written.

INDIVIDUALIZED DAILY READING

▶5 Have the Students Read for Information/Document IDR Conferences

Remind the students that one of the purposes of reading expository nonfiction is to learn information about a topic. Explain to the students that today they will read articles and other expository nonfiction independently, and put self-stick notes beside interesting facts and information they are learning. At the end of IDR they will share some of the facts they have learned with their group.

Distribute several self-stick notes to each student and have the students read independently for up to 30 minutes. Circulate among the students and ask individuals to read a passage to you and tell you what it is about. Use the "IDR Conference Notes" record sheet to conduct and document individual conferences.

At the end of IDR have the students review the facts that they noted and choose four of the most interesting facts to share with their group. Have them use "Heads Together" to share what their article or text is about and their four interesting facts.

Day 4

Materials

- "The Debate on Banning Junk Food Ads" (see pages 320–321)
- *Student Response Book* pages 40–41
- *Assessment Resource Book*
- *Student Response Book*, IDR Journal section

Strategy Lesson

In this lesson, the students:

- *Use text structure* to explore articles
- Explore how articles can inform by highlighting pros and cons
- Read independently for up to 30 minutes
- Include one another and contribute to group work

▶ **1 Review "The Debate on Banning Junk Food Ads"**

Have pairs sit in their groups of four. Review that in the previous lesson the students heard and discussed the article "The Debate on Banning Junk Food Ads." Ask and briefly discuss:

Q *What is this article about?*

Have a few volunteers share what they remember.

Review that news articles and other kinds of expository nonfiction are organized to inform their readers in a particular way. Review that it is common for writers to inform the reader by highlighting the pros and cons of an issue. This technique helps readers learn about both sides of the issue and gain a deeper understanding of it.

Explain that today the students will reread "The Debate on Banning Junk Food Ads" individually and then think and talk about how the article is organized in a way that highlights pros and cons.

Reread "The Debate on Banning Junk Food Ads" and Discuss in Groups

Ask the students to turn to *Student Response Book* pages 40–41. Explain that the students will read the article quietly to themselves and then use "Heads Together" to talk about what they noticed. Ask them to consider the following questions as they reread:

Q *What arguments does the article make for banning junk food advertising?*

Q *What arguments does the article make against banning junk food advertising?*

After the students have had a chance to reread, use "Heads Together" to have them discuss the pros and cons they found in the article.

Teacher Note

As the students work, circulate and check in with individual students. Support struggling students by asking questions such as:

Q *What information did you find out in the part you just read?*

Q *After reading [that ads can cause people to make unhealthy choices], are you convinced that junk food ads should be banned? Why do you think that?*

> **CLASS COMPREHENSION ASSESSMENT**
>
> Circulate among the students and ask yourself:
>
> **Q** *Do the students understand the article?*
>
> **Q** *Are they able to identify pros and cons in the article?*
>
> **Q** *Are they able to explain their thinking clearly?*
>
> Record your observations on page 19 of the *Assessment Resource Book.*

Discuss Pros and Cons as a Class

Signal for the students' attention and facilitate a whole-class discussion about the pros and cons in "The Debate on Banning Junk Food Ads" by asking questions such as:

Q *According to the article, why might stopping junk food advertising on TV be good for kids? What did you read that makes you agree?*

Q *According to the article, why shouldn't we ban junk food advertising on TV? What did you read that makes you think so?*

Q *Are you more persuaded by the arguments for or against regulating junk food ads? Explain your thinking.*

Students might say:

"I think banning the ads is a good idea because it might help kids eat less junk food."

"In addition to what [Leigh] said, if people start eating better when they're young, they might be healthier as adults, too."

"I disagree with what [Emmanuel] said because if kids don't see the ads, they won't learn how to choose healthy foods."

"I agree with [Mari] because if the ads are banned, people won't have all the information."

Review that highlighting pros and cons is one way authors organize articles and other kinds of expository nonfiction to inform their readers. Encourage the students to start noticing how articles they read independently are written and to look for examples of articles that inform by highlighting pros and cons.

Explain that next week the students will hear more news articles and think and talk about how they are organized.

▶4 Reflect on Working in Groups

Help the students reflect on how they worked together during "Heads Together" by asking:

Q *How did you contribute to the group conversation during "Heads Together"?*

Q *How did your group do with making sure everyone was included in the conversation?*

Q *What problems did you have? How did you try to deal with those problems? What can your group do to avoid those problems next time?*

INDIVIDUALIZED DAILY READING

 5 **Read for Information/Record Facts in Their IDR Journals**

Remind the students that they have been reading articles and other expository texts and noticing what they are learning. Explain that today the students will continue to read expository nonfiction independently and then they will record several pieces of information they have learned.

Have the students read articles and other expository nonfiction texts for up to 30 minutes.

At the end of IDR, have the students write in their IDR Journals about what they read. Ask each student to write the title, the author's name, and five or six things she learned from the reading.

After sufficient time, signal for the students' attention and briefly discuss questions such as:

Q *What did you read today?*

Q *What information did you learn from your reading?*

Q *What surprised you about the article you read?*

Q *What questions do you have for [Machyl] about what [he] read?*

EXTENSION

Research Advertising

You might have the students find more information about advertising directed at children. You and your students can find more information on such websites as www.pbskids.org/dontbuyit and www.justthink.org.

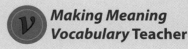 *Making Meaning Vocabulary* **Teacher**

Next week you will revisit this week's reading to teach Vocabulary Week 16.

The Debate on Banning Junk Food Ads

Advertising Works

Food companies spend millions of dollars on TV advertising each year. The reason is simple: advertising works. It's especially effective with children. A 2006 study found that each year, children between the ages of eight and twelve see 50 hours of junk food ads on TV, and teenagers see 40 hours. About 90 percent of all food ads during children's viewing times are devoted to junk food—none are for fruit and vegetables.

What's Junk?

Junk food may taste good, but it's low in nutritional value. For example, a sugary donut doesn't have as many nutrients as an apple. Many people argue that one way to help people, especially children, to choose more nutritious foods is to regulate, or control, the messages they receive about food from advertising. Others argue that regulating advertising will simply create more problems.

Pros

Good Habits Start Young

Some countries already regulate TV advertising for junk food. England introduced the Children's Food Bill in 2006, which bans junk food advertising during children's TV shows. They say that TV advertising encourages bad eating habits among young people, because young people are more easily influenced than adults by advertising. One study found that children aged twelve and younger who watched junk food ads often asked their parents to buy the foods they had seen advertised. Young people are especially affected by junk food ads when their favorite cartoon characters, celebrities, or superheroes are telling them to buy it.

Junk food is a slang term for food with little nutritional value. It includes food that is high in fat, sugar, or salt (or all three). These foods make up a large portion of foods we see advertised on TV.

A child who develops unhealthy habits is also likely to keep on making unhealthy choices as an adult. So it makes sense to control the messages that young people receive. This gives them a better chance at having a healthy future.

Good health is a big concern to many people today. Worldwide, hundreds of millions of people have serious problems related to an unhealthy diet, such as diabetes and heart disease. A common problem in the United States is obesity. It's estimated that nearly 200 million adults and 7 million children are overweight or obese. Limiting junk food ads may be one way to help people make choices that will prevent obesity and other health problems.

> "In England foods such as olive oil, honey, and cheese are labeled as junk food."

Cons

Giving Food a Bad Name

There are some big problems with creating rules about junk food advertising. For example, how do we decide exactly what is junk food and what is not? In England, foods such as olive oil, honey, and cheese have been banned from advertising during certain hours because they are labeled "junk food." These foods have nutritional value, but they are also high in fat, salt, or sugar. Calling these foods "junk food" makes it more difficult for people to understand what makes up a healthy, balanced diet.

To make things even more complicated, some ads for fast food now emphasize more nutritious choices—for example, fruit and milk with children's meals. Some promote health and fitness, too. If all fast food ads were banned from children's TV, these healthy messages would be, as well.

Some parents feel that they have the right to decide what is best for their children, and that regulating TV ads takes away that right. It is up to the parent to say "yes" or "no" when a child asks for something he or she has seen advertised on TV. What the parent says helps the child to learn about how advertising affects the people who see it.

Regulating TV ads takes away some of the information parents and children have access to. They need that information in order to make their own decisions. Making decisions is the consumer's right, not the right of the government.

England's Children's Food Bill bans junk food ads during children's TV shows and on children's channels.

Week 2

Overview

UNIT 7: ANALYZING TEXT STRUCTURE

Expository Nonfiction

"All-girls' and All-boys' Schools: Better for Kids"

This article discusses the benefits of separating students into all-boys' and all-girls' schools.

"Do Kids Really Need Cell Phones?"

This article discusses the benefits of equipping young children with cell phones.

ALTERNATIVE RESOURCES

Weekly Reader, www.weeklyreader.com

Just Think, www.justthink.org

Comprehension Focus

- Students *use text structure* to explore nonfiction articles.

- Students explore how articles can inform by investigating one side of an issue.

- Students explore author's point of view.

- Students read independently.

Social Development Focus

- Students take responsibility for their own learning during group work.

- Students include one another and contribute to group work.

- Students explain their thinking.

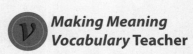

Making Meaning Vocabulary Teacher

If you are teaching Developmental Studies Center's *Making Meaning Vocabulary* program, teach Vocabulary Week 16 this week. For more information, see the *Making Meaning Vocabulary Teacher's Manual.*

Day 1

Materials

- "All-girls' and All-boys' Schools" (see pages 334–335)
- *Student Response Book* pages 38–43
- "Reading Comprehension Strategies" chart

Read-aloud

In this lesson, the students:

- *Use text structure* to explore articles
- Identify what they learn from an article
- Read independently for up to 30 minutes
- Take responsibility for their own learning during group work

▶1 Get Ready to Work Together

Have pairs sit in their groups of four. Remind the students that they used "Heads Together" in their groups last week and thought about how they were including one another and contributing to the group work. Explain that they will continue to work in groups in the coming week and that you would like them to think about how they are taking responsibility for their own learning during group work. Ask:

Q *What can be challenging about taking responsibility for your own learning during group work?*

Q *During "Heads Together" today, how can you make sure you are participating fully and learning everything you can about what is being discussed?*

Students might say:

"Sometimes it can be challenging if everyone's talking but you don't get what they're talking about."

"I agree with [Susan]. We can take responsibility by stopping and asking the other people in the group to explain if we don't understand."

"In addition to what [Alejandro] said, we can make sure to say what we think so other people in the group can think about it, too."

Encourage the students to pay attention to how they are taking responsibility for their own learning today, and tell them that you will check in with them to see what they noticed.

 Review and Introduce "All-girls' and All-boys' Schools"

Remind the students that they read two articles last week, "Copycats: Why Clone?" and "The Debate on Banning Junk Food Ads," and discussed how the articles were organized to inform readers in a particular way. Have the students turn to their copies of the articles on *Student Response Book* pages 38–41 and ask:

Q   *What do you remember about how "Copycats: Why Clone?" and "The Debate on Banning Junk Food Ads" are organized?*

Explain that today the students will hear and read an article about all-girls' and all-boys' schools. Explain that this article is written from one point of view. Invite the students to think about how the article is written as you read it.

3 **Preview and Read Aloud**

Ask the students to turn to *Student Response Book* pages 42–43 and explain that this is a copy of the article they will read today, "All-girls' and All-boys' Schools: Better for Kids." Review that last week the students skimmed the title and section headings to help them think about what information might be in the articles they read. Have the students quietly read the title and section headings. Ask and briefly discuss:

Q   *Based on the title and section headings, what information do you think might be in this article?*

Have a few students share.

Ask the students to follow along in their *Student Response Books* as you read the article aloud. Explain that you will stop during the reading to have the students use "Heads Together" to discuss what they are learning. Read aloud, stopping as described on the next page.

Suggested Vocabulary

interact with: come in contact with (p. 334)

coeducational/coed: with boys and girls in school together (p. 334)

segregated: kept separate (p. 335)

gaining favor: becoming more popular (p. 335)

ELL Vocabulary

English Language Learners may benefit from discussing additional vocabulary, including:

are more confident: feel better about themselves (p. 334)

academically: in school (p. 334)

develops: grows and changes (p. 334)

instruction: teaching (p. 334)

graduates: people who finish school (p. 334)

enthusiastic: excited (p. 335)

their academic abilities: how well they do in school (p. 335)

their personalities: what kind of people they are (p. 335)

head start: chance to get ahead (p. 335)

getting on board: (idiom) deciding something is a good idea (p. 335)

Read the introduction and the first section, "Together or Apart?" aloud twice. Ask and briefly discuss:

Q *What have you found out so far?*

Continue reading. Stop after:

> **p. 335** "Likewise, female students in all-girls' schools scored better in math and science than did their female peers in coed classrooms."

Have the students use "Heads Together" to discuss what they have heard. After a minute or two, signal for their attention. Without sharing as a class, reread the last sentence and continue reading. Follow this procedure at the next two stopping points:

> **p. 335** "Since the switch, the average has soared to 80 percent."

> **p. 335** "…they're more likely to feel enthusiastic about speaking up in class, asking questions, and joining in class discussions."

Continue reading to the end of the article.

4 ▶ Discuss the Reading

First in groups, and then as a whole class, have the students discuss:

Q *What does the article say about how having all-boys' and all-girls' classrooms affects students' test scores?*

Q *What are some reasons the article gives for having all-boys' and all-girls' schools?*

Q *What did you find out about all-boys' and all-girls' schools that surprised you?*

Students might say:

"Kids in all-boys' and all-girls' schools can do better on tests."

"The article says that boys and girls might not be as shy in class if they're in separate classes."

"I was surprised the article said that boys' and girls' brains are different."

Explain that tomorrow the students will reread the article and discuss how it is written.

5 ▶ Reflect on Working in Groups

Help the students reflect on how they took responsibility for their own learning during group work by asking:

Q *What did you learn about the article as you talked with your group members?*

Q *If you didn't understand something, what did you do?*

◀ Teacher Note

If the students have difficulty answering these questions, reread sections of the article to help them remember what they heard.

INDIVIDUALIZED DAILY READING

 Use Comprehension Strategies to Read Articles and Other Expository Texts

Direct the students' attention to the "Reading Comprehension Strategies" chart, review each strategy with the students, and remind them that these are the strategies they have learned so far this year. Ask them to notice which strategies they use and where they use them during their reading today. At the end of IDR, they will share in their groups of four.

Have the students read articles and other expository texts independently for up to 30 minutes.

 At the end of independent reading, have each student share his reading and a strategy he used—the name of the strategy and where he used it with his group. Have students who cannot think of a comprehension strategy they used discuss what they read.

Signal for the students' attention, and as a whole class, discuss questions such as:

Q *How did making inferences about [the effect of global warming on the polar bear population] help you make sense of the text?*

Q *[Jackie] said [she] was able to visualize [the hardships a gold miner faced as he panned for gold during the gold rush]. How did visualizing help you make sense of your text?*

Q *How did recognizing the pros and cons of [receiving a weekly allowance] help you understand the article you read?*

Reading Comprehension Strategies

- *recognizing text features*

Day 2

Strategy Lesson

In this lesson, the students:

- *Use text structure* to explore articles
- Explore how articles can inform by investigating one side of an issue
- Explore author's point of view
- Read independently for up to 30 minutes
- Include one another in group work

1 ▶ **Review "All-girls' and All-boys' Schools" and Introduce Author's Point of View**

Remind the students that they have been reading articles and thinking about how the articles inform readers. Review that yesterday the students read the article "All-girls' and All-boys' Schools: Better for Kids." Ask them to turn to the article on *Student Response Book* pages 42–43. Ask and briefly discuss:

Q *What do you remember about this article?*

Review that articles and other kinds of expository nonfiction are organized to inform their readers in a particular way. Review that the articles the students read last week, "Copycats: Why Clone?" and "The Debate on Banning Junk Food Ads," were written to highlight the pros and cons of an issue.

Point out that "All-girls' and All-boys' Schools: Better for Kids" informs readers by investigating one side of an issue instead of giving information about both sides. Explain that many articles in newspapers, in magazines, and on websites investigate one side of an issue to help readers understand a particular point of view or opinion, but do not inform readers about different points of view.

Explain that in order to help readers understand why all-boys' and all-girls' schools are a good idea, the author of "All-girls' and All-boys' Schools: Better for Kids" made choices about what to include in the

Materials

- "All-girls' and All-boys' Schools" (see pages 334–335)
- *Student Response Book* pages 42–43
- "Reading Comprehension Strategies" chart

article. Explain that today the students will think and talk about how the article informs readers about the benefits of all-boys' and all-girls' schools.

2 ▶ Reread the Article and Highlight Evidence in Pairs

Explain that the author of "All-girls' and All-boys' Schools: Better for Kids" gives examples, or evidence, to support the opinion that all-girls' and all-boys' schools are good for students. Ask the students to follow along as you reread "Together or Apart?" and the first paragraph of "Different Brains, Different Gains" aloud. Point out that the first section introduces the benefits of all-girls' and all-boys' schools, and the next section gives the reader evidence of those benefits.

Read aloud and have the students underline in their *Student Response Books* the sentence "Because of differences like these, males and females learn different subjects in different ways." Explain that the fact that boys and girls learn differently is evidence the author gives that separate boys' and girls' schools are good for students.

Explain that the students will read the rest of the article in pairs and underline three other examples, or pieces of evidence, the author gives to support this point of view.

 Have pairs spend several minutes working together to find and underline evidence in the article.

 When most pairs have finished, signal for the students' attention. Have partners discuss what they underlined with the other pair in their group of four.

3 ▶ Discuss the Article as a Class

When most of the students have had time to talk in their groups, facilitate a whole-class discussion about the evidence in the article by asking questions such:

Q *What evidence did you and your partner underline that supports the point of view that all-boys' and all-girls' schools are a good idea?*

Teacher Note ▶

Other evidence that supports the point of view that all-girls' and all-boys' schools are a good idea includes:

- "The researchers found that male students from all-boys' schools scored better in reading and writing than male graduates of coeducational schools."

- "Before then, an average of only about 65 percent of students would pass final exams each year. Since the switch, the average has soared to 80 percent."

- "Without the pressure of worrying about how they might look to members of the opposite sex, they can feel free to be themselves."

Q *How does ["male students from all-boys' schools scored better in reading and writing than graduates of coeducational schools"] help support the point of view that all-boys' and all-girls' schools are a good idea?*

Q *What other evidence did you find that [having separate all-boys' and all-girls' schools helps students do better in school]?*

Q *What questions can we ask [Annette] about [her] thinking?*

Students might say:

"We underlined, 'Boys increased their average scores in reading from about 20 percent to 66 percent.'"

"If kids are getting better test scores, that shows they are doing better in school."

"I underlined the same things as [Mariel]. I agree that [when the author says kids might try new things, it shows that all-boys' and all-girls' schools help kids be more confident]."

"In addition to what [Lenny] said, I think if kids feel less shy in class and ask more questions, they might be less shy with other kids, too."

4 ▶ Discuss the Author's Point of View

Review that the author of "All-girls' and All-boys' Schools: Better for Kids" takes the point of view that that all-boys' and all-girls' schools are better for kids. Remind the students that the author does not mention any evidence that does not support that point of view. Ask and briefly discuss:

Q *How did you feel about all-boys' and all-girls' schools after reading this article? What in the article made you feel that way?*

Q *Did the author convince you that all-boys' and all-girls' schools are a good idea? Why or why not?*

Explain that tomorrow the students will hear and discuss another article that investigates one side of an issue.

Reflect on Group Work

Share examples of successes or problems you observed as the students worked in their groups of four. Ask and briefly discuss:

Q *What did you do to make sure everyone was included in your group discussion?*

INDIVIDUALIZED DAILY READING

 Have the Students Read Articles and Other Expository Texts/Document IDR Conferences

Direct the students' attention to the "Reading Comprehension Strategies" chart, review each strategy with the students, and remind them that they have been using these strategies to help them make sense of their independent reading. Ask them to continue to notice which strategies they use and where they use them during their reading today. At the end of IDR, they will share with the whole class.

Have the students read articles and other expository texts independently for up to 30 minutes.

Use the "IDR Conference Notes" record sheet to conduct and document individual conferences.

At the end of independent reading, have each student share her reading and a strategy she used—the name of the strategy and where she used it—with the class.

Ask and briefly discuss questions such as:

Q *What did you infer about the author's purpose in the article about [why children should not watch television]? How did inferring about the author's purpose help you make sense of the text?*

Reading Comprehension Strategies

- *recognizing text features*

Q *What did you visualize when you read about [the life cycle of the monarch butterfly]? How did visualizing help you make sense of your text?*

Q *Which comprehension strategy have you found the most helpful when you are reading independently?*

EXTENSION

Read and Discuss Other Articles That Investigate One Side of an Issue

Have the students identify articles written from one point of view in magazines or on websites. Have the students read the articles in pairs and discuss whether or not they find the authors' evidence convincing. Most public library cards give students access to searchable periodical databases. Consult with your local librarian or visit your local library's website to find out more.

All-girls' and

Better for Kids

Out in the world, males and females live, work, and interact with one another. But at an increasing number of schools, the classrooms are filled with all boys or all girls. Life isn't separated into male and female sides, so why should schools be?

TOGETHER OR APART?

Because male and female students think, learn, and behave differently from one another, it makes sense that they would do better at schools that understand these differences. Research has shown that students at all-boys' or all-girls' schools are more confident, more willing to try new things, and might even perform better academically than students at coeducational schools.

DIFFERENT BRAINS, DIFFERENT GAINS

You might not realize it, but your brain develops differently from the brain of a classmate of the opposite sex. For example, the area of a girl's brain that understands language is one of the first areas to develop. In a boy's brain, other areas develop first, such as the part that makes sense of math. Because of differences like these, males and females learn different subjects in different ways.

An all-boys' or all-girls' school can focus its instruction to meet the needs of either male or female students, not both at the same time. This helps students to make quicker, stronger progress. For example, one Michigan study compared graduates of all-boys' and all-girls' high schools with

In 1972, a new law came into effect stating that all U.S. public schools should be coeducational. However, the law was changed in 2002 to allow all-boys' and all-girls' public schools.

All-boys' Schools

graduates of coeducational schools. The researchers found that male students in all-boys' schools scored better in reading and writing than male graduates of coeducational schools. Likewise, female students in all-girls' schools scored better in math and science than did their female peers in coed classrooms.

Shy students may feel happier about participating in an all-boys' or all-girls' class. Taking part in classroom discussions helps them get more out of the lesson.

POSITIVE PROOF IN TEST RESULTS

In 2000, the principal of Thurgood Marshall Elementary School in Seattle, Washington, decided to separate the students at his school into all-boys' or all-girls' classrooms. He hoped that this would improve the behavior of students. Not only did behavior improve, but academic results did, too. Boys increased their average scores in reading from about 20 percent to 66 percent. In writing, they scored the highest in their state. An inner-city high school in Montreal, Canada, also made the switch from coed to all-boys' and all-girls' classrooms in 2000. Before then, an average of only about 65 percent of students would pass final exams each year. Since the switch, the average has soared to 80 percent.

BUILDING CONFIDENCE

Supporters of all-boys' and all-girls' classrooms argue that in those environments, the students are less distracted. This makes it easier for all students to focus on the lesson.

Students who feel shy around people of the opposite sex could benefit the most from all-boys' or all-girls' schools. Without the pressure of worrying about how they might look to members of the opposite sex, they can feel free to be themselves. For example, they might explore subjects they wouldn't normally explore and join clubs or sports teams. Shy students are more likely to feel more comfortable in an all-boys' or all-girls' class, so they're more likely to feel enthusiastic about speaking up in class, asking questions, and joining in class discussions.

Many people argue that an all-boys' or all-girls' education could make it more difficult for young people to learn how to relate to members of the opposite sex. It's true that we live in a world where males and females live and work with one another, not segregated as in boys' or girls' schools. But many graduates of these schools say that they feel confident not only about their academic abilities, but they're also more confident in their personalities. And this confidence can give graduates a head start in building friendships with the opposite sex.

AN INCREASINGLY POPULAR OPTION

All-boys' and all-girls' classes and schools are gaining favor across the United States. In 1995, only three public schools in the United States offered this option. Today, there are more than 250. School districts, parents, and students are increasingly getting on board with all-boys' and all-girls' education as a great way to boost students' scores and confidence.

Day 3

Materials

- "Do Kids Really Need Cell Phones?" (see pages 346–347)
- *Student Response Book* pages 42–45
- *Student Response Book,* IDR Journal section

Read-aloud

In this lesson, the students:

- *Use text structure* to explore articles
- Identify what they learn from an article
- Read independently for up to 30 minutes
- Take responsibility for their own learning during group work

1 **Review "All-girls' and All-boys' Schools" and Introduce "Do Kids Really Need Cell Phones?"**

Have pairs sit in their groups of four. Have the students turn to pages 42–43 in their *Student Response Books*. Review that this week they read "All-girls' and All-boys' Schools: Better for Kids" and thought and talked about the author's point of view. Ask and briefly discuss:

Q *What is the author's point of view in the article? What evidence does the author give to support that point of view?*

Explain that today the students will hear and read another article written from one point of view.

2 **Preview the Article and Read Aloud**

Ask the students to turn to *Student Response Book* pages 44–45 and explain that "Do Kids Really Need Cell Phones?" is the article they will be reading today. Have the students quietly skim the title and section headings. Ask and briefly discuss:

Q *Based on the title and section headings, what information do you think might be in this article?*

Have a few students share.

Ask the students to follow along as you read the article aloud. Explain that you will stop during the reading to have them use "Heads Together" to discuss what they are learning. Invite the students to think about the author's point of view as they listen. Read the text aloud, stopping as described below. Do not read the boxed text at this time.

Suggested Vocabulary

lifeline: something that can save you in an emergency (p. 346)

mothers in the labor force: mothers who work outside the home (p. 346)

be dependent on: require; need (p. 347)

devices: machines (p. 347)

reliant on: dependent on (p. 347)

belongings: things that someone owns (p. 347)

opt for: choose (p. 347)

ELL Vocabulary

English Language Learners may benefit from discussing additional vocabulary, including:

catchy ringtones: fun sounds phones make when they ring (p. 346)

resist: say "no" to (p. 346)

stay in contact with: talk to (p. 346)

are familiar with this technology: know how to use cell phones (p. 347)

definitions: what words mean (p. 347)

personal possessions: things that belong to someone (p. 347)

preteen: aged 10 to 12 (p. 347)

prepaid plan: paying for a certain number of cell phone minutes ahead of time so you can only use that many (p. 347)

Read the section headed "Benefits Beyond the Cool Factor" twice, asking the students to listen for information they might have missed the first time. Continue reading the article.

Stop after:

p. 346 "This means that it is more important than ever to have a way of keeping in touch with family—and a way of getting help in an emergency."

Have the students use "Heads Together" to discuss what they have heard. After a minute or two, signal for their attention. Without sharing as a class, reread the last sentence and continue reading. Follow this procedure at the next two stopping points:

> **p. 347** "…and, in turn, help them feel confident when they grow up and begin working."

> **p. 347** "Learning responsibility in this way helps children to respect other people's belongings, too."

Continue reading to the end of the article.

 Point out the "Easy to Set Controls and Limits" text box and have the students follow along as you read it aloud. Briefly discuss first in groups, and then as a class, what the students learned from the text box.

▶ 3 Discuss the Reading as a Class

Facilitate a discussion about the article by asking questions such as:

Q *What does the article say about how many children have and will have cell phones?*

Q *What are some reasons the article gives for young children having cell phones?*

Q *What information that the author included surprised you?*

Teacher Note ▶

If the students have difficulty answering these questions, reread sections of the article to help them remember what they heard.

Students might say:

"It said 6 million kids had phones in 2006."

"The article said that if kids have cell phones, they will be able to get help in an emergency."

"I agree with [LaShauna]. The article also said that cell phones might be able to help kids with their school work."

"I was surprised that so many kids are home alone after school."

Explain that tomorrow the students will reread the article and discuss how it is written.

Reflect on Working in Groups

Help the students reflect on how they took responsibility for their own learning during group work by asking:

Q *What did you do to take responsibility for yourself during the group work today?*

Q *What is something new you learned from the article as you talked with your group members?*

INDIVIDUALIZED DAILY READING

5 ▶ Read Independently/Write in Their IDR Journals

Have the students read articles and other expository texts for up to 30 minutes.

As the students read, circulate among them. Observe their reading behavior and engagement with the text. Ask individual students questions such as:

Q *What is your [article/book] about?*

Q *What do you already know about this topic? What new information are you learning?*

Q *What comprehension strategies are you using to help you understand what you're reading?*

At the end of independent reading, have each student write in his IDR Journal about his reading and a strategy he used—the name of the strategy and where he used it. Have students who cannot think of a strategy write about their reading. Have a few students share their writing with the class.

Materials

- "Do Kids Really Need Cell Phones?" (see pages 346–347)
- *Student Response Book* pages 44–45
- *Assessment Resource Book*

Guided Strategy Practice

In this lesson, the students:

- *Use text structure* to explore articles
- Explore how articles can inform by investigating one side of an issue
- Explore the author's point of view
- Read independently for up to 30 minutes
- Explain their thinking

▶ 1 Review "Do Kids Really Need Cell Phones?"

Remind the students that they have been reading articles that explore pros and cons and articles that investigate one side of an issue and thinking about how the articles are written. Review that the article the students heard yesterday, "Do Kids Really Need Cell Phones?" investigates one side of an issue.

Ask them to turn to the article on *Student Response Book* pages 44–45. Ask and briefly discuss:

Q *What is "Do Kids Really Need Cell Phones?" about?*

Q *What is the author's point of view in "Do Kids Really Need Cell Phones?" How do you know that?*

Remind the students that earlier in the week, they reread "All-girls' and All-boys' Schools: Better for Kids" and found evidence in the article to support the author's point of view. Explain that today the students will reread "Do Kids Really Need Cell Phones?" in groups and think and talk about how the information in the article supports the author's point of view.

 Note

Prior to having the students look for and underline evidence in the article, reread it to your English Language Learners. Stop frequently to check for understanding.

2 ▶ Reread and Briefly Discuss "Do Kids Really Need Cell Phones?"

Have the students gather in their groups of four and explain that a volunteer in each group will read the article aloud to the rest of the group. Explain that the students will follow along and listen for evidence that supports the point of view that cellular phones benefit young children and their parents, and then groups will use "Heads Together" to talk about the evidence they heard in the article.

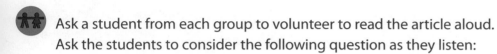 Ask a student from each group to volunteer to read the article aloud. Ask the students to consider the following question as they listen:

Q *What information does the author include in the article to support the point of view that it's a good idea for young children to have cellular phones?*

◀ **Teacher Note**

If more than one student wants to read aloud, suggest that the students take turns reading sections of the article aloud. If most students are reluctant to read aloud, ask the students to reread the article to themselves silently. Support your English Language Learners as needed.

3 ▶ Underline Evidence of the Author's Point of View and Discuss in Groups

Without having the students share as a class, explain that they will quietly scan the article in their own *Student Response Books* and underline three pieces of evidence that support the author's point of view. Then they will use "Heads Together" to talk about what they underlined.

Have the students spend a few minutes looking for and underlining evidence in the article.

◀ **Teacher Note**

Evidence in the article that supports the point of view that cell phones are good for kids includes:

- "Cell phones allow children to stay in contact with family."

- "One way to ensure that young people are familiar with this technology is to allow them to use cell phones now."

- "Owning a tool such as a cell phone can be a great way for a child to learn responsibility."

4 ▶ Discuss Evidence in Groups and as a Class

After the students have had a chance to underline evidence in the article, use "Heads Together" to have them discuss what they underlined and why. Remind them to explain their thinking as they share.

CLASS COMPREHENSION ASSESSMENT

Circulate among the students and ask yourself:

Q *Do the students understand the article?*

Q *Are they able to identify evidence in the article that supports the author's point of view?*

Q *Are they able to explain their thinking clearly?*

Record your observations on page 20 of the *Assessment Resource Book.*

When most of the students have had time to talk in their groups, facilitate a whole-class discussion about evidence that supports the author's point of view in "Do Kids Really Need Cell Phones?" Discuss questions such as:

Q *[Clarice] underlined ["Cell phones allow children to dial 911 or call their parents if there is an accident or emergency."]? Did you underline that sentence? What made you choose that one?*

Q *What other evidence did you find that [cell phones help kids be safer]?*

Q *Who agrees with what [Ronnie] said? Why? Who disagrees with what [Ronnie] said? Why?*

Q *Do you agree with the author's point of view based on the evidence in the article? Explain your thinking.*

Q *What can you add to what [Genevieve] said?*

Students might say:

"I underlined that sentence, too, because I think being safe is the most important reason to have a cell phone."

"I underlined 'Today, about 40 percent of twelve-year-old students are alone at home after school.'"

"I disagree with what [Mara] said because even if kids are home alone, they probably have a phone in the house."

"In addition to what [Pedro] said, I agree with the author's point of view because kids can learn a lot from having a cell phone."

Review that in the last weeks the students have explored how articles can inform readers by investigating one or both sides of an issue. Emphasize that it is important when reading articles for readers to ask themselves whether they are finding out about all sides of an issue or not. Encourage the students to notice the author's point of view in their independent reading.

Explain that next week, the students will read and discuss more expository nonfiction.

 ## Reflect on Explaining Their Thinking

Help the students reflect on how they did listening and explaining their thinking to the group by asking:

Q *What helped you explain your thinking clearly to your group?*

Q *If you didn't understand something someone else said, what did you do?*

INDIVIDUALIZED DAILY READING

 ## Think About How Authors Write Articles

Remind the students that they have been thinking about different ways that articles inform readers about topics and issues. Encourage the students to think about the author's purpose, or what the author is trying to tell readers, in the articles they read today.

Have the students read independently for up to 30 minutes.

As they read, circulate among them. Ask individual students questions such as:

Q *What is your text about?*

Q *What do you notice about how the author chose to write this piece?*

At the end of independent reading, have a few volunteers share what they read and how the articles are written. Have students who read books rather than articles share several things they learned from the reading.

EXTENSION

Research and Write an Article on Cell Phones for Kids

Have the students generate questions they have for the author after reading the article, and then have them conduct research to answer their own questions. Then, you might have the students work in groups to write an article either from the same or the opposing point of view, based on their research.

Most library cards give students access to searchable research and periodicals databases. Consult with your local librarian or visit your local library's website to find out more.

Teacher Note

Being a Writer, a writing curriculum from Developmental Studies Center, provides lessons that will help your students write in a variety of genres.

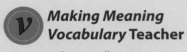

Making Meaning Vocabulary **Teacher**

Next week you will revisit this week's reading to teach Vocabulary Week 17.

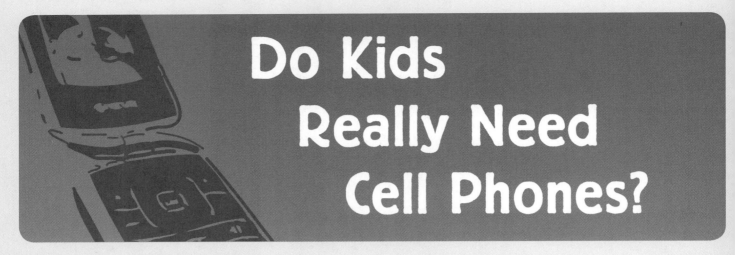

Do Kids Really Need Cell Phones?

Benefits Beyond the Cool Factor

There are more than 2 billion cell phone users worldwide—and the trend is catching on among eight- to twelve-year-olds. With bright colors and catchy ringtones, cell phones are hard for young people to resist.

But why does a person as young as eight years old need a cell phone? He or she is likely to come up with a list of reasons why, including, "All my friends have them." However, for very young kids, there are many benefits to having cell phones, beyond the obvious "cool" factor.

A Cell Phone Is a Lifeline

In an emergency, a cell phone can be a lifeline. Cell phones allow children to dial 911 or call their parents if there is an accident or emergency. Cell phones allow children to stay in contact with family. Children, parents, and other caregivers are often in different places throughout the day, and things often don't go as expected. For example, if soccer practice ends early or a parent is stuck in traffic, a cell phone can let everyone know how plans have changed.

As our lives become busier, the number of students at home alone after school is increasing. Between 1970 and 2002, the number of children in the United States with mothers in the labor force increased from about 39 percent to 63 percent. Today, about 40 percent of twelve-year-old students are alone at home after school.* This means that it is more important than ever to have a way of keeping in touch with family—and a way of getting help in an emergency.

*Source: U.S. Dept. of Commerce, U.S. Census Bureau, 2002.

Cell phones can help the day run smoothly by keeping family members in touch with one another.

Easy to Set Controls and Limits

Many people worry that cell phones put young children in danger. Bullies or even criminals might use the phones to contact children, and the Internet features of cell phones put children even more at risk. There is also the chance that children can run up high cell phone charges.

However, many cell phones now have parental controls. For example, it's possible to place limits on who can call and be called with some phones. Many cell phones don't have Internet access or text messaging. Some have Global Positioning System (GPS) tracking so that parents can find their child easily, using another cell phone or a website.

Parents can also opt for a prepaid plan so that their child can't go over spending limits. So, it's possible for children to get the benefits of cell phone use without the risks.

Workplaces around the world are becoming more and more reliant on technology.

Preparing for Working with Technology

In the near future, many jobs will be dependent on cell phones and similar devices. Many people predict that mobile devices such as cell phones will be as important in the future as the computer has been in the last twenty years. One way to ensure that young people are familiar with this technology is to allow them to use cell phones now.

Using a cell phone isn't limited to text messaging and talking any more. For example, cell phones can be helpful when doing schoolwork. On a standard cell phone, students can check the Internet for definitions and spellings of tricky words, take photos and make short videos for school projects, and listen to audio books using an MP3 player. Carrying out a variety of tasks using cell phones can help boost young people's confidence around technology—and, in turn, help them feel confident when they grow up and begin working.

Cell Phones Teach Responsibility

Owning a tool such as a cell phone can be a great way for a child to learn responsibility. Because cell phones are valuable and can be used in different ways, children must learn to use them wisely—for example, making sure they don't lose them, keeping them charged, and using them only when they are not in school. These things help young people learn to treat personal possessions with care. Learning responsibility in this way helps children to respect other people's belongings, too.

An Unstoppable Trend

Researchers say that about 6 million of the 20 million American children between eight and twelve years old had cell phones by the end of 2006. Researchers also predict that, by 2010, there will be 10.5 million preteen cell phone users. If young children don't already own cell phones, it's likely that they will in the future. The best way for young people to benefit from this technology is to learn to use it responsibly today.

Week 3

Overview

UNIT 7: ANALYZING TEXT STRUCTURE

Expository Nonfiction

"How to Make an Origami Cup"

This functional text is a set of step-by-step instructions for making a cup using the paper-folding art of origami.

"Ashton Hammerheads Schedule for July, 2008"

This sample of a functional text presents a schedule in a calendar format for a professional sports team.

"Frontier Fun Park" Ticket Prices

This sample of a functional text gives individual and family ticket prices for an amusement park.

ALTERNATIVE RESOURCES

As an alternative resource for these lessons, you might gather appropriately leveled functional texts such as advertisements, charts, graphs, recipes, or instructions. You can find functional texts in places such as newspapers, magazines, cookbooks, or on the Internet.

Comprehension Focus

- Students explore functional texts.

- Students identify what they learn from functional texts.

- Students explore how functional texts inform readers.

- Students read independently.

Social Development Focus

- Students take responsibility for their learning and behavior.

- Students listen respectfully to others' thinking.

DO AHEAD

- Prior to Day 1, prepare a sheet of chart paper with the title "Functional Texts."

- Collect a variety of functional texts for the students to examine and read on Day 3. (See the Teacher Note on page 354.)

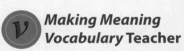

Making Meaning
Vocabulary Teacher

If you are teaching Developmental Studies Center's *Making Meaning Vocabulary* program, teach Vocabulary Week 17 this week. For more information, see the *Making Meaning Vocabulary Teacher's Manual.*

Day 1

Materials

- "How to Make an Origami Cup" (see page 357)
- "Ashton Hammerheads Schedule for July, 2008" (see page 358)
- "Functional Texts" chart, prepared ahead, and a marker
- *Student Response Book* pages 46–47
- "Self-monitoring Questions" chart
- Self-stick note for each student

Read-aloud

In this lesson, the students:

- Explore functional texts
- Identify what they learn from a functional text
- Read independently for up to 30 minutes
- Take responsibility for their learning and behavior

▶1 Get Ready to Work Together

Have partners sit together. Remind the students that in the last weeks they have been working on taking responsibility for themselves as they work in pairs and small groups. Ask and briefly discuss:

Q *What is one thing you like about working with a partner?*

Q *How can you be responsible as you work with others this week?*

Encourage the students to notice how they take responsibility for their behavior and learning.

▶2 Review Articles and Introduce Functional Texts

Review that so far this year, the students have heard and read different kinds of expository nonfiction. Review that in the last two weeks they read articles and thought about how articles can be organized to inform readers. Ask and briefly discuss:

Q *What did you find out about how authors can organize articles to inform readers?*

Explain that this week the students will explore another kind of expository nonfiction called functional texts. Explain that functional texts inform readers in a different way. They help readers do things in everyday life. Some examples of functional texts are street signs, labels, recipes, instructions, and schedules.

 Point out one or two functional texts in the classroom, and then have the students use "Turn to Your Partner" to discuss:

Q *What other functional texts do you see in our classroom?*

Have several volunteers point out the functional texts they noticed. As they share, record the functional texts they found in the classroom on the "Functional Texts" chart. Briefly discuss how each functional text is helpful.

> **Students might say:**
>
> "I see the class meeting rules. Having the rules posted reminds us to act on them."
>
> "The calendar for the cafeteria tells us what's for lunch. We can find out if we want to eat the school lunch on a certain day."
>
> "The map on our bulletin board let's us know how to leave the classroom if there is a fire."

Explain that later in the week the students will explore functional texts they find outside the classroom. Today and tomorrow they will look at several sample functional texts written to help them understand how functional texts are organized.

Teacher Note

If the students have difficulty answering the question, offer some suggestions like those in the "Students might say" note, and then ask the students what other examples of functional texts they see in the classroom.

▶3 Examine and Discuss "How to Make an Origami Cup"

Have the students turn to *Student Response Book* page 46. Read the title, "How to Make an Origami Cup," aloud and explain that these are directions for making a cup out of folded paper. Explain that a set of directions for making something is a type of functional text.

Ask the students to follow along as you read aloud the directions for making the cup, giving the students a moment to look at the diagram for each step before reading the next step.

Teacher Note

English Language Learners will benefit from previewing the functional texts before you read them aloud to the class. You might summarize the purpose of and information communicated by the functional text and point out and explain organizational features such as titles, diagrams, and legends.

Suggested Vocabulary

diagonal: an imaginary line connecting two opposite corners of a four-sided shape (p. 357)

 Give pairs a few moments to look over the directions together and have them discuss:

Q *What makes these directions easy to understand?*

Have volunteers share.

> *Students might say:*
>
> "The steps are numbered so you know what to do first."
>
> "The directions have pictures so you know how it's supposed to look as you're folding."
>
> "In addition to what [Carlos] said, there are arrows showing which way to fold the paper."

Point out that instructions often are organized into numbered steps and contain labeled diagrams to make them easy for readers to follow.

 4 ▶ Read and Discuss "Ashton Hammerheads Schedule for July, 2008"

Explain that the students will look at another kind of functional text. Have them turn to *Student Response Book* page 47. Read the title "Ashton Hammerheads Schedule for July, 2008" aloud and explain that this is a sample game schedule for a professional baseball team. Explain that schedules are often presented as calendars to help readers find the information they want quickly.

Call the students' attention to the legend, and explain that it shows the symbols for different game promotions. The legend also explains the color coding used for home and away games. Explain that legends are often found in functional texts because they give readers extra information without making the page too crowded.

Ask the students to follow along as you read aloud a few of the days from the calendar, referring to the legend as necessary.

Suggested Vocabulary

raffle: game where one person's ticket is picked randomly out of all the tickets and that person wins a prize (p. 358)

ELL Vocabulary

English Language Learners may benefit from discussing additional vocabulary, including:

fans: people who goes to see a team play (p. 358)
away game: game played away from the team's home city or home baseball park (p. 358)

When you are finished, give the students a few moments to reread the schedule quietly to themselves, and then briefly discuss, first in pairs, and then as a class:

Q *What information does this schedule give you?*

Q *What makes this schedule easy to use?*

Students might say:

"The title has the date in it so you know which month it's for."

"You can tell right away from the colors if it's a home or away game."

"The picture of the cap means that you might get a free hat if you go to that game."

"It says the time if the game is at a different time from usual."

Point out that the title, the legend, and the color-coding help make it easy for readers to understand the calendar.

5 Practice Using the Functional Text

Help the students explore how a reader might use the schedule by asking and briefly discussing as a class questions such as:

Q *If you want to go to a game in the afternoon and get a free t-shirt, which game could you go to? How do you know that?*

Q *Do the Hammerheads have more home or away games in July? How do you know that?*

Q *If you want a chance to win tickets to the League Championship, which game should you go to? How do you know that?*

Explain that because the game schedule and the instructions for the origami cup give different information, they are organized in different ways to help the reader make sense of them. The origami cup instructions are organized into numbered steps and include labeled diagrams to help readers make the cup more easily. The game schedule is organized as a calendar and includes a legend and color-coding to help readers find information quickly and make decisions about which game to go to. Tell the students that reading functional texts carefully and noticing how they are organized helps readers understand and use them more easily.

Teacher Note

If the students have difficulty coming up with ideas, offer some examples—maps, calendars, TV listings or channel guides, utility bills, driving directions, report cards, to-do lists, public transportation schedules, brochures, receipts, game directions, newspaper classifieds, food wrappers, tickets, sheet music, and business cards.

 6 ▶ Brainstorm and Prepare to Collect Functional Texts

Explain that later in the week, the students will bring functional texts to school and that they will have time to discuss them. Briefly review the "Functional Texts" chart and then have the students use "Think, Pair, Share" to think about and discuss:

Q *What other functional texts can you think of that you might find at home, in the newspaper, or in other places outside of school?*

After a few moments, have several volunteers share, and record their answers on the "Functional Texts" chart.

Teacher Note

Before Day 3, collect a variety of functional texts to make available for students who are unable to bring their own.

Ask the students to collect two or three functional texts at home or elsewhere outside of school and tell them when they will be expected to bring the functional texts to school. Remind them to ask permission to bring in functional texts that don't belong to them.

 ELL Note

Encourage your English Language Learners to collect functional texts in their native languages.

Explain that tomorrow the students will look at another functional text and talk about how it is organized to inform readers.

Save the "Functional Texts" chart for use during this week.

Reflect on Taking Responsibility

Ask and briefly discuss:

Q *What did you do to act in a responsible way when you worked with your partner today? Why is that important to do?*

INDIVIDUALIZED DAILY READING

 ## Practice Self-monitoring and Rereading

Refer to the "Self-monitoring Questions" chart and review the questions on it. Remind the students that they have been practicing checking their comprehension as they are reading.

Explain that one of the best techniques for helping them comprehend what they are reading is to go back and reread. Tell them that rereading a text helps them understand more deeply and helps clarify misunderstandings. Explain that today they will practice rereading expository nonfiction and articles at their appropriate reading levels, and share what they read in pairs.

Distribute a self-stick note to each student. Ask the students to place a self-stick note on the page where they will begin reading today. Have the students read independently for 10 minutes.

 Stop the students after 10 minutes and have them use "Turn to Your Partner" to have partners tell each other what they have learned in the part of the text that they just read.

After partners have shared for a few minutes, signal for the students' attention. Ask them to turn back to the page with the self-stick note and reread the part they just read.

 Stop the students after 10 minutes and have them use "Turn to Your Partner" to have partners tell each other about any new details they learned from the rereading.

> **Self-monitoring Questions**
>
> - What is happening in my story right now?
> - Does the reading make sense?

At the end of independent reading, have the students briefly share their experiences of how rereading helped them understand. Ask questions such as:

Q *What information did you learn when you reread that you missed during the first reading?*

Q *How might rereading help you understand expository nonfiction?*

Encourage the students to continue to reread texts, especially if the text is complicated and contains a lot of factual information.

EXTENSION

Make Origami Cups

Distribute an 8" x 8" paper square to each student. Have the students make origami cups using the instructions on *Student Response Book* page 46. Consider having them test their cups to see if the cups hold water. When the students have finished making their cups, facilitate a whole-class discussion using questions such as:

Q *Were the instructions easy to follow and understand?*

Q *If you had trouble making your cup, what was it about the instructions that made it challenging?*

Q *How could the author have made these instructions easier to use?*

How to Make an Origami Cup

Now you can learn to make a handy cup using only a sheet of paper!
Begin with a square piece of paper and follow the instructions below:

Step 1:

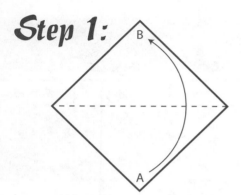

Fold your square on the diagonal,
matching up corners **A** and **B**.

Step 2:

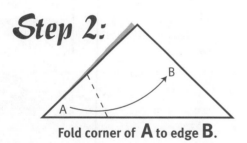

Fold corner of **A** to edge **B**.

Step 3:

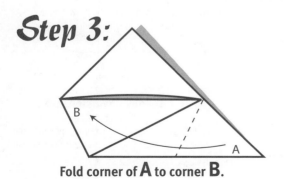

Fold corner of **A** to corner **B**.

Step 4:

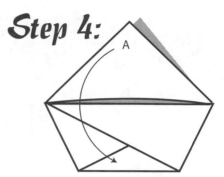

Take the top flap (flap **A**) and fold down
toward you. Turn the cup over and repeat
the step with the other remaining flap.

Step 5:

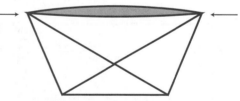

Gently push sides in to form your cup.
If you followed the instructions above, your cup
should look like this and be able to hold water.
Enjoy your cup!

Ashton Hammerheads Schedule
for July, 2008

Sunday	Monday	Tuesday	Wednesday	Thursday	Friday	Saturday
		1 vs Glen Hill @ Bank Park	2 vs Flourbell @ Fair Stad 12:30 p.m.	3	4 vs Ardmore	5 vs Plymouth 12:15 p.m.
6 vs Plymouth	7 vs Paulsboro	8 vs Paulsboro	9 vs Paulsboro 12:30 p.m.	10	11 vs Mt Holly @ Holly Stad 9:00 p.m.	12 vs Mt Holly @ Holly Stad
13 vs Mt Holly @ Holly Stad 3:00 p.m.	14 vs Beverley @ Bev Stad 9:00 p.m.	15 vs Beverley @ Bev Stad 9:00 p.m.	16 vs Springfield @ Spring Bank 1:30 p.m.	17	18 vs Bridgeport @ Broomall	19 vs Bridgeport @ Broomall 2:30 p.m.
20 vs Ridley Crew @ Broomall 1:30 p.m.	21	22 vs Wishton	23 vs Wishton	24 vs Oreland 12:15 p.m.	25 vs Oreland 9:00 p.m.	26 vs Chester
27 vs Chester 1:15 p.m.	28 vs Glenolden @ Wales Park	29 vs Paulsboro @ Wales Park 2:00 p.m.	30 vs Paulsboro @ Wales Park	31 vs Paulsboro @ Wales Park		

Hammerheads t-shirt day
(free t-shirt for first 1500 fans)

Hammerheads cap day
(free baseball cap for all fans under fifteen)

**League Championship
ticket raffle**
(all fans entered into a drawing for 4 free
tickets to the League Championship game)

☐ = Hammerheads Home Game   ▨ = Hammerheads Away Game

All games begin at 6:00 p.m. unless otherwise indicated.

Tickets $25

Day 2

Read-aloud

In this lesson, the students:

- Identify what they learn from a functional text
- Explore how functional texts inform readers
- Read independently for up to 30 minutes
- Take responsibility for their learning and behavior

1 ▶ Review Functional Texts

Refer to the "Functional Texts" chart and review that yesterday the students noticed functional texts in the classroom and brainstormed functional texts they might find outside the classroom. They also looked at two sample functional texts—instructions for making an origami cup and a baseball team schedule—and they thought about how functional texts give readers information.

Ask and briefly discuss:

Q *What helped make the information in the origami cup instructions easy to understand and use? The information in the baseball team schedule?*

Students might say:

"The instructions had steps to follow."

"The schedule was a calendar so you could find days right away."

"On the calendar, the days were different colors so you could tell the home games."

Explain that today the students will read another functional text and think about how it is organized to inform readers.

2 ▶ Introduce "Frontier Fun Park" Ticket Prices

Have the students turn to *Student Response Book* page 48 and explain that this is a sample of a ticket price list from an amusement

Materials

- "Frontier Fun Park" ticket prices (see page 364)
- "Functional Texts" chart from Day 1
- *Student Response Book* page 48
- Self-stick note for each student

◀ **Teacher Note**

If the students have difficulty recalling what they noticed, have them refer to the functional texts on pages 46–47 of the *Student Response Book*.

park. Point out that the list is divided into sections for single-day and one-week passes to Frontier Fun Park and that there are passes for individual people and for families. Give the students a moment to look over the price list. Ask and briefly discuss:

Q *How might this list help someone who is buying tickets?*

 3 Read Aloud and Discuss "Frontier Fun Park" Ticket Prices

Have the students follow along on *Student Response Book* page 48 as you read "Frontier Fun Park" ticket prices aloud.

Suggested Vocabulary

attractions: rides or other activities (p. 364)

consecutive: in a row (p. 364)

highest priority: most important thing (p. 364)

liable: legally responsible (p. 364)

ELL Vocabulary

English Language Learners may benefit from discussing additional vocabulary, including:

thrilling: exciting (p. 364)

discount on all purchases: lower price for everything you buy (p. 364)

 Briefly discuss, first in pairs, and then as a class:

Q *What information does this functional text give readers?*

Q *What makes it easy to use?*

Students might say:

"Each kind of pass has a name that tells what it is."

"It has a section for single-day passes and another part for 1-week passes."

"The adults and kids prices are in columns, so they are easy to read."

"The information about the roller coaster helps because if you are under 4 feet you shouldn't buy a Pine Mountain pass."

Point out that the names for the different kinds of tickets, the columns, the sections, and the text box help organize the information in this functional text so readers can understand and use it.

▶ 4 Use and Analyze the Functional Text

Help the students explore how a reader might use the ticket price list by asking and briefly discussing questions such as:

Q *How much would it cost for two adults who want to ride the Pine Mountain roller coaster to go to the Frontier Fun Park for one day if they don't have children with them? How do you know that?*

Q *One adult and three children want to go to the Frontier Fun Park for one day. The adult doesn't want to ride Pine Mountain, but the children do. How much will their tickets cost? How do you know that?*

Q *If a family of two adults and two children wants to go to the park for two days, is it better for them to get a 1-day Family Pass each day or to get a 1-week Family Pass? If they want to go to the park for three days? How do you know that?*

Students might say:

"The 1-day Pine Mountain Pass is $50. It's two of those, so $100."

"It will cost $160—$40 for the adult plus 3 x $40 for the kids."

"Even if the family is only going for three days, the 1-week Family Pass costs less than three 1-day Family Passes."

Facilitate a whole-class discussion about how the functional text informs readers using questions such as:

Q *How does this functional text help readers make decisions about which tickets to buy?*

Q *Do you think it includes enough information to help readers make decisions? Why or why not?*

◀ Teacher Note

If the students have difficulty answering the questions, have them work in pairs before discussing the answers as a class. Circulate and offer support as necessary.

FACILITATION TIP

Continue to focus on **responding neutrally** with interest during class discussions by refraining from overtly praising or criticizing the students' responses. Instead, build the students' intrinsic motivation by responding with genuine curiosity and interest, for example:

- *Interesting—say more about that.*

- *What you said makes me curious. I wonder…*

- *You have a point of view that's [similar to/different from] what [Janna] just said. How is it [similar/different]?*

Students might say:

"You can find out how much different kinds of tickets will cost."

"In addition to what [Margot] said, you can compare how much different kinds of tickets cost. Then you know which ones are the cheapest to buy."

"It helps readers make decisions because they know what is included with each ticket."

"I disagree with what [Roberto] said. It tells you what's included with different tickets, but you might not know if you're going to buy anything at the Frontier Cabin Outdoor Superstore. You don't know how much money you will save."

Review that in the last two days, the students read three sample functional texts and thought about how the texts are organized to give readers information. Point out that functional texts don't always answer all the questions readers have. Emphasize that it is important for readers to read functional texts carefully and ask themselves whether the texts include all the information they need.

Explain that tomorrow the students will share functional texts they collected from outside the classroom and discuss how they are organized to give readers information. Remind them to bring the functional texts they have collected to school.

INDIVIDUALIZED DAILY READING

 5 ▶ **Continue to Practice Self-monitoring and Rereading**

Remind the students that one of the best techniques for helping them comprehend complicated and factual text is to go back and reread. Explain that today the students will continue to practice rereading expository nonfiction and share what they read in pairs.

Distribute a self-stick note to each student. As they did in the previous lesson, have the students open to where they will start reading today, and ask them to place a self-stick note on that page. Explain that today the students will read for 15 minutes.

 Stop the students after 15 minutes and have them use "Turn to Your Partner" to talk in pairs about what they have learned in the part of the text that they just read.

After a few minutes, signal for their attention and ask them to turn back to the page with the self-stick note and reread the part they just read.

 Stop the students after 15 minutes and have them use "Turn to Your Partner" to talk in pairs about any new details they learned from the rereading.

At the end of independent reading, have the students share their experiences of how rereading helped them understand.

Remind the students to continue to reread texts if they are not understanding what they are reading or if the text is complicated and contains a lot of factual information.

FRONTIER FUN PARK

Home of the Legendary PINE MOUNTAIN

At 460 feet, Pine Mountain is the nation's highest roller coaster!
We think it's the world's greatest, most thrilling roller coaster ever!
You must be more than 4 feet tall to ride the Pine Mountain.

SINGLE-DAY PASSES

	Adults (Age 10+)	Children (Ages 3–9)
1-DAY BASIC PASS	$40.00	$30.00

Includes entry to all main attractions (does not include Pine Mountain roller coaster)

	Adults (Age 10+)	Children (Ages 3–9)
1-DAY PINE MOUNTAIN PASS	$50.00	$40.00

Includes entry to all main attractions, including Pine Mountain roller coaster

1-DAY PINE MOUNTAIN FAMILY PASS $140.00

(Up to 2 adults and 2 children aged 3–9)
Includes entry to all main attractions, including Pine Mountain roller coaster

1-DAY PINE MOUNTAIN PLUS FAMILY PASS $160.00

(Up to 2 adults and 2 children aged 3–9)
Includes entry to all main attractions, including Pine Mountain roller coaster, plus a 20% discount on all purchases from the Frontier Cabin Outdoor Superstore

ONE-WEEK PASSES

1-WEEK PINE MOUNTAIN FAMILY PASS $320.00

(Up to 2 adults and 2 children aged 3–9)
Includes entry to all main attractions, including Pine Mountain roller coaster, for 7 consecutive days

Disclaimer
The safety of our guests is Frontier Fun Park's highest priority. However, the Frontier Fun Park will not be liable for any injuries, damages, or losses that occur in connection with the Fun Park's activities.

Day 3

Guided Strategy Practice

In this lesson, the students:

- Share functional texts collected outside the classroom
- Identify what they learn from functional texts
- Explore how functional texts inform readers
- Read independently for up to 30 minutes
- Listen respectfully to others' thinking

Materials

- "Functional Texts" chart and a marker
- Variety of functional texts
- *Assessment Resource Book*
- "Self-monitoring Questions" chart

▶1 Review and Get Ready to Work Together

Review that so far this week the students have read three sample functional texts and thought about how the functional texts are organized to give readers information. Explain that today the students will share and discuss in small groups the functional texts they collected and continue to think about how functional texts are organized to help readers understand and use them.

Review that the students have been working on acting responsibly when they work in pairs and groups. Ask and briefly discuss:

Q *How did your group of four act responsibly when you worked together last week?*

Explain that today the students will work in the groups of four they worked with last week. Remind the students that it will be important to listen respectfully when other people share their functional texts with the group. Ask:

Q *What can you do to be respectful when others are sharing their functional texts?*

Have a few volunteers share their thinking. Explain that you will check in with the class later to see how they did.

> *Students might say:*
>
> "I can look at the person who is talking."
>
> "You can listen quietly and not interrupt."
>
> "I can pay attention to what they're saying in case I have questions about it."

2 Share and Discuss Functional Texts in Groups and as a Class

Teacher Note ▶

Distribute samples of functional texts that you have collected to any students who did not bring in their own.

Have the students sit with their groups of four. Give the students a few moments to silently examine the functional texts they collected, keeping the following questions in mind.

Q *What information does this functional text give you?*

Q *What makes the functional text easy for readers to understand and use?*

Q *What do you find most interesting about it?*

ELL Note

English Language Learners will benefit from telling you about what information is included in their functional text before they share in their groups. You might also consider providing prompts for them to use when they share (for example, "This functional text is called…," "It tells readers…," and "I think it is interesting because…").

Explain that each student will choose one functional text to share with her group. Explain that the person sharing will briefly explain what the functional text is, what information it includes, what makes it easy for readers to use, and what she finds most interesting about it. Encourage the students to ask each other questions after they share. Remind them to listen respectfully as others in the group share.

 Give the students several minutes to work in their groups.

CLASS COMPREHENSION ASSESSMENT

Circulate among the groups as they work. Randomly select students to observe and ask yourself:

Q *Are the students able to identify what they learn from functional texts?*

Q *Are the students able to identify how information in functional texts is organized to inform readers?*

Record your observations on page 21 of the *Assessment Resource Book*.

When most groups are finished, signal for the students' attention. Ask volunteers to share some examples of functional texts with the class. Add any new functional texts to the "Functional Texts" chart.

 Review the Week and Expository Text

Remind the students that functional texts are expository texts that give readers information and help them function in their everyday lives. Refer to the "Functional Texts" chart, and review that this week the students explored samples of functional texts in their *Student Response Books* and real-world functional texts from inside and outside the school. Review that reading functional texts carefully and thinking about how they are organized helps readers make sense of them. Encourage the students to continue to notice and think about functional texts in their everyday lives.

Explain that next week the students will hear and read an expository text that is similar to a school textbook and think about how it is organized to give readers information.

Reflect on Listening Respectfully to Others' Thinking

Ask and briefly discuss:

Q *How did it make you feel to have others in your group listen respectfully while you were sharing?*

Q *How did listening to others' thinking help you?*

INDIVIDUALIZED DAILY READING

 Review and Practice Self-monitoring with Expository Nonfiction

Refer to the "Self-monitoring Questions" chart and review the following questions:

- What is happening in my story right now?

- Does the reading make sense?

- What am I puzzled about?

- How many words on the page I just read are new to me?

- How many words don't I know?

- Would it be better to continue reading this book or get a new book?

Remind the students that they have been using the questions to help them track whether they are comprehending what they are reading. When they do not understand, they may need to reread, use a comprehension strategy, or get a different text.

Have the students read articles and other expository texts at their appropriate reading levels independently for 10 minutes. Stop them at the end of 10 minutes and have them monitor their comprehension by thinking about the questions on the chart. Ask and discuss the following questions:

Q *If you don't understand what you are reading, what might you do?*

Q *If you don't know more than five words on a page, what might you do?*

Students might say:

"If I don't understand what I am reading, I can reread and see if that helps."

"In addition to what [Nancy] said, if I still don't understand after I reread, I should get a new book that I can understand."

"If I can't read more than five words on a page, the book is probably too hard for me and I should get another book."

Have the students decide if they can understand what they are reading or if they should get a new book, and ask the students who need new books to each choose one. Have the students read independently for another 15 minutes.

At the end of the reading time, ask and briefly discuss:

Q *What will you do the next time you read independently if you do not understand what you are reading?*

EXTENSION

Create a Functional Texts Bulletin Board

Continue to have the students bring in examples of functional texts. Ask the students to share the texts with the class. Have them point out how their functional texts are organized to inform readers. Have each student glue his functional text to a large sheet of construction paper and label the features that help organize the information and make it easy to use. (For example, a menu might be labeled "The menu is divided into appetizers, entrees, and desserts" and "The spicy dishes are marked with a pepper.") Have the students hang their posters on a class bulletin board.

Day 4

Materials

- "Class Meeting Ground Rules" chart
- "Self-monitoring Questions" chart

---

*Class Meeting
Ground Rules*

- *one person talks
at a time*

- *listen to one another*

Class Meeting

In this lesson, the students:

- Have a class meeting to discuss working in groups of four
- Read independently for up to 30 minutes
- Take responsibility for their learning and behavior

▶1 Gather for a Class Meeting

Post the "Class Meeting Ground Rules" chart where everyone can see it. Explain that today the students will have a class meeting to check in on how they are doing building a reading community. Review the procedure for coming to a class meeting.

Have the students move to their places for the meeting, with partners sitting together, and ask them to make sure they can see their classmates.

▶2 Discuss the Challenges of Working in Groups of Four

Briefly review the class meeting ground rules. Explain that the purpose of this class meeting is to talk about working in groups of four.

Ask and discuss questions such as:

Q *What has gone well for you working in your group of four?*

Q *What has been challenging about working in a group of four?*

Q *[Ramón] said it's challenging to make sure everyone is included in the discussions. What might be challenging about including one another in your group discussions?*

Q *[May Chin] said that [she] finds it challenging to contribute ideas to the discussion. What might be challenging about contributing to the group work?*

Encourage the students to be honest while protecting everyone's feelings by not using names when discussing challenges. Use "Turn to Your Partner" as needed during this discussion to increase participation, especially if you are hearing from only a few students. You can also use "Turn to Your Partner" if many students want to speak at the same time.

If the students have difficulty answering these questions, stimulate their thinking with examples like those in the "Students might say" note and then repeat the questions.

> **Students might say:**
>
> "If one person speaks for a long time, the other kids in the group might not get a chance to share."
>
> "When one person is sharing, they might feel bad if the other people in the group aren't listening."
>
> "In addition to what [Martha] said, you might have a different idea than everyone else and feel shy about sharing."

3 ▶ Discuss Solutions

Have the students use "Think, Pair, Share" to think about and discuss:

Q *What are some ways you can try to make sure that everyone is included and that you contribute your own ideas during group work?*

Q *Why is it important for everyone in the group to share their thinking?*

> **Students might say:**
>
> "You can ask anyone who hasn't shared if they have anything to share."
>
> "If one person speaks for a long time, you can remind them that we want everyone to have time to share."
>
> "I agree with [Victor], and we can ask each other questions about what we are sharing. That way we'll feel more comfortable contributing ideas because we'll know that people are interested in what we have to say."
>
> "In addition to what [Janet] said, if you listen carefully to what other people share, you might get ideas about what you want to share."

Teacher Note

Remind the students to connect their comments to comments made by others by using the discussion prompts they learned in previous lessons:

- *I agree with _____ because…*
- *I disagree with _____ because…*
- *In addition to what _____ said, I think…*

Explain that you would like the students to use some of their suggestions the next time they work in groups of four. Remind them that you will be checking in with them to see how they are doing.

4 ▶ Reflect on the Ground Rules and Adjourn the Meeting

Briefly discuss how the students felt they did with following the ground rules during the class meeting. Review the procedure for returning to their desks, and adjourn the meeting.

INDIVIDUALIZED DAILY READING

5 ▶ Have the Students Practice Self-monitoring/ Document IDR Conferences

Continue to have the students monitor their comprehension. Remind them that it is important to stop to think about what they are reading and use the questions to help them track whether they are understanding their reading. When they do not understand what they are reading, they may need to reread, use a comprehension strategy, or get a different text.

Have the students read articles and other expository texts at their appropriate reading levels independently for up to 30 minutes.

Circulate among the students and ask individual students to read a passage to you, tell you what it is about, and tell you which questions they are using to help them monitor their comprehension. Use the "IDR Conference Notes" record sheet to conduct and document individual conferences.

At the end of the reading time, have a whole-class discussion about how the students used the self-monitoring questions to track their reading comprehension.

Self-monitoring Questions

- *What is happening in my story right now?*

- *Does the reading make sense?*

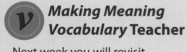

Making Meaning Vocabulary Teacher

Next week you will revisit this week's reading to teach Vocabulary Week 18.

Week 4

Overview

UNIT 7: ANALYZING TEXT STRUCTURE

Expository Nonfiction

Survival and Loss: Native American Boarding Schools*
(Developmental Studies Center, 2008)

In the late 1800s and early 1900s, the U.S. government forcibly educated Native American children at off-reservation boarding schools. This book briefly describes the origin of the schools and looks closely at the impact of school life on the children and on Native American culture at large.

* This book is also used in Week 5.

ALTERNATIVE BOOKS

The Great Depression by Elaine Landau

The Settling of Jamestown by Janet Riehecky

Comprehension Focus

• Students hear and discuss expository text.

• Students identify what they learn from expository text.

• Students read independently.

Social Development Focus

• Students develop the group skills of including one another, contributing to group work, and using prompts in small group discussions.

• Students explain their thinking.

DO AHEAD

• Prior to Day 1, make a transparency of the "Native American Land" maps (BLM27).

• Prior to Day 1, decide which of the students' social studies textbooks you would like them to read this week during IDR. If the textbooks are challenging for your students, plan to read the textbooks aloud with the students before having them read independently.

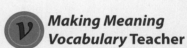

**Making Meaning
Vocabulary Teacher**

If you are teaching Developmental Studies Center's *Making Meaning Vocabulary* program, teach Vocabulary Week 18 this week. For more information, see the *Making Meaning Vocabulary Teacher's Manual.*

Day 1

Read-aloud

In this lesson, the students:

- Hear expository text read aloud
- Identify what they learn from expository text
- Read independently for up to 30 minutes
- Explain their thinking
- Use discussion prompts in small group discussions

About Reading Textbooks

The students spent the first three weeks of Unit 7 analyzing text structure to help them make sense of articles and functional texts, two kinds of expository nonfiction. The focus of the final two weeks of Unit 7 is on analyzing text structure in textbooks. The students hear and read a book written to resemble textbooks the students might read in school. This week the students hear the book read aloud and identify and discuss what they learn from the text. Next week the students analyze parts of the book in depth and explore several text structures commonly used to organize the information in textbooks: cause and effect, compare and contrast, and chronology. This week's and next week's lessons on exploring how expository texts are organized lay the foundation for work that the students will do in middle school and high school. Mastery of these concepts is not expected at this point. The goal, as with all the reading comprehension strategies, is for the students to be able to use the strategy to make sense of their independent reading.

 Discuss Reading Textbooks

Have pairs sit in their groups of four. Remind the students that they have been reading articles and functional texts and thinking about how expository nonfiction can inform readers. Explain that in the coming weeks the students will look at another kind of expository nonfiction—textbooks—and work in groups and as a class to explore how textbooks are written.

Materials

- *Survival and Loss* (pages 2–5)
- World map
- Transparency of "Native American Land" maps (BLM27)
- *Student Response Book* page 49
- (Optional) Wall map of the United States
- Textbooks for students to read during IDR
- Self-stick note for each student

Point out that textbooks are a kind of expository text that the students read often in school. Ask:

Q *What kinds of textbooks have you been reading this year?*

Q *What can be hard about reading textbooks?*

Explain that the students will hear a textbook read aloud and think about and discuss how textbooks can be organized to give readers information. They will use what they learn to help them make sense of their own textbooks. They will also have opportunities to explain their thinking in their groups and use discussion prompts in groups.

 Introduce *Survival and Loss*

Tell the students that the book you will read aloud over the next few days is titled *Survival and Loss: Native American Boarding Schools*. Show the cover and explain that this is a book written to be similar to textbooks the students read in school.

Explain that *Survival and Loss: Native American Boarding Schools* is about schools built in the late 1800s and early 1900s for children from Native American tribes. If necessary, explain that *Native American* is another word for *American Indian* and that a boarding school is a school where students live away from home.

To provide historical background, refer to a world map and explain that beginning in the 1400s, people from countries in Europe began traveling to North America by boat looking for new land and opportunity. As greater numbers of settlers came to North America, life became more and more difficult for Native Americans. Many Native Americans died from diseases the settlers brought from Europe and from the destruction of their way of life. Those who were left had less and less land to live on.

By the mid-1800s, all the Native American tribes in the United States had been forced to live on small areas of land called reservations, which were set aside by the U.S. government. Show the "Native American Land" maps (BLM27) on the overhead and point out the differences in the amount of land occupied by Native American tribes in 1775 and 1894. Explain that on the reservations the tribes didn't have enough land to support themselves. The boarding ▶

schools were built because the government thought that if Native American children were educated to fit in to the world outside the reservations, they could get better jobs and help support their tribes.

Note

Prior to each read-aloud lesson this week, show your English Language Learners the sections you will be reading. Point out the text features and summarize the information in the text, making sure your students have at least a surface-level understanding of the information.

3 ▶ **Introduce the Reading and Read the Introduction**

Show the table of contents of *Survival and Loss* and ask the students to turn to their own copy of it on *Student Response Book* page 49. Read the chapter titles and section headings aloud. Ask:

Q *What topics do you think you will hear about in this book?*

Have one or two volunteers share their thinking.

Explain that today the students will hear the Introduction and Chapter 1 of the book. Explain that you will stop periodically during the reading and have them discuss what they have learned from the book up to that point.

4 ▶ **Read Aloud with Brief Section Introductions**

Read the Introduction and Chapter 1 (pages 2–5) following the procedure described on the next page.

 ⋯⋯⋯⋯⋯

Suggested Vocabulary

fashioned: made (p. 2)

present-day Oklahoma: the area that is known today as the state of Oklahoma (p. 4)

geography: layout of the land (p. 4)

confrontations: fights (p. 4)

ELL Vocabulary

English Language Learners may benefit from discussing additional vocabulary, including:

had never learned the ways of civilization: did not think or act like people from Europe (p. 2)

citizens: people who live in a country and have legal rights and the protection of the government (p. 2)

tensions began to build: people started to get angry (p. 4)

game: animals hunted for food (p. 5)

Read the first two paragraphs of the Introduction aloud and then reread them, asking the students to listen for information they might have missed the first time. Ask and briefly discuss:

Q *What did you hear on the second reading that you missed the first time?*

Continue reading to the end of the Introduction. Point out and read the sidebar "Naming the Native Peoples" on page 2.

Read Chapter 1's title, "Broken Promises," and first section heading, "The Trail of Tears," aloud. Explain that the first section of Chapter 1 tells how East Coast Native American tribes were forced to leave their homelands and move west to make room for European settlers. Show the "Cherokee Removal Routes" map on page 4 and explain that one tribe, the Cherokee tribe, was moved from the area that is now Georgia to the area that is now Oklahoma.

Read "Trail of Tears" aloud, showing the photograph and reading the caption. Stop after:

> **p. 4** "This journey became known as the Trail of Tears."

Ask:

Q *What did you find out in the part you just heard?*

Have one or two students share what they found out. Then continue reading to the end of the section. Stop after:

> **p. 4** "…the population of white settlers grew."

Ask and briefly discuss:

Q *What was life like for the Eastern tribes in Oklahoma?*

Students might say:

"I think it was hard for them because the land in Oklahoma wasn't like the land they were used to."

"I agree with what [Skyler] said. The crops they were used to growing didn't grow on the land."

"In addition to what [Tina] said, it was hard because the U.S. government kept taking land away from the Native Americans when more settlers came."

◀ **Teacher Note**

This week's read-aloud contains a lot of factual information that the students might have difficulty following. To support the students, you will briefly introduce each section before you read it. This will help to focus the students' listening on the main ideas discussed in that section.

Teacher Note ▶

You may want to point out the Plains states on a wall map of the United States (Colorado, Iowa, Kansas, Minnesota, Montana, Nebraska, New Mexico, North Dakota, Oklahoma, South Dakota, Texas, Wyoming) and indicate roughly where the tribes mentioned in the text lived. The Arapaho lived in parts of Colorado, Kansas, Nebraska, and Wyoming. The Cheyenne lived in parts of North and South Dakota, Wyoming, Nebraska, Colorado, and Kansas. The Crow lived in Montana and Wyoming. The Sioux lived in the Dakotas, Minnesota, Nebraska, and Wyoming.

Teacher Note

If necessary, review the following discussion prompts:

* *I agree with _____, because…*
* *I disagree with _____, because…*
* *In addition to what _____ said, I think…*

Tell the students that the next section, "The Reservations," discusses how the U.S. government tried to prevent conflict between Western, or Plains, Native American tribes and the European settlers who were moving west onto their land.

Read "The Reservations" aloud, showing the photograph and reading the caption. Ask:

Q *What happened to the Plains tribes as the settlers moved west?*

Have a few volunteers share what they found out.

5 ▶ **Discuss the Reading**

Explain that you will reread from part of the first chapter of the book and will have the students use "Heads Together" to discuss their thinking in groups. Reread from "The Trail of Tears," beginning on page 3 with "In 1836, the U.S. government tried to resolve its 'Indian problem'…" and stopping after "This journey became known as the Trail of Tears."

 Have the groups use "Heads Together" to discuss the following question. Encourage the students to use the discussion prompts during their conversation and remind them to refer to the information in the reading to support their thinking.

Q *Why do you think it is called the Trail of Tears? Explain your thinking.*

When most groups are finished, signal for attention and have a few volunteers share with the class. Be ready to refer to the text to help the students support their thinking.

> ***Students might say:***
>
> "I think it's called the Trail of Tears because so many people died on the journey."
>
> "I agree with [Sadie] because it says in the book that 4,000 people died."
>
> "In addition to what [Sterling] said, I think it was called the Trail of Tears because the Native Americans were sad to leave their land."

Use the same procedure to have the students discuss the following question. Again, encourage them to use discussion prompts to respond to one another, both in their small group discussions and in the whole-class discussion.

Q *Do you think the Eastern and Plains Native American tribes were treated fairly by the U.S. government? Explain your thinking.*

Students might say:

"I don't think the tribes were treated fairly. The government gave them land and then took it away."

"I agree with what [Carlos] said. The book says the reservations kept getting smaller."

"I disagree with [Janet] because I think the government had to make room for the settlers and the Native Americans didn't want to cooperate."

Explain that tomorrow the students will hear and discuss the next two chapters of the book.

6 ▶ Reflect on Group Work

Ask and briefly discuss:

Q *How did you do with explaining your thinking in your group?*

Q *How did the discussion prompts help you participate in your group discussion?*

INDIVIDUALIZED DAILY READING

7 ▶ Practice Self-monitoring and Rereading Textbooks

Tell the students that for the next two weeks they will read their social studies textbook during IDR. Explain that they will focus on how they are making sense of the information in the textbook.

Remind the students that they have been practicing checking their comprehension as they are reading. Review with the students that one of the best techniques for helping them comprehend what they are reading is to go back and reread. Explain that this is especially true when they are reading textbooks. Tell them that rereading a textbook helps them understand more deeply and clarify misunderstandings. Explain that today they will practice rereading their social studies textbook and share what they read in pairs.

Distribute a self-stick note to each student. Ask the students to open their textbooks to a chapter that looks interesting to them and to place a self-stick note on that page. Have the students read independently for 10 minutes.

 Stop them after 10 minutes and have them use "Turn to Your Partner" to talk in pairs what they have learned in the part of the text that they just read.

After a few minutes, signal for the students' attention. Ask them to turn back to the page with the self-stick note and reread the part they just read.

 Stop the students after 10 minutes and use "Turn to Your Partner" to have partners tell each other about any new details they learned from the rereading.

At the end of independent reading, have the students share with the class their experiences of how rereading helped them understand. Briefly discuss questions such as:

Q *What information did you learn when you reread that you had missed during the first reading?*

Q *How might rereading help you understand textbooks and other expository nonfiction?*

EXTENSION

Research the Trail of Tears

Interested students may want to do further research on the Trail of Tears. You can find information on many websites, including www.nps.gov, www.pbs.org, and www.nationaltota.org. The students also can search elsewhere on the Internet using keywords such as "Trail of Tears" and "Indian Removal Act."

Day 2

Read-aloud

In this lesson, the students:

- Hear expository text read aloud
- Identify what they learn from expository text
- Read independently for up to 30 minutes
- Include others in group work
- Use discussion prompts in small group discussions

Materials

- *Survival and Loss* (pages 6–13)
- Textbooks for students to read during IDR
- "Reading Comprehension Strategies" chart
- (Optional) Wall map of the United States

▶1 Review and Introduce the Reading

Have groups sit together. Show the cover of *Survival and Loss: Native American Boarding Schools* and review that the part of the book the students heard yesterday told how life changed for Native Americans as more and more European settlers came to the United States. Ask and briefly discuss:

Q *What have you found out so far about how the U.S. government treated Native Americans in the 1800s?*

Explain that the part of the book the students will hear today talks about how Native Americans continued to lose land to the settlers and about what life was like on the reservations. Explain that you will stop periodically during the reading and have them discuss what they have learned from the book up to that point.

▶2 Read Aloud with Brief Section Introductions

Read Chapters 2 and 3 (pages 6–13) as described on the next page.

Suggested Vocabulary

treaty: agreement (p. 6)

sacred: religious (p. 6)

bison: buffalo (p. 9)

self-sufficient: able to support themselves (p. 9)

fast: not eat food (p. 10)

Americanize Native American children: make Native American children more like European Americans (p. 12)

defenseless: not able to defend themselves (p. 13)

ELL Vocabulary

English Language Learners may benefit from discussing additional vocabulary, including:

settlements: places where people live (p. 6)

nearing completion: almost finished (p. 6)

protest the broken treaty: complain about the government not doing what it agreed to (p. 7)

admitted defeat: said that they lost (p. 7)

distributed rations of food: handed out certain amounts of food (p. 8)

ceremonies: special ways of celebrating important times (p. 10)

lodges: small houses made out of wood poles covered with animal skins (p. 10)

scarce: hard to find (p. 10)

reluctantly: even though he didn't want to (p. 13)

Teacher Note

You may want to show the transcontinental railroad route on a wall map of the United States. Explain that the railroad was built starting from Omaha, Nebraska, in the Plains and from Sacramento, California, in the West and that the railroad was completed when the tracks met in Promontory, Utah, which is north and slightly east of Salt Lake City. Point out New York City and San Francisco on the map, and explain that the railroad ultimately connected the East and West coasts.

Teacher Note

You may want to show the area covered by the Treaty of Fort Laramie on a wall map of the United States. The territory included the western half of South Dakota and adjacent parts of North Dakota, Wyoming, and Nebraska.

Read the Chapter 2 title, "Lost Land, Lost Independence," and the first section heading, "Coast to Coast," aloud. Explain that the first section of Chapter 2 tells how the building of the transcontinental, or cross-country, railroad caused Native American tribes to lose land. Ask the students to listen for how the building of the railroad caused Native Americans to lose land.

Read "Coast to Coast" aloud, showing the photograph and reading the caption on page 6. Ask:

Q *Why did the building of the railroad cause Native Americans to lose land?*

Have one or two volunteers share their thinking.

Tell the students that the next section, "Chief Red Cloud and the Treaty of Fort Laramie," talks about how the U.S. government took back land it had promised to the Sioux tribe.

Read "Chief Red Cloud and the Treaty of Fort Laramie" aloud, showing the photograph and reading the caption. Ask:

Q *What did you find out in the part you just heard?*

Have a couple of students share what they found out.

Read the next section heading, "Wards of the State," aloud and explain that this section talks about what happened when the U.S. government decided to take over the reservations. Read "Wards of the State" aloud. Ask:

Q *What did it mean for Native Americans to become wards of the state?*

Have volunteers share their thinking.

Read the Chapter 3 title, "Life on the Reservations," and the first section heading, "Lost Traditions," aloud. Explain that the first section of Chapter 3 tells more about life on the reservations. Read "Lost Traditions" aloud, including the quote by Geronimo. Ask:

Q *How were the Native Americans' traditional ways of life different from life on the reservations?*

Have one or two volunteers share their thinking.

Tell the students that the next two sections, "Pushed Toward the Classroom" and "The Boarding School Solution" talk about how Native American children were pushed further and further away from their traditional ways of being educated. Read "Pushed Toward the Classroom" and "The Boarding School Solution" aloud, stopping to show the photographs and read the caption and quotes. Then have the students use "Heads Together" to discuss:

Q *What did you find out in the sections you just heard about how education changed for Native American children?*

Have a few volunteers share what they found out.

Teacher Note

As groups talk, listen for evidence that the students are discussing the book and understanding it. If necessary, reread parts of the text to help the students recall what they heard.

Students might say:

"Before they lived on the reservations, Native American children learned just by watching the grownups and playing games."

"I found out that the U.S. government built schools on the reservations but the children didn't stay in school."

"Captain Pratt thought that Native American children should be taken away from their tribes and be sent to boarding schools."

"I found out that the U.S. government gave Captain Pratt an old army fort so he could build a school."

"In addition to what [Meredith] said, Captain Pratt convinced Spotted Tail to send the children from his tribe to Captain Pratt's school."

3 **Discuss the Reading**

Explain that you will reread from the section from Chapter 2 about Chief Red Cloud and the students will discuss what they heard, in groups and as a class. Reread from "Chief Red Cloud and the Treaty of Fort Laramie," beginning on page 7 with "When Red Cloud traveled to Washington, D.C., to protest the broken treaty…" and stopping after "…Red Cloud realized that Native Americans could never win a full-scale war against the settlers."

 Have the students use "Heads Together" to discuss the following question. Remind them to include everyone in the discussion and to refer to information in the text to support their thinking.

Q *Why do you think Red Cloud changed his mind about fighting the settlers?*

When most groups are finished, have volunteers share with the class. Be ready to reread sections of the text to help the students support their thinking. Encourage the students to use discussion prompts to respond to one another.

Students might say:

"I think when he saw how many settlers there were in the East, he realized he didn't have enough soldiers to fight them."

"In addition to what [Jonathan] said, I think Chief Red Cloud thought the Native Americans could never win because the Europeans had the power to build big cities."

"I disagree with what [Yuan] said. I think he changed his mind because when he found out the U.S. government lied, he realized Native Americans would never be treated fairly."

FACILITATION TIP

Continue to build the students' intrinsic motivation during class discussions by **responding neutrally** with genuine curiosity and interest rather than with praise or criticism, for example:

- *Interesting—say more about that.*

- *What you said makes me curious. I wonder…*

- *You have a point of view that's [similar to/different from] what [Jackson] just said. How is it [similar/different]?*

Explain that tomorrow the students will hear and discuss the next part of the book.

4 Reflect on Group Work

Ask and briefly discuss:

Q *What did your group do to make sure everyone was included?*

Q *If everyone wasn't included, what do you want to do differently next time so everyone can participate?*

Q *Why is it important to include everyone when you are working in groups?*

INDIVIDUALIZED DAILY READING

5 Use Comprehension Strategies to Read Textbooks

Explain to the students that in addition to rereading to help them understand a text, using the reading comprehension strategies they have been learning this year will also help them make sense of it. Explain that today the students will continue to read their social studies textbook and check to see which comprehension strategy they are using to help them understand what they are reading.

Direct the students' attention to the "Reading Comprehension Strategies" chart, review each strategy with the students, and remind them that these are the strategies they have learned so far this year. Ask them to notice which strategies they use and where they use them during their reading today. At the end of IDR, they will share with their group.

Have the students read their social studies textbook independently for up to 30 minutes.

At the end of independent reading, have each student share her reading and a strategy she used—the name of the strategy and where she used it—in her group of four. Have students who cannot think of a comprehension strategy they used discuss what they read.

> *Reading Comprehension Strategies*
>
> - *recognizing text features*

Signal for the students' attention. As a whole class, discuss questions such as:

Q *How did making inferences about [the causes of the Civil War] help you make sense of the text?*

Q *[Jackie] said [she] was able to visualize [the hardships and oppression slaves felt prior to the Emancipation Act]. How did visualizing help you make sense of the text?*

Q *What questions do you have for [Marion] about [his] thinking?*

EXTENSIONS

Research Native American Chiefs

Interested students may want to do further research on Chief Red Cloud or another Native American chief, such as Sitting Bull, Crazy Horse, Seattle, or Geronimo.

For Chief Red Cloud, you can find information on websites such as www.sagehistory.net/gildedage/documents/RedCloud.htm and www.pbs.org.

For Chief Sitting Bull, you can find information on websites such as www.pbs.org and www.biographi.ca.

The students can also search elsewhere on the Internet using the chiefs' names as keywords.

Explore and Discuss Expository Text Features

Show and read the expository text features in Chapters 2 and 3, reading any text aloud. Show the picture of Chief Spotted Tail and his wife on page 13. Ask and discuss:

Q *How do you think Chief Spotted Tail and his wife felt about sending their children and all the other children of the tribe to Carlisle School?*

Day 3

Read-aloud

In this lesson, the students:

- Hear expository text read aloud
- Identify what they learn from expository text
- Read independently for up to 30 minutes
- Contribute to group work
- Include one another during group work

▶1 Review and Get Ready to Work Together

Have groups sit together. Show the cover of *Survival and Loss: Native American Boarding Schools* and review that the part of the book the students heard yesterday told how the United States government took over the reservations, how life on a reservation was different from Native American tribes' traditional ways of life, and how education began to change for Native American children. Ask and briefly discuss:

Q *What do you remember finding out in the part of the book you heard yesterday?*

▶2 Introduce the Reading and Read Aloud with Brief Section Introductions

Explain that the part of the book the students will hear today talks about what life was like for Native American children who were sent to the boarding schools. Explain that you will stop periodically during the reading and have them discuss what they have learned from the book up to that point.

Read Chapters 4 and 5 (pages 14–21) as described on the next page.

Materials

- *Survival and Loss* (pages 14–21)
- Textbooks for students to read during IDR
- *Student Response Book,* IDR Journal section
- (Optional) Wall map of the United States

ELL

Suggested Vocabulary

wailed: cried (p. 14)

immersed: surrounded (p. 14)

dormitories: school buildings where many students live together (p. 16)

deliberately: on purpose (p. 17)

tom-toms: Native American drums (p. 17)

cash economy: system in which people use money to buy things (p. 21)

ELL Vocabulary

English Language Learners may benefit from discussing additional vocabulary, including:

program: plan (p. 14)

anxious: nervous (p. 14)

in such close quarters: so close together (p. 16)

immunity: ability to fight off diseases (p. 16)

for their own good: because it would be better for them (p. 18)

Read the Chapter 4 title, "Boarding School Life," and the first two section headings, "The Journey" and "'Before' and 'After,'" aloud. Explain that these sections tell about what it was like for Native American children to travel to the Carlisle School and what happened when the children arrived there.

Read "The Journey" and "'Before' and 'After'" aloud. Ask and briefly discuss:

Q *How do you think the children felt when they arrived at school? What did you hear that makes you think that?*

Have one or two volunteers share their thinking.

Tell the students that the next two sections, "New Names" and "Unfamiliar Routines," talk about what life was like for students at Carlisle and many of the other boarding schools.

Read "New Names" and "Unfamiliar Routines" aloud, including the sidebar titled "What's in a Name?" on page 16. Show the photographs on page 15 and read the caption; then ask:

Q *What made it difficult for Native American children to live at the boarding schools?*

Teacher Note ▶

You may want to point out the location of the Carlisle School on a wall map of the United States. The school was in Carlisle, Pennsylvania, west and slightly south of Harrisburg, the state capital.

Teacher Note ▶

Show the photographs and read any captions, sidebars, and quotes as you come to them during today's read-aloud.

Have a couple of students share their thoughts.

> **Students might say:**
>
> "They weren't even allowed to speak their own language."
>
> "In addition to what [Crane] said, I think it was difficult because they got English names that didn't mean anything to them."
>
> "I think it was difficult because the food they ate made them sick."
>
> "In addition to what [Winston] said, the children got sick because the dormitories were crowded and they weren't immune to a lot of diseases."

Read the next two section headings, "Runaways" and "Keeping Culture Alive," aloud. Explain that these sections talk about students who tried to escape from the boarding schools and students who stayed at school but tried to hold on to their traditional ways of life.

Read "Runaways" and "Keeping Culture Alive" aloud. Ask:

Q *What did you find out in the sections you just heard?*

Have volunteers share what they found out.

Read the Chapter 5 title, "Lessons and Learning," and the section headings "Entering a Strange World" and "New Skills" aloud. Explain that Chapter 5 tells more about how Native American children were taught at the schools and which subjects they learned. Read Chapter 5 aloud and then have the students use "Heads Together" to discuss:

Q *What did you find out about what Native American children learned at the boarding schools?*

Have one or two volunteers share what they discussed in their groups.

3 ▶ Discuss the Reading

Have the students use "Heads Together" to discuss the following question. Encourage the students to include one another and contribute ideas during the group discussion. Ask:

Q *Why do you think some children ran away from the schools? What did you hear that makes you think that?*

Teacher Note

Circulate as groups work. Support students who are having difficulty answering the question by rereading passages from Chapters 4 and 5 aloud and having the students listen for information about what life was like for Native American children at the schools. Ask questions such as:

Q *In the part you just heard, what did you find out about what life was like for the Native American children?*

Q *Do you think [having their names changed] made the students want to run away? Why do you think that?*

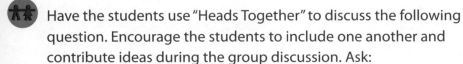

When most groups are finished, signal for attention. Have a few volunteers share their thinking. Remind the students to use discussion prompts to respond to one another.

Facilitate a discussion about Chapter 5, using the following question. Encourage the students to continue to include one another and contribute ideas to the discussion. Ask:

Q *Do you think what the children learned at the schools helped them? Explain your thinking.*

As students respond, encourage them to refer to the text to support their thinking. Be ready to reread from the text to help them.

> ***Students might say:***
>
> "I don't think it helped them because they spent so much time learning how to farm, but the land on the reservations wasn't good for farming."
>
> "I disagree with what [Clara] said. I think if they learned about farming, they could leave the reservation when they grow up and farm somewhere else."
>
> "In addition to what [Kenji] said, I don't think the teachers could help the children learn very well because the teachers didn't speak Native American languages."
>
> "I agree with what [Piper] said. I don't think what the children learned made sense to them."

Explain that tomorrow the students will hear and discuss the last two chapters of the book.

▶4 Reflect on Group Work

Review that today the students focused on contributing their thinking during group work. Ask and briefly discuss:

Q *What did you do to make sure everyone in your group felt comfortable sharing their thinking?*

Q *Why is it important to contribute your thinking to the group discussion?*

INDIVIDUALIZED DAILY READING

 Read Textbooks/Record Facts in Their IDR Journals

Remind the students they have been reading their social studies textbook and monitoring what they are learning. Explain that today the students will continue to read their social studies textbook independently, and then they will record several pieces of information they have learned.

Have the students read their social studies textbook for up to 30 minutes.

At the end of IDR, have the students write in their IDR Journals about what they read. Ask the students to write the title of the chapter they read and five or six things they learned from their reading.

After sufficient time, signal for the students' attention and briefly discuss questions such as:

Q *What did you read today?*

Q *What information did you learn from your reading?*

Q *What inferences did you make about [Reconstruction after the Civil War]?*

Q *What questions do you have for [Bonnie] about [her] thinking?*

EXTENSION

Explore and Discuss Expository Text Features

Show the text features in Chapters 4 and 5, reading any text aloud. Draw the students' attention to the "before" and "after" pictures on page 15. Ask and discuss questions such as:

Q *Why do you think Captain Pratt took these pictures of students when they arrived at Carlisle School?*

Q *What might someone looking at the pictures think about the school?*

Day 4

Materials

- *Survival and Loss* (pages 22–26)
- Textbooks for students to read during IDR
- *Assessment Resource Book*

Read-aloud

In this lesson, the students:

- Hear expository text read aloud
- Identify what they learn from expository text
- Read independently for up to 30 minutes
- Contribute to group work
- Explain their thinking

▶ 1 Review and Introduce the Reading

Have groups sit together. Show the cover of *Survival and Loss: Native American Boarding Schools* and review that the part of the book the students heard yesterday described life at the boarding schools. Ask and briefly discuss:

Q *What do you remember finding out in the part of the book you heard yesterday?*

Explain that the part of the book the students will hear today tells what happened to the Native American boarding schools and discusses the effect the schools had on the students and on Native American culture. Explain that you will stop periodically during the reading and have the students discuss what they have learned from the book up to that point.

▶ 2 Read Aloud with Brief Section Introductions

Read Chapters 6 and 7 (pages 22–26), stopping as described on the next page.

Suggested Vocabulary

suppress Native American ways: stop Native Americans from living as they did in their tribes (p. 24)

humiliated: ashamed (p. 25)

ELL Vocabulary

English Language Learners may benefit from discussing additional vocabulary, including:

its Native American policies had failed: the government's plans to make Native Americans more like European Americans did not work (p. 22)

experts: people who are known for being good at what they do (p. 22)

nutrients: things in food that make the food healthy (p. 22)

damaged: hurt (p. 24)

faced prejudice: were treated unfairly because of their race (p. 24)

had lost the ability to communicate altogether: did not know how to talk anymore (p. 24)

final blow: the last and worst thing that happened (p. 25)

exclude them: keep them out (p. 26)

Read the Chapter 6 title, "Boarding Schools in Question," and the first two section headings, "A Good Investment?" and "The Meriam Report," aloud. Explain that these sections tell about why the United States government began to think the boarding schools weren't a good idea. Have the students listen for information about problems at the schools.

Read "A Good Investment?" and "The Meriam Report" aloud. Ask:

Q *What were some of the problems at the boarding schools?*

Have a few volunteers share.

Tell the students that the next section, "Closed for Good," talks about the closing of the schools in the early 1900s.

Read "Closed for Good" aloud, showing the photograph and reading the caption on page 23. Ask:

Q *What did you find out about the closing of the schools?*

Have a couple of students share what they found out.

Read the Chapter 7 title, "Long-term Effects," and the first section heading, "Effects on the Students," aloud. Explain that this section talks about what happened to children who went to the boarding schools. Read "Effects on the Students" aloud. Ask and briefly discuss:

Q *What did you find out about the effects of the schools on the students?*

Have one or two students share their thoughts.

Read the next two section headings, "Effects on Native American Culture as a Whole" and "Hope for the Future," aloud and explain that these sections talk about what effect the boarding schools had on all Native Americans and how Native Americans have tried to regain their rights.

Read "Effects on Native American Culture as a Whole" and "Hope for the Future" aloud, including the sidebar text on page 26. Ask:

Q *What did you find out in the sections you just heard?*

Have volunteers share what they found out.

3 ▶ Discuss the Reading

Review that Captain Pratt and the U.S. government got the idea for educating Native American children at boarding schools because they thought it was important for the children to be "Americanized." Have the students use "Heads Together" to discuss the following question. Remind them to explain their thinking.

Q *Why did Captain Pratt and the U.S. government want Native American children to be Americanized? Explain your thinking.*

Teacher Note

If necessary, briefly discuss the meaning of "Americanize."

Teacher Note

If the students have trouble answering the question, call for their attention and have a couple of volunteers share what their groups have talked about so far, or suggest ideas such as those in the "Students might say" section. Then have groups continue working.

CLASS COMPREHENSION ASSESSMENT

Circulate among the groups as they work. Randomly select groups to observe and ask yourself:

Q *Are the students able to identify what they've learned from the book?*

Q *Are they able to explain their thinking during small group discussions?*

Record your observations on page 22 of the *Assessment Resource Book.*

Students might say:

"Captain Pratt thought it would be good for Native American children to live in the English-speaking world. He thought if they were away from their tribes, they would be more like European Americans."

"In addition to what [Charmaine] said, I think the government wanted to help Native American children fit into society more so the children could grow up and help support their tribes. They taught subjects like English and farming so the students would be able to make a living."

"I disagree with what [Chantel] said. I think a lot of people thought the Native Americans were savages and their way of life was not as good as the American way of life. So the U.S. government tried to wipe out Native American ways of life by Americanizing the kids."

"I think the government wanted the Native Americans to be Americanized so they wouldn't get in the way of all the settlers. I think that because there were so many problems with Native Americans attacking settlers and fighting over the land."

"In addition to what [Beto] said, I think the government wanted Native American tribes to take care of themselves so it wouldn't have to support them. I think that because the government had to give people on the reservations food and money in order for them to survive."

When most groups are finished, signal for attention. Have volunteers share their thinking with the class.

Facilitate a brief discussion using the following question. Encourage the students to use the discussion prompts they have learned as they participate in the discussion. Ask:

Q *What do you think of the idea of trying to Americanize Native American children at the boarding schools? Explain your thinking.*

As students respond, encourage them to refer to the text to support their thinking. Be ready to reread from the text to help them.

> ***Students might say:***
>
> "I don't think it was a good idea because the children didn't want to go to the schools, I don't think it was fair to make them go. I think that because so many of them ran away and others didn't cooperate at the schools."
>
> "In addition to what [Cameron] said, I don't think it was a good idea because the children had everything taken away from them. They didn't even get to keep their names."
>
> "I agree with what [Thanh] said. The children at the schools weren't happy or healthy and when they went back to their tribes they didn't fit in."
>
> "I disagree with what [Carmen] said. I think it was a good idea because the government was trying to help Native Americans fit in so they could take care of themselves."

Explain that next week the students will hear and read parts of the book again and explore how the text is organized to give readers information.

 ## Reflect on Group Work

Share your observations of how the students did with explaining their thinking in their groups and in the class discussion. Explain that the students will have more opportunities to explain their thinking in the coming weeks.

INDIVIDUALIZED DAILY READING

 5 ▶ **Have the Students Practice Self-monitoring/ Document IDR Conferences**

Continue to have the students read their textbooks and monitor their comprehension. Remind the students that it is important to stop to think about what they are reading. When they do not understand what they are reading, they may need to reread the textbook to help them make sense of it. In addition, encourage them to continue to use the reading comprehension strategies they have learned so far this year to help them make sense of the text.

Have the students read their textbooks independently for up to 30 minutes.

Circulate among the students and ask individuals to read a passage to you and tell you what it is about. If a student is confused by any part of the textbook, have him reread that section. If several students are struggling, read the section aloud to the whole class and briefly discuss what they have learned.

Use the "IDR Conference Notes" record sheet to conduct and document individual conferences.

At the end of the reading time, have a whole-class discussion about what the students learned from the textbook.

EXTENSIONS

Explore and Discuss Expository Text Features

Point out the "Native American Land" maps on pages 24–25 and show them on the overhead (BLM27). Read the legends of both maps aloud. Review that maps are a text feature often found in expository nonfiction. Ask and discuss questions such as:

Q *Looking at the maps, what statements can you make about Native American land? How do you know that?*

Q *How do these maps give readers information?*

Read and Discuss the Appendices in *Survival and Loss: Native American Boarding Schools*

Show and read the appendices "The Word 'No'" (page 27) and "Major Events in Native American History" (page 28). Then show the Glossary (page 29) and Index (page 30) in the back of *Survival and Loss: Native American Boarding Schools.* Discuss the function of each section by asking questions such as:

Q *How do you think the [passage written by Zitkala-Sa] might help a reader make sense of this book?*

Q *What do you notice about the ["Major Events in Native American History" timeline]? How might a reader use it?*

Q *What information does the [Glossary] provide? How is that helpful to a reader?*

Q *How do you think the [Index] might help a reader?*

Making Meaning Vocabulary Teacher

Next week you will revisit this week's reading to teach Vocabulary Week 19.

Week 5

Overview

UNIT 7: ANALYZING TEXT STRUCTURE

Expository Nonfiction

Survival and Loss: Native American Boarding Schools*
(Developmental Studies Center, 2008)

In the late 1800s and early 1900s, the U.S. government forcibly educated Native American children at off-reservation boarding schools. This book briefly describes the origin of the schools and looks closely at the impact of school life on the children and on Native American culture at large.

* This book was also used in Week 4.

ALTERNATIVE BOOKS

The Great Depression by Elaine Landau

The Settling of Jamestown by Janet Riehecky

Comprehension Focus

- Students *use text structure* to explore expository text.

- Students explore how information is organized in textbooks.

- Students explore text structures such as cause and effect, chronological, and compare and contrast relationships in expository text.

- Students read independently.

Social Development Focus

- Students take responsibility for their own learning during group work.

DO AHEAD

- Prior to Day 1, prepare a sheet of chart paper with the title "Relationships in Expository Text." See Step 2 on page 406.

- Prior to Day 1, decide which of the students' social studies textbooks you would like them to read this week during IDR. If the textbooks are challenging for your students, plan to read the textbooks aloud with the students before having them read the textbooks independently.

- Prior to Day 2, choose a passage from the students' social studies textbook for the class to read during IDR.

- Make copies of the Unit 7 Parent Letter (BLM16) to send home with the students on the last day of the unit.

Making Meaning
Vocabulary Teacher

If you are teaching Developmental Studies Center's *Making Meaning Vocabulary* program, teach Vocabulary Week 19 this week. For more information, see the *Making Meaning Vocabulary Teacher's Manual.*

Day 1

Materials

- *Survival and Loss*
- *Student Response Book* pages 49–51
- "Relationships in Expository Text" chart and a marker
- Social studies textbook for each student to read during IDR
- *Student Response Book,* IDR Journal section

Strategy Lesson

In this lesson, the students:

- *Use text structure* to explore expository text
- Explore how information can be organized in expository text
- Explore chronological relationships in expository text
- Read independently for up to 30 minutes
- Take responsibility for their own learning during group work

▶1 Review *Survival and Loss*

Have pairs sit in their groups of four. Explain that for the last several weeks the students have been working on how to be responsible group members. They have been making an effort to include everyone in their group discussions, using discussion prompts, and contributing their thinking and ideas to their small group discussions. Ask the students to continue to take responsibility for their learning during their small group discussions this week.

Remind the students that last week they heard *Survival and Loss: Native American Boarding Schools,* a book written like many social studies textbooks. Show the cover and then have the students turn to their copy of the table of contents from *Survival and Loss: Native American Boarding Schools* on *Student Response Book* page 49. Ask the students to read the table of contents silently and then have them use "Heads Together" to briefly review what they learned in each chapter.

Signal for attention. As a class, discuss the question on the following page.

Q *What are some things you learned about Native American boarding schools from* Survival and Loss: Native American Boarding Schools?

Explain that it can be helpful in understanding textbooks to think about how the information is organized. Tell the students that they will use *Survival and Loss: Native American Boarding Schools* this week to explore three different ways information can be organized in nonfiction text. They will then use this information to help them make sense of their own textbooks.

◀ **Teacher Note**

If the students struggle with this question, consider rereading sections of the book and asking the question again.

▶2 Discuss and Notice Chronological Relationships

Referring to the table of contents from *Survival and Loss: Native American Boarding Schools* on *Student Response Book* page 49, explain that the author made deliberate choices when deciding what the chapters would be about and their order in the book.

Read the chapter titles aloud and point out that time is used to organize the text—the book opens in the mid-1800s with the U.S. government forcing Native American tribes onto reservations ("Broken Promises" and "Lost Land, Lost Independence"), explores how conditions on the reservations led to the creation of the first boarding school ("Life on the Reservations"), describes how children lived and what they learned at the boarding schools ("Boarding School Life" and "Lessons and Learning"), explains the closing of the schools ("Boarding Schools in Question"), and traces the effects of the schools from then to the present day ("Long-term Effects"). Explain that when events are written in the order in which they occurred, they are organized *chronologically*.

Have the students turn to *Student Response Book* pages 50–51, where the first part of Chapter 1, "The Trail of Tears," is reproduced. Explain that this is another example of information organized chronologically. Ask the students to follow along as you read the text aloud. Ask them to notice how the authors use time to organize the information. Briefly discuss the following question:

Q *What do you notice about how the author uses time to organize information in this passage?*

Teacher Note

This lesson and the following lessons on exploring how expository texts are organized lay the foundation for work that the students will continue to do in subsequent grades. Mastery of these concepts is not expected at this point. Also note that for clarity the terms "chronological relationships," "cause and effect relationships," and "compare and contrast relationships" are used to describe the expository text structures of chronology, cause-effect, and compare-contrast.

Students might say:

"I notice that the passage starts in 1836 and ends in 1838."

"In addition to what [Michael] said, it describes how some tribes fought against leaving their homelands, then tells what the U.S. government did to make them leave."

If necessary, point out that the passage describes events in the order that they happened in time, from the two-year warning in 1836 to the forced removal of the Cherokees in 1838.

Teacher Note ▶

Save the "Relationships in Expository Text" chart for use throughout the week.

On the sheet of chart paper entitled "Relationships in Expository Text," write *chronological*. Point out that recognizing chronological relationships can help the students make sense of the nonfiction texts they read. Explain that you will add to the chart in the coming days as the students explore other ways information can be organized.

Explain that the students will explore other kinds of relationships in *Survival and Loss: Native American Boarding Schools* tomorrow. Encourage them to look for chronological relationships in expository text they read independently.

Save the "Relationships in Expository Text" chart for use later this week.

INDIVIDUALIZED DAILY READING

▶ 3 **Read Textbooks/Record Facts in Their IDR Journals**

Remind the students they have been reading textbooks and monitoring what they are learning. Explain that today the students will read their social studies textbook independently and then they will record several pieces of information they have learned.

Have the students read their social studies textbook for up to 30 minutes.

At the end of IDR, have the students write in their IDR Journals about what they read. Ask the students to write the title of the chapter they read and five or six things they learned from their reading.

After sufficient time, signal for the students' attention. Briefly discuss questions such as:

Q *What did you read today?*

Q *What information did you learn from your reading?*

Q *Did you notice if the text was organized in chronological order? If so, what did you learn in that section of the textbook?*

Q *What questions do you have for [Joanie] about [her] thinking?*

Day 2

Materials

- *Survival and Loss*
- "Relationships in Expository Text" chart from Day 1 and a marker
- *Student Response Book* pages 52–55
- *Student Response Book*, IDR Journal section

 Note

Prior to today's lesson, consider reviewing the reading with your English Language Learners, making sure they understand the material.

Strategy Lesson

In this lesson, the students:

- *Use text structure* to explore expository text
- Explore how information can be organized in expository text
- Explore cause and effect relationships in expository text
- Read independently for up to 30 minutes
- Take responsibility for their own learning during group work

1 ▶ **Review the "Relationships in Expository Text" Chart**

Have pairs sit in their groups. Remind the students that they read a passage from Chapter 1 of *Survival and Loss: Native American Boarding Schools* yesterday and thought about chronological relationships in the reading. Direct their attention to the "Relationships in Expository Text" chart and review that chronological relationships are one way expository text can be organized. Explain that the students will explore another way information can be organized today.

2 ▶ **Discuss and Notice Cause and Effect Relationships**

Ask the students to turn to *Student Response Book* pages 52–53, where the section "Wards of the State" from Chapter 2 of *Survival and Loss: Native American Boarding Schools* is reproduced.

Ask the students to follow along as you read the first two paragraphs of the section aloud. Read the first two paragraphs of "Wards of the State" aloud slowly and clearly.

Ask:

Q *What effect did being made wards of the state have on Native Americans? What sentence tells you that?*

Students might say:

"Being made wards of the state made it so Native Americans could not to take care of themselves."

"I agree with [Jamie] because the book says 'they no longer had the resources they needed to make a living.'"

Review for the students that being made wards of the state had an effect on Native Americans; it made them unable to make a living and forced them to depend on the government.

Point out that cause and effect relationships, or relationships in which one thing causes another thing to happen or affects another thing, are often found in expository text. Explain that being made wards of the state caused the effect of making Native Americans unable to take care of themselves.

On the "Relationships in Expository Text" chart, write *cause and effect*. Direct the students' attention to the third paragraph of the "Wards of the State" section and ask them to follow along as you read the rest of the section aloud, slowly and clearly. Ask and briefly discuss:

Q *What cause and effect relationships do you notice in the part you just heard?*

Students might say:

"The reservations were on land no one else wanted because the soil was bad. The effect of that was that the Native Americans could not use the land for farming."

"In addition to what [Jeffrey] said, the Native Americans couldn't farm because they didn't know how to farm like European Americans."

"A lot of bison were killed during the building of the railroad. That caused the effect that there were not enough bison for Native Americans to hunt."

◀ Teacher Note

If the students have difficulty answering this question, suggest some ideas like those in the "Students might say" note.

Direct the students to *Student Response Book* pages 54–55, where the passage entitled "The Reservations" is reproduced. Ask them to silently reread the passage to themselves. Then have the students use "Heads Together" to discuss any cause and effect relationships they notice.

After a few minutes, signal for the students' attention. Have a few volunteers share with the class.

Remind the students that the purpose of exploring relationships in expository text is to help them better understand texts they read independently by recognizing how the texts are organized. Encourage them to look for cause and effect and chronological relationships in expository text they read independently.

3 ▶ Reflect on Group Work

Help the students reflect on their work together by asking:

Q *What did you do to take responsibility during "Heads Together" today?*

Q *What problems did you have in your group? How did you try to solve those problems? What can you do next time to avoid those problems?*

Explain that the students will continue to explore relationships in *Survival and Loss: Native American Boarding Schools* tomorrow.

INDIVIDUALIZED DAILY READING

4 ▶ Read Textbooks/Record Facts in Their IDR Journals

Have pairs sit in their groups of four. Remind the students they have been reading textbooks and monitoring what they are learning. Explain that today the students will all read the same section of their social studies textbook independently and then, as they did in the previous lesson, record several pieces of information they have learned.

Teacher Note ▶

Cause and effect relationships found in this passage include: the discovery of gold in California (cause), which resulted in the westward migration of white settlers hoping to make their fortunes (effect) and the passage of settlers through Native American land (effect); the disrespectful treatment of the land by settlers (cause), which resulted in confrontations between Native Americans and settlers (effect); the increase in violent confrontations between Native Americans and settlers (cause), which led to the passage of the Indian Appropriations Act (effect) and the creation of the reservations (effect); the U.S. government promising the same land to more than one tribe (cause), which resulted in the tribes fighting over available resources (effect). Some students might struggle recognizing cause and effect relationships. If your students struggle, point out the cause and effect relationships mentioned here.

Teacher Note ▶

Prior to this activity, select a passage for the students to read.

Have all the students read the same section of their social studies textbook for up to 30 minutes.

At the end of IDR, have the students write in their IDR Journals about what they read. Ask the students to write the title of the chapter they read and five or six things they learned from their reading.

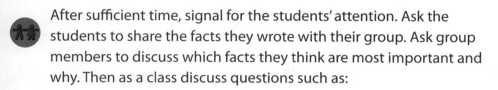 After sufficient time, signal for the students' attention. Ask the students to share the facts they wrote with their group. Ask group members to discuss which facts they think are most important and why. Then as a class discuss questions such as:

Q *What information do you think is important in what you read today? Why?*

Q *How did your group include everyone today?*

Q *What ideas did you contribute to the discussion?*

Materials

- *Survival and Loss*
- *Student Response Book* pages 56–61
- "Relationships in Expository Text" chart
- Social studies textbooks for students to read during IDR
- Self-stick note for each student
- (Optional) Transparency of "Double-entry Journal About *Survival and Loss: Native American Boarding Schools*" (BLM28)

Teacher Note

This lesson may require an extended class period.

Strategy Lesson/Guided Strategy Practice

In this lesson, the students:

- *Use text structure* to explore expository text
- Explore how information can be organized in expository text
- Explore compare and contrast, cause and effect, and chronological relationships in expository text
- Use a double-entry journal to record their thinking
- Read independently for up to 30 minutes
- Take responsibility for their own learning during group work

▶ 1 Discuss and Notice Compare and Contrast Relationships

Have groups sit together. Remind the students that they will continue to take responsibility for their learning during their group work today by contributing ideas and including everyone.

Remind the students that they have learned about chronological and cause and effect relationships in expository text and that yesterday they discussed a cause and effect relationship between the Native Americans becoming wards of the state and the tribes' ability to support themselves. Ask and briefly discuss:

Q *How did being made wards of the state affect Native Americans living on the reservations?*

Remind the students that before European settlers came to North America, Native Americans lived very differently. Ask and briefly discuss:

Q *How was the way Native Americans lived on their own land different from the way they lived on the reservations?*

If necessary, remind the students that before Native American tribes were forced onto reservations, they were very connected to their land. Their traditions reinforced their connection to the land and their appreciation of nature's gifts. They lived by hunting wild animals and by cultivating whatever crops grew naturally in the area where they lived. They built houses and made tools and other goods out of wood, animal skins, reeds, and other materials that came from the land. Most reservation land, on the other hand, could not sustain crops and had few natural resources. Native Americans were unable to hunt or farm enough to make a living, and because they were not able to live off the land, their traditions no longer made sense. Point out that this is an example of another relationship that can be found in expository text: the compare and contrast relationship, in which the author describes the similarities and/or differences between two things.

Point out that in much the same way that life on the reservations was different for Native Americans from life on their own land, life at the boarding schools was different for Native American children from life at home with their tribes.

Ask the students to turn to *Student Response Book* pages 56–58, where two sections from Chapter 4 of *Survival and Loss: Native American Boarding Schools* are reproduced. Ask the students to follow along as you read the section entitled "'Before' and 'After'" aloud. Read it aloud slowly and clearly. Then ask:

Q *How were the clothes and customs forced on the children when they arrived at the Carlisle School [similar to/different from] what they were used to? What sentences tell you that?*

Students might say:

"It was different because they weren't allowed to wear or keep anything they brought with them, even their special necklaces. It says, 'Everything was placed in a pile and burned.'"

"In addition to what [Stanley] said, it was different because they were used to loose clothing, and the clothes they were given to wear were very stiff and uncomfortable."

"The boys were used to having long hair, and when they got to school, their hair was cut short."

ELL Note

Consider reviewing this material with your students prior to today's lesson.

◀ **Teacher Note**

If the students have difficulty answering this question, suggest some ideas like those in the "Students might say" note.

Teacher Note ▶

The passage discusses the contrast between the day-to-day life the children were used to and the routine at the boarding schools.

Teacher Note

If the students have difficulty identifying relationships, identify a few together as a class. Some examples: "The Carlisle school opened in 1879.... By 1902, there were 25 boarding schools in 15 states..." (chronological); "The report was embarrassing for the U.S. government... By the 1930s, most of the boarding schools, including Carlisle, had been closed for good." (cause and effect); "At the time of the Meriam Report, almost 80 percent of Native American school-aged children were in boarding schools.... By the 1930s, most of the boarding schools, including Carlisle, had been closed for good." (compare and contrast).

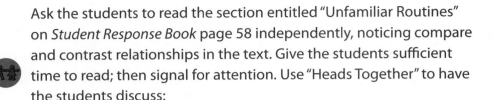

Ask the students to read the section entitled "Unfamiliar Routines" on *Student Response Book* page 58 independently, noticing compare and contrast relationships in the text. Give the students sufficient time to read; then signal for attention. Use "Heads Together" to have the students discuss:

Q *What compare and contrast relationships did you notice in this passage?*

On the "Relationships in Expository Text" chart, add *compare and contrast*. Review all the items on the chart and explain that the students will get more practice in recognizing chronological, cause and effect, and compare and contrast relationships today.

2 Identify Relationships and Record in Double-entry Journals

Explain that the students will individually read Chapter 6 of *Survival and Loss: Native American Boarding Schools,* reproduced on *Student Response Book* pages 59–60, and look for examples of cause and effect, chronological, and compare and contrast relationships. They will discuss in groups the examples they found and then record the examples on the "Double-entry Journal About *Survival and Loss: Native American Boarding Schools*" on *Student Response Book* page 61. Remind the students that they used double-entry journals in previous lessons. Ask them to turn to page 61 and point out that the three different relationships are given in the left-hand column. The students will record examples from the text for each relationship in the right-hand column. (If necessary, model this using a transparency of the "Double-entry Journal About *Survival and Loss: Native American Boarding Schools*"—see Teacher Note.)

As the students work, circulate and ask them the following questions to help them think about relationships in the text:

Q *What caused the U.S. government to send Lewis Meriam and his team to report on reservation and boarding school conditions?*

Q *What happened with the boarding schools between 1879 and 1902?*

Q *How did the number of students who attended the Carlisle School compare with the number of students who graduated?*

Q *How did what the U.S. government hoped the boarding schools would accomplish compare with what actually happened?*

▶3 **Discuss the Double-entry Journals**

When most groups have had time to discuss examples of relationships and the students have had time to record the examples in their own double-entry journals, signal for their attention. Facilitate a whole-class discussion by asking:

Q *What is an example of a [cause and effect/chronological/compare and contrast] relationship in the reading? How do you know?*

Q *How does recognizing that relationship help you understand what this text is saying about why the boarding schools closed?*

Q *How did you take responsibility for your own learning during this lesson?*

Explain that tomorrow the students will have an opportunity to look for cause and effect, chronological, and compare and contrast relationships in expository texts they read independently.

INDIVIDUALIZED DAILY READING

▶4 **Practice Self-monitoring and Rereading Textbooks**

Remind the students that they have been practicing checking their comprehension as they are reading. Review with the students that one of the best techniques for helping them comprehend what they are reading is to go back and reread. Remind the students that this is especially true when they are reading textbooks. Explain that today they will practice rereading their social studies textbook and share what they read in pairs.

FACILITATION TIP

Continue to focus on **responding neutrally** with interest during class discussions by refraining from overtly praising or criticizing the students' responses. Instead, build the students' intrinsic motivation by responding with genuine curiosity and interest, for example:

• *Interesting—say more about that.*

• *What you said makes me curious. I wonder…*

• *You have a point of view that's [similar to/different from] what [Justine] just said. How is it [similar/different]?*

Distribute a self-stick note to each student. Ask the students to open their textbooks to where they will start reading today and to place a self-stick note on that page. Have the students read independently for 10 minutes.

 Stop the students after 10 minutes and have them use "Turn to Your Partner" to talk in pairs about what they have learned in the part of the text that they just read.

After a few minutes, signal for the students' attention. Ask them to turn back to the page with the self-stick note and reread the part they just read.

 Stop the students after 10 minutes and have them use "Turn to Your Partner" to have partners tell each other about any new details they learned from the rereading.

Encourage the students to stop and reread when they read independently in the future.

Independent Strategy Practice

In this lesson, the students:

- *Use text structure* to explore expository text read independently
- Explore how information can be organized in expository text
- Explore cause and effect, chronological, and compare and contrast relationships in expository text
- Take responsibility for their own learning during group work

Materials

- Social studies textbook for each student
- "Relationships in Expository Text" chart
- Self-stick notes for each student
- *Assessment Resource Book*
- Unit 7 Parent Letter (BLM16) for each student

1 Review the "Relationships in Expository Text" chart

Remind the students that over the past several days they have been exploring relationships in expository text. Direct their attention to the "Relationships in Expository Text" chart and remind the students that expository text can be organized around chronological, cause and effect, and compare and contrast relationships.

Explain that today the students will practice recognizing these relationships as they read their own social studies and/or science textbooks independently.

> **Relationships in Expository Text**
>
> - chronological
> - cause and effect
> - compare and contrast

2 Read Textbooks Independently Without Stopping

Distribute several self-stick notes to each student. Have the students flip through their textbooks and stop either at the next chapter they are to read or one that looks interesting to them. Ask them to mark where they will start reading today with a self-stick note, then read independently for 10–15 minutes.

3 Think About Relationships and Prepare to Reread

Stop the students and ask them to think quietly to themselves for a moment about the following questions:

Q *What is your reading about?*

Q *Did you notice cause and effect relationships in your reading? If so, what is the cause and what is the effect?*

Q *Did you notice chronological, or time, relationships in your reading? If so, what is the time frame?*

Q *Did you notice compare and contrast relationships in your reading? If so, what is being compared?*

Explain that the students will reread the same section beginning at the self-stick note. As they reread, they will mark any cause and effect, chronological, and compare and contrast relationships they notice with self-stick notes. Encourage them to think about how recognizing these relationships helps them understand what they are reading.

4 Reread Independently and Mark with Self-stick Notes

Have the students reread independently for 10 minutes, marking as they read. Circulate and look for evidence that the students are recognizing relationships as they read.

CLASS COMPREHENSION ASSESSMENT

Circulate and observe the students as they reread and ask yourself:

Q *Do the students notice how their texts are organized?*

Q *Do they recognize cause and effect, chronological, and compare and contrast relationships in their reading?*

Record your observations on page 23 of the *Assessment Resource Book.*

Discuss Readings as a Class

Signal for the students' attention. Have a few volunteers share with the class what they read by saying a few words about the topic and then reading a passage they marked. As the students share passages, facilitate a discussion by asking:

Q *What kind of relationship do you think [Mindy] marked there? Why do you think so?*

Q *What questions can we ask [Mindy] about the passage [she] read?*

Q *[Mindy], how does recognizing that compare and contrast relationship help you better understand the topic you're reading about?*

Remind the students that the purpose for studying relationships in expository text is to help them make sense of their own independent reading. Encourage them to continue to look for these relationships as they read expository text during IDR and throughout the school day.

Reflect on Taking Responsibility

Ask and briefly discuss:

Q *What did you do to take responsibility for your learning this week?*

Q *What do you want to continue to work on the next time you work with a partner or in a group?*

Teacher Note

This is the last week in Unit 7. If you feel your students need more experience with analyzing expository text before moving on, you may want to repeat Weeks 4 and 5 of this unit with an alternative book. Alternative books are listed on the Weeks 4 and 5 Overview pages.

You will reassign partners for Unit 8.

INDIVIDUAL COMPREHENSION ASSESSMENT

Before continuing with Unit 8, take this opportunity to assess individual students' progress in reading and making sense of expository nonfiction. Please refer to pages 44–45 in the *Assessment Resource Book* for instructions.

SOCIAL SKILLS ASSESSMENT

Take this opportunity to assess your students' social skill development using the Social Skills Assessment record sheet on pages 2–3 of the *Assessment Resource Book*.

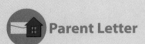

Parent Letter

Send home with each student the Parent Letter for this unit (see "Do Ahead," page 403). Periodically, have a few students share with the class what they are reading at home.

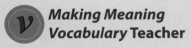

Making Meaning Vocabulary Teacher

Next week you will revisit this week's reading to teach Vocabulary Week 20.

Determining Important Ideas and Summarizing

FICTION AND NARRATIVE NONFICTION

During this unit, the students make inferences to understand text. They also think about important and supporting ideas in a text and use important ideas to summarize. During IDR, the students explore the important ideas in their independent reading. Socially, they give reasons for their opinions, discuss opinions respectfully, reach agreement, and give feedback in a caring way.

Week 1 *Letting Swift River Go* by Jane Yolen

Week 2 *A River Ran Wild* by Lynne Cherry

Week 3 *Harry Houdini: Master of Magic* by Robert Kraske

Week 4 "Mrs. Buell" in *Hey World, Here I Am!* by Jean Little

Week 5 Student-selected text

Week 1

Overview

UNIT 8: DETERMINING IMPORTANT IDEAS AND SUMMARIZING
Fiction and Narrative Nonfiction

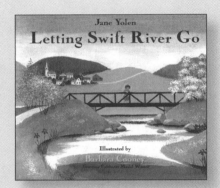

Letting Swift River Go
by Jane Yolen, illustrated by Barbara Cooney
(Little, Brown, 1992)

In this story based on actual events, a woman recalls her childhood in the Swift River Valley and the flooding of the valley to form a reservoir.

ALTERNATIVE BOOKS

Bill Pickett: Rodeo-Ridin' Cowboy by Andrea D. Pinkney

Pink and Say by Patricia Polacco

Comprehension Focus

- Students *make inferences* to understand text.

- Students *think about important and supporting ideas* in a text.

- Students read independently.

Social Development Focus

- Students take responsibility for their learning and behavior.

- Students develop the group skills of giving reasons for their opinions and reaching agreement.

DO AHEAD

- Prior to Day 1, decide how you will randomly assign partners to work together during the unit.

- Make a transparency of "Excerpt 1 from *Letting Swift River Go*" (BLM29).

- Make a transparency of "Excerpt 2 from *Letting Swift River Go*" (BLM30).

- Prepare to model distinguishing between important and supporting ideas (see Day 4, Step 1 on page 438).

Making Meaning Vocabulary Teacher

If you are teaching Developmental Studies Center's *Making Meaning Vocabulary* program, teach Vocabulary Week 20 this week. For more information, see the *Making Meaning Vocabulary Teacher's Manual.*

Day 1

Read-aloud

Materials

- *Letting Swift River Go*
- "Reading Comprehension Strategies" chart
- Small self-stick notes for each student

Being a Writer™ **Teacher**

You can either have the students work with their *Being a Writer* partner or assign them a different partner for the *Making Meaning* lessons.

Teacher Note ▶

You might model the prompt by saying, "Wildfires are not all bad. The reason I think this is that wildfires burn down a lot of dead trees so there's space for new ones to grow" or "Richard Wright succeeded in spite of racism. The reason I think this is that he managed to check out books from the library even though blacks couldn't get a library card, and he became a great reader and writer."

In this lesson, the students:

- *Make inferences* as they hear a story
- Read independently for up to 30 minutes
- Give reasons for their opinions

1 Pair Students and Learn a Prompt for Supporting Opinions

Randomly assign partners and have them sit together. Review that the students have practiced several social skills, including asking clarifying questions, confirming that they understand another person's thinking by repeating back what they heard, and using prompts to add to a discussion. Explain that in the next few weeks, they will focus on explaining their thinking more clearly by giving reasons for their opinions.

Write the following prompt on the board: "The reason I think this is _____." Tell the students that you would like them to use this prompt when they answer a question or give an opinion during a book discussion.

Point out that this skill is not new to the students. Whenever they have answered the questions *Why do you think so?* and *What in the text makes you think that?* they practiced giving reasons for their opinions. Now the focus is on consciously using the prompt without waiting to be asked to explain their thinking.

2 Introduce *Letting Swift River Go*

Review that the students have been making inferences to help them make sense of poems, stories, and books. Explain that you would like them to continue to think about making inferences as they hear a new book today.

Tell the students that you will read *Letting Swift River Go.* Show the cover of the book and read the names of the author and illustrator aloud.

Explain that the story is based on an actual event. In the late 1920s, people living in the Swift River Valley of central Massachusetts were made to move out of their homes, and the valley was flooded to create a reservoir. Explain that a *valley* is a low area surrounded by hills or mountains, and that a *reservoir* is an artificial lake, often connected to a river, where a large amount of water is stored.

In the story, a woman named Sally Jane recalls her life in the valley as a young girl and what happened when the valley was flooded.

 Read *Letting Swift River Go* Aloud

Read the book aloud, showing the illustrations and stopping as described on the next page.

Suggested Vocabulary

mumblety-peg: a game in which players flip a knife so the blade will stick in the ground (p. 6)

harvested ice: cut and gathered blocks of ice (p. 12; refer to the illustration)

eiderdowns: quilts filled with duck feathers (p. 12)

"woodpeckers": (idiom) workers who cut down trees (p. 19)

caissons: watertight chambers used for underwater construction work (p. 24)

ELL Vocabulary

English Language Learners may benefit from discussing additional vocabulary, including:

blacktop: road covered with black asphalt (p. 4)

We could trade water for money…new houses…a better life: We could get paid to move away so a reservoir could be built. (p. 14)

So it was voted…to drown our towns that the people in the city might drink: People voted to create a reservoir where the towns were to provide water for the city (p. 14)

headstones: markers at graves identifying who is buried there (p. 17; refer to the illustration)

sacred ground: holy place that should be treated with respect (p. 17)

it had more breath than we did: we couldn't keep up with it (p. 23)

dammed rivers: rivers whose waters are held back by dams or big walls (p. 26)

 Note

To build background knowledge about reservoirs, you may need to explain that reservoirs are usually created to provide water to cities or to supply power to generators. To make a reservoir in an area where people are living, the government purchases the people's properties and helps them relocate. You may also want to read or paraphrase the Author's Note on page 3 of the book.

Read the first page of the story twice and continue reading to page 14. Stop after:

p. 14   "But then everything began to change."

 Have the students use "Turn to Your Partner" to discuss:

Q *What did you learn about Sally Jane's life in the valley as a young girl?*

Without sharing as a class, reread the first sentence on page 14 and continue reading to the bottom of the page:

p. 14   "So it was voted in Boston to drown our towns that the people in the city might drink."

 Have the students use "Turn to Your Partner" to discuss:

Q *What happened in the part of the story you just heard?*

 Without sharing as a class, reread the last sentence and continue reading. Follow the same procedure at the remaining stops:

p. 23   "I never heard where Georgie went, never even got to say good-bye."

p. 27   "It took seven long years."

p. 32   "I looked down into the darkening deep, smiled, and did."

FACILITATION TIP
During this unit, we invite you to continue practicing **responding neutrally** with interest during class discussions. This week, continue to respond neutrally by refraining from overtly praising or criticizing the students' responses. Try responding neutrally by nodding, asking them to say more about their thinking, or asking other students to respond.

4 Discuss the Story as a Class

Facilitate a discussion of the story, using the questions that follow. Be ready to reread passages to help the students recall what they heard. Remind them to use "The reason I think this is _____" and the discussion prompts they have learned to add to one another's thinking.

Q *What happens in this story?*

Q *How does Sally Jane feel about her life in the valley before it was flooded? What in the book makes you think that?*

Students might say:

"I think Sally Jane liked living there. The reason I think this is she got to be with her friends, and she had fun."

"I agree with [Abe]. Sally Jane went fishing and camped out and did a lot of fun stuff."

"In addition to what [Katia] said, I think Sally Jane felt safe in her town. The reason I think this is she didn't have to worry about walking around by herself."

Remind the students that at the end of the story Sally Jane, now grown up, goes rowing on the reservoir with her father. Reread page 30 and ask:

Q *What do you infer from this passage about how Sally Jane feels as she remembers her life in the valley? Explain your thinking.*

Reread page 11 and ask:

Q *What did Sally Jane's mother mean when she said, "You have to let them go, Sally Jane"?*

As the students make inferences about the story, point them out (for example, "The story does not directly say that Sally Jane had a happy life before the valley was flooded, but you inferred that from clues in the story").

 ## Reflect on Giving Reasons for Opinions

Facilitate a brief discussion about how the students did using the prompt to give reasons for their opinions. Share your own observations, and explain that you would like the students to continue to focus on giving reasons for their opinions throughout the week.

Reading Comprehension
Strategies

- recognizing text
features

INDIVIDUALIZED DAILY READING

 ## Review the "Reading Comprehension Strategies" Chart

Distribute several self-stick notes to each student. Direct the students' attention to the "Reading Comprehension Strategies" chart and remind them that these are the strategies they have learned so far this year. Ask them to notice which strategies they use and where they use them during their reading today. Explain that they will use self-stick notes to mark places in their book where they use a strategy and that they should write the name of the strategy on the self-stick note. At the end of independent reading, they will share in pairs one of the passages they marked and the strategy they used. Ask them to be prepared to talk about how the strategy helped them understand what they read.

Have the students read independently for up to 30 minutes, marking with self-stick notes places in their reading where they use a comprehension strategy.

As the students read, circulate among them. Ask individual students questions such as:

Q *What is your book about?*

Q *What strategies are you using as you read?*

Q *How does this passage help you [visualize]? How does [visualizing] this passage help you understand the story?*

 At the end of independent reading, have each student share with her partner a passage she marked and the strategy she used to make sense of it. Remind the students to ask clarifying questions and to use the prompt "The reason I think this is _____" to support their thinking.

As partners share, circulate and listen to their conversations and make notes. You might want to share some of your observations or have a few volunteers share with the class.

Day 2

Guided Strategy Practice

In this lesson, the students:

- *Make inferences* as they hear a story
- *Think about what is important* in the text
- Use "Think, Pair, Write"
- Read independently for up to 30 minutes
- Give reasons for their opinions

About Determining Important and Supporting Ideas

The focus of the next two weeks is on *determining important and supporting ideas*, a strategy that helps readers understand and retain what they read. In the *Making Meaning* program, the focus is on helping the students distinguish between important and supporting ideas in text, rather than having them identify the one "main idea." The students explore these ideas through teacher modeling, partner and class discussions, and referring to the text to justify their opinions. The goal, as with all the reading comprehension strategies, is for the students to be able to use the strategy to make sense of their independent reading. (For more about determining important ideas, please see volume 1, page xvi.)

1 ▸ Use "Think, Pair, Write" to Think About What Is Important

Review that the students heard *Letting Swift River Go* and made inferences to figure out what happens in the story and why. Explain that today they will use inferences in a new way—to help them think about what is important to understand and remember in the story.

Explain that you will reread the first part of *Letting Swift River Go* aloud and the students will use "Think, Pair, Write" to take notes about what they think is important in the story.

Have the students turn to "Think, Pair, Write About *Letting Swift River Go*" on *Student Response Book* page 62. Explain that during the reading you will stop several times. At the first two stops, you will model thinking about what is important so the students can see an

Materials

- *Letting Swift River Go* (pages 4–19)
- *Student Response Book* page 62
- "Reading Comprehension Strategies" chart
- Small self-stick notes for each student

◄ **Teacher Note**

You may need to remind the students that "Think, Pair, Write" is a technique in which they think quietly for a moment, talk in pairs about their thinking, and then individually write their ideas.

example before trying it on their own. At the last two stops, they will think about what is important, turn to their partner to share their thinking, and write their own ideas in their *Student Response Books.*

▶2 Reread Pages 4–13 and Model Thinking About What Is Important

Read page 4 of the story twice, and stop at the bottom of the page.

Model thinking quietly for a moment; then think aloud about what seems important in the passage. (For example, you might say, "What seems most important to understand and remember in this passage is that the world felt safe to Sally Jane when she was a child.")

Model writing a note about this on the board where all the students can see it. Ask the students to write the same note in their own *Student Response Books.* Emphasize that thinking about what's important sometimes means saying in a few words what the author says over several sentences or pages.

Repeat this procedure with pages 5–13 of the story.

▶3 Reread Pages 14–19 with "Think, Pair, Write"

Remind the students that at the next two stops they will practice thinking about what is important on their own and share their thinking in pairs.

Reread the first sentence on page 14 and continue reading to the bottom of the page. Stop after:

> **p. 14** "So it was voted in Boston to drown our towns that the people in the city might drink."

Ask:

Q *What seems most important to understand and remember in the part I just read?*

Give the students 5–10 seconds to think, and then have them share briefly in pairs. After a moment, ask the class to listen again for what

Teacher Note

Circulate as partners talk and notice whether they are able to identify important ideas in the passage. Important ideas include that Boston did not have water, that the Swift River Valley had lots of water, and that people in Boston decided to make a reservoir where the towns were.

If the students have difficulty, reread parts of the passage to individual students and ask questions such as:

Q *What is this part mainly about?*

Q *If you had to tell what this part is about in one sentence, what would you say?*

seems most important to understand or remember, and then reread the passage aloud.

Have the students record on *Student Response Book* page 62 what they think is most important to understand or remember in the passage. Then have a few volunteers share what they wrote with the class.

Facilitate a brief class discussion by asking:

Q *Why does that idea seem most important?*

Q *What other ideas seemed most important as you listened to the passage? Why?*

Reread the last sentence on page 14 and continue reading to the next stopping point:

> **p. 19** "They were stacked like drinking straws along the roads, then hauled away."

Ask:

Q *What seems most important to understand and remember in the part I just read?*

 Again, have the students think, and then briefly share in pairs. Reread the passage aloud and have the students record on *Student Response Book* page 62 what they think is most important to understand or remember in the passage.

Have a few volunteers share what they wrote with the class. Then facilitate a brief class discussion by asking:

Q *Why does that idea seem most important?*

Q *What other ideas seemed most important as you listened to the passage? Why?*

Tell the students that *thinking about what is important* is a strategy good readers use to help them identify and remember the essential ideas in a text. Explain that in the next lesson you will read the rest of the story and the students will continue to think about what's important.

◀ **Teacher Note**

Students may have different ideas about what is important in a passage. Encourage them to explain their thinking and to refer to the text to support their opinions.

◀ **Teacher Note**

Again, circulate as partners talk and notice whether they are able to identify important ideas in the passage. Important ideas include that people began to prepare for the reservoir by moving graves and cutting down trees.

4 Reflect on "Think, Pair, Write"

Facilitate a brief discussion of how the students did giving reasons for their opinions when they talked in pairs during "Think, Pair, Write."

INDIVIDUALIZED DAILY READING

5 Discuss Reading Comprehension Strategies

Have the students continue to use self-stick notes to mark places they use reading comprehension strategies. Refer to the "Reading Comprehension Strategies" chart and review the strategies.

Have the students read independently for up to 30 minutes.

As the students read, circulate among them. Ask individual students questions such as:

Q *What strategies are you using as you read?*

Q *How does [making inferences] in this passage help you understand the story?*

At the end of independent reading, have each student share with his partner a passage he marked and the strategy he used to make sense of it. Remind the students to give reasons for their thinking and to ask each other clarifying questions.

As partners share, circulate and listen to their conversations and make notes. You might want to share some of your observations or have a few volunteers share with the class.

Allow time for any student who has finished a book to record it in the "Reading Log" section of his *Student Response Book*.

ELL Note

You might want to model this activity for your English Language Learners and preview the questions you will ask prior to having these students read.

EXTENSION

Learn More About Jane Yolen

Jane Yolen has written numerous books, short stories, and poems. Have the students do an author study—reading and discussing some of her work. Titles to consider include these novels, picture books, and poetry and story collections: *The Devil's Arithmetic; Briar Rose; Sacred Places; Merlin; Snow, Snow: Winter Poems for Children; Owl Moon;* and *When I Was Your Age: Original Stories About Growing Up.*

Day 3

Materials

- *Letting Swift River Go* (pages 19–32)
- *Student Response Book* page 62
- Small self-stick notes for each student
- "Reading Comprehension Strategies" chart

Guided Strategy Practice

In this lesson, the students:

- *Make inferences* as they hear a story
- *Think about what is important* in a text
- Use "Think, Pair, Write"
- Read independently for up to 30 minutes
- Give reasons for their opinions

▶1 Review Giving Reasons for Opinions

Explain that today the students will again use "Think, Pair, Write" to help them think about what is important in a text. Remind them to practice giving reasons for their opinions, using "The reason I think this is _____."

▶2 Review Thinking About What Is Important

Remind the students that in the previous lesson they heard the first part of *Letting Swift River Go* again and used "Think, Pair, Write" to think about what is important in the story. Have the students open to *Student Response Book* page 62 and review the important ideas they recorded. Ask:

Q *What are some important ideas we identified in the first part of* Letting Swift River Go?

Explain that today you will reread the rest of the story aloud, stopping three times. As you did yesterday, you will model thinking about what is important at the first stop. At the next two stops, the students will use "Think, Pair, Write" to think about what is important in the passage they just heard, share their thinking in pairs, and write their own ideas on *Student Response Book* page 62.

Reread Pages 19–32 with Modeling and "Think, Pair, Write"

Remind the students that in the last part of the story they heard, workers began to prepare for the reservoir by moving graves to new cemeteries and cutting down brush and trees. Reread page 19; then continuing reading to page 23. Stop after:

> **p. 23** "I never heard where Georgie went, never even got to say good-bye."

Model thinking quietly for a moment; then think aloud about what seems important in the passage. (For example, you might say, "What seems most important to understand and remember in this part of the story is that the families in the valley had to move away, and Sally Jane was separated from her friends.")

Model writing a note about this where everyone can see it (for example, "The families had to move away from the valley, and Sally Jane was separated from her friends"). Ask the students to write the same note in their own *Student Response Books.*

Ask the students to think about what is most important in the next passage you read. Continue reading, slowly and clearly, and stop after:

> **p. 27** "It took seven long years."

Ask:

Q *What is most important to understand and remember in the part I just read?*

 Give the students 5–10 seconds to think; then have them share briefly in pairs. After a few moments, ask the class to listen again for what seems most important to understand or remember, and reread the passage aloud.

Have the students record what they think is most important to understand or remember in the passage on *Student Response Book* page 62, and then have a few volunteers share what they wrote with the class.

Teacher Note

Important ideas in this passage include that workers built a dam and dike in the valley, that Sally Jane's town didn't seem like her town anymore, and that water from the dammed rivers took seven years to cover the valley.

Facilitate a brief class discussion by asking:

Q *Why does that idea seem most important?*

Q *What other ideas seemed most important as you listened to the passage? Why?*

Reread the last sentence on page 27 and continue reading to the next stopping point:

> **p. 32** "I looked down into the darkening deep, smiled, and did."

 Again, have the students think, and then briefly share in pairs. Reread the passage aloud and have the students record on *Student Response Book* page 62 what they think is most important to understand or remember in the passage.

Have a few volunteers share what they wrote with the class; then facilitate a brief class discussion by asking:

Q *Why does that idea seem most important?*

Q *What other ideas seemed most important as you listened to the passage? Why?*

Remind the students that thinking about what is important in a story helps them identify what is essential to understand and remember. Explain that in the next lesson they will think more about what is important in *Letting Swift River Go*.

Teacher Note

Important ideas in this passage include that many years later Sally Jane visited the reservoir with her father, that she remembered her pleasant life in the valley, and that she was able to follow her mother's advice that there are some things you have to let go.

 4 ▶ Reflect on "Think, Pair, Write"

Facilitate a brief discussion about how the students did working in pairs during "Think, Pair, Write." Ask:

Q *How did you and your partner do giving reasons for your thinking about what was important today?*

Q *Did others change your mind about what was important in a passage after you heard their thinking? Tell us about that.*

INDIVIDUALIZED DAILY READING

 5 ▸ **Discuss Reading Comprehension Strategies/
Document IDR Conferences**

Have the students continue to place self-stick notes where they
use reading comprehension strategies. Refer to the "Reading
Comprehension Strategies" chart and review the strategies they
have learned this year.

Ask and briefly discuss:

Q *Which of these strategies have you used in your independent
reading this week? How did [questioning] help you understand
what you were reading?*

Remind the students that using these strategies will help them
understand and enjoy what they are reading. However, if they are
having difficulty using these strategies and comprehending the text
they are reading, they should think about selecting a different text.

Have the students read independently for up to 30 minutes.

Use the "IDR Conference Notes" record sheet to conduct and
document individual conferences.

 At the end of independent reading, have each student share with
her partner a passage she marked and the strategy she used to
help make sense of it. Remind the students to give reasons for their
thinking and to ask each other clarifying questions.

> *Reading Comprehension
> Strategies*
>
> *- recognizing text
>   features*

Day 4

Materials

- *Letting Swift River Go*
- Transparency of "Excerpt 1 from *Letting Swift River Go*" (BLM29)
- Transparency pens in two colors
- *Student Response Book* page 63
- Transparency of "Excerpt 2 from *Letting Swift River Go*" (BLM30)
- *Assessment Resource Book*
- "Reading Comprehension Strategies" chart and a marker
- Small self-stick notes for each student
- *Student Response Book,* IDR Journal section

Guided Strategy Practice

In this lesson, the students:

- *Distinguish between important ideas and supporting ideas* in a story
- Use "Think, Pair, Write"
- Read independently for up to 30 minutes
- Reach agreement

▶1 Model Distinguishing Between Important and Supporting Ideas

Review that in previous lessons the students heard you reread *Letting Swift River Go* and used "Think, Pair, Write" to think about the important ideas in the story.

Place the transparency of "Excerpt 1 from *Letting Swift River Go*" on the overhead projector. Point out that this passage comes from the very beginning of the story, and read it aloud. Remind the students that in a previous lesson they discussed the important idea in the passage—that Sally Jane felt safe as a child. Explain that the first sentence expresses the important idea in the passage ("When I was six years old the world seemed a very safe place"). Underline the sentence on the transparency.

Using a different colored pen, underline the second sentence in the passage ("The wind whispered comfortably through the branches of the willow by my bedroom window") and explain that this sentence is a detail about the safe world Sally Jane lived in. Explain that details, examples, or descriptions that tell more about the important ideas are called *supporting ideas.*

Ask:

Q *What else in this passage supports the important idea that the world seemed like a safe place to Sally Jane?*

Have a few volunteers share their thinking with the class, and underline the supporting ideas on the transparency.

> **Students might say:**
>
> "I think 'Mama let me walk to school all alone' is a supporting idea. The reason I think this is that it's an example of how safe it was in the town."
>
> "I agree with [Tracy]. In addition, I think where she walked—'past the Old Stone Mill,' for example—is a supporting idea. It's a detail."

Point out that readers don't usually remember every word or detail as they read, so they need to be thinking about what ideas are the most important to understand and remember. Good readers need to be able to tell the difference between important ideas and supporting details as they read. Explain that today the students will practice identifying important and supporting ideas in another passage from *Letting Swift River Go*.

2 ▶ **Agree on One Important and One Supporting Idea**

Have the students turn to *Student Response Book* page 63. Point out that this is the part of the story in which the men and women of the Swift River Valley gather in Grange Hall to listen to the men from Boston. Read the excerpt aloud slowly and clearly as the students follow along.

Explain that the students will read the excerpt and think quietly about one important and one supporting idea in the passage. They will then discuss their thinking in pairs. Partners will come to agreement on one important and one supporting idea and underline these in their *Student Response Books*. The students may use two different colored pens, or a pencil and a pen, to distinguish between the important and supporting ideas they underline.

◀ **Teacher Note**

If the students have difficulty identifying supporting ideas, review that supporting ideas are details, examples, and descriptions that tell more about an important idea. Ask:

Q *Where in the passage are other details about Sally Jane's safe world?*

 Note

English Language Learners may benefit from extra support to make sense of the excerpt. Show and discuss the illustration on page 15 again. Read the excerpt aloud as the students follow along, and stop periodically to talk about what is happening. The students may benefit from an explanation of the following words and passages:

- "Grange Hall"
- "Boston had what Papa called 'a mighty long thirst,' and no water to quench it."
- "So it was voted in Boston to drown our towns that the people in the city might drink."

Teacher Note

Initially, students often have difficulty distinguishing between important and supporting ideas. Having the students identify only one important idea and one supporting idea helps to focus their thinking.

CLASS COMPREHENSION ASSESSMENT

Circulate as the pairs work and notice which sentences the students underline. Ask yourself:

Q *Are the students able to identify an important idea in the passage?*

Q *Are they able to identify a supporting idea?*

Q *Is there evidence that they see the difference between important and supporting ideas in the passage?*

Record your observations on page 24 of the *Assessment Resource Book.*

3 **Discuss Important and Supporting Ideas as a Class**

When the students finish their partner work, place the transparency of "Excerpt 2 from *Letting Swift River Go*" on the overhead projector. Facilitate a discussion using the following questions. Remind the students to give reasons for their opinions.

Q *What is an important idea in this part of the story? Why do you think that information is important?*

Q *Do others agree that this information is important? Why or why not?*

Students might say:

"I think 'nobody asked us kids' is important. The reason I think this is that the kids lived in the town, too, but nobody was thinking about them."

"I disagree with [Raúl]. I don't think it's important that the kids weren't there. The stuff about why they decided to drown the town is what's important."

"I think 'the city of Boston, sixty miles away, needed lots of water' is important. The reason I think this is it explains why they made the reservoir."

Q *What is a supporting idea? Why do you think that information is supporting?*

Students might say:

"I think 'good water, clear water, clean water, cold water' is supporting. The reason I think this is because I think those are just details about the water."

"I thought 'Boston had what Papa called a mighty long thirst' was supporting. The story already said that Boston 'needs lots of water,' so what Papa said is just repeating that."

As the students share, underline the important and supporting information on the transparency, using different colored pens.

Ask:

Q *Over the past couple of days we've been talking about important ideas in* Letting Swift River Go. *Now that you've thought about some of the important ideas, what would you say this story is about?*

4 ▶ Add to the "Reading Comprehension Strategies" Chart

Direct the students' attention to the "Reading Comprehension Strategies" chart and add *determining important ideas* to it. Remind the students that distinguishing between important and supporting information can help them better understand and remember what they've read and that the goal is for them to use the strategy as they read independently.

Tell the students that they will continue to think about important and supporting information in the coming weeks.

5 ▶ Reflect on Reaching Agreement

Facilitate a brief discussion about how the students worked together. Ask:

Q *How did you and your partner do agreeing on one important and one supporting idea?*

Q *What did you do if you didn't agree at first?*

Reading Comprehension Strategies

- recognizing text features

INDIVIDUALIZED DAILY READING

 ## 6 ▶ Write About Reading Comprehension Strategies in Their IDR Journals

Ask the students to continue to use self-stick notes to mark passages where they use reading comprehension strategies to make sense of what they are reading.

Have the students read independently for up to 30 minutes.

At the end of independent reading, have the students write in their IDR Journals about a strategy they used and how it helped them understand their reading. Have a few students share their writing with the class.

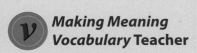

Making Meaning Vocabulary **Teacher**

Next week you will revisit this week's reading to teach Vocabulary Week 21.

Week 2

Overview

UNIT 8: DETERMINING IMPORTANT IDEAS AND SUMMARIZING
Fiction and Narrative Nonfiction

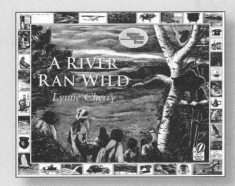

A River Ran Wild
by Lynne Cherry
(Voyager, 2002)

This book traces the history of the Nashua River in Massachusetts from its discovery by Native Americans through its near destruction from pollution to its later reclamation.

ALTERNATIVE BOOKS

The Mary Celeste by Jane Yolen

Come Back, Salmon by Molly Cone

Comprehension Focus

- Students *make inferences* to understand text.

- Students *think about important and supporting ideas* in a text.

- Students read independently.

Social Development Focus

- Students take responsibility for their learning and behavior.

- Students develop the group skills of giving reasons for their opinions and reaching agreement.

DO AHEAD

- Make transparencies of the "Excerpt from *A River Ran Wild*" (BLM31–BLM32).

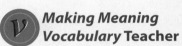

Making Meaning Vocabulary Teacher

If you are teaching Developmental Studies Center's *Making Meaning Vocabulary* program, teach Vocabulary Week 21 this week. For more information, see the *Making Meaning Vocabulary Teacher's Manual.*

Day 1

Materials

- *A River Ran Wild*
- Small self-stick notes for each student

Teacher Note

This week, the students focus again on the key comprehension strategies of *making inferences* and *determining important ideas*. This practice will help to prepare them for *summarizing,* which is the focus of the later weeks of this unit. As always, the goal is for the students to use the strategies to make sense of what they read independently.

ELL Note

You might make the book available to your English Language Learners before the read-aloud so they can preview the illustrations and maps.

Read-aloud

In this lesson, the students:

- *Make inferences* as they hear a nonfiction text
- Read independently for up to 30 minutes
- Give reasons for their opinions

▶1 Review Giving Reasons for Opinions

Ask partners to sit together. Review that last week the students used the prompt "The reason I think this is _____" to give reasons for their opinions. Explain that you would like them to continue using the prompt as they talk in pairs and with the whole class this week.

▶2 Introduce *A River Ran Wild*

Show the cover of *A River Ran Wild* and read the title and the author's name aloud. Explain that this nonfiction book traces the history of the Nashua River in Massachusetts from thousands of years ago to modern times. Show the opening spread and explain that these are maps of the area of New England where the Nashua River is located. The left page shows the area as it was when the Native Americans inhabited the land, and the right page shows the area in the 1900s. Explain that as they listen you would like the students to think about how the river and valley changed over the years and why they changed.

▶3 Read *A River Ran Wild* Aloud

Read the book aloud, showing the illustrations and stopping as described on the next page.

Suggested Vocabulary

thatch their dwellings: build homes using thin sticks for the walls and roof (p. 10)

trading post: store in the wilderness where people trade for food and supplies (p. 12)

pelts: animal skins (p. 14)

sawmills: buildings where machines saw logs into lumber (p. 14)

grist mills: buildings where machines grind grain such as corn or wheat (p. 16)

industrial revolution: period of change in which machines are used more and more to do work previously done by hand (p. 18)

pulp: a mixture of ground-up wood, water, and other matter from which paper is made (p. 18)

decomposed: rotted or decayed (p. 22)

petitions: documents signed by many people that request government officials to take an action or change a policy (p. 26)

greenway: path lined with trees (p. 31)

ELL Vocabulary

English Language Learners may benefit from discussing additional vocabulary, including:

cattails: tall plants with long fuzzy ends that look similar to a cat's tail (p. 10)

wilderness: wild area that has very few people living in it (p. 14)

trespass: go onto another person's property without permission (p. 16)

dye: a substance used to color cloth and paper (p. 18)

pollution: harmful materials that damage the air, water, or soil (p. 21)

descendant: child, grandchild, great-grandchild, etc. of someone (p. 24)

mourned: felt sorrow or grief (p. 24)

sewer: pipe or ditch that carries waste materials (p. 26)

process the waste: make their garbage less harmful (p. 26)

foul it: make it dirty (p. 28)

Stop after:

p. 10   "The river, land, and forest provided all they needed."

 Have the students use "Turn to Your Partner" to discuss:

Q   *What did you learn about the river valley in the part of the story you just heard?*

Without sharing as a class, reread the last sentence and continue reading to the next stop. At each of the following stops, have the students use "Turn to Your Partner" to share very briefly what they have learned. Then reread the last sentence and continue.

p. 16 "Deer still came to drink from the river, and owls, raccoons, and beaver fed there."

p. 22 "The Nashua was slowly dying."

p. 26 "Finally, new laws were passed and the factories stopped polluting."

Continue reading to the end of the story.

▶ **4** **Discuss the Reading as a Class**

Facilitate a discussion of the story using the following questions. Be ready to reread passages aloud and show illustrations again to help the students recall what they heard. Remind them to use "The reason I think this is _____" and the other discussion prompts they have learned to add to one another's thinking.

Q *What was the way of life of the Native Americans who settled along the river, and how did it change?*

Students might say:

"They got everything they needed from the river and forests. When Europeans came, they cut down the forests so the Native Americans couldn't hunt like before."

"I agree with [Hallie]. The reason I think this is that the Native Americans asked the animals they killed to forgive them, which shows how they respected nature. But the settlers destroyed nature and ruined things for the Indians."

"In addition to what [Angel] said, I think the settlers' fences made it hard for the Native Americans to hunt like before. The settlers took over the land and pushed them out."

FACILITATION TIP

For the rest of the unit, continue to focus on **responding neutrally** with interest during class discussions by refraining from overtly praising or criticizing the students' responses. Instead, build the students' intrinsic motivation by responding with genuine curiosity and interest, for example:

• *Say more about that.*

• *Explain your thinking further.*

• *You have a point of view that's [similar to/different from] what [Hanan] said. How is it [similar/ different]?*

• *Do you agree or disagree with [Erica]? Why?*

• *What question do you have for [Erica] about [her] thinking?*

Show the illustration on page 19. Ask:

Q *What effect did machines and factories have on the river during the industrial revolution?*

Q *How did the river become clean again?*

> **Students might say:**
>
> "Some politicians shut down all the factories."
>
> "I disagree with [Luke]. The reason I think this is the story said that a Native American and a woman named Marion decided to do something about the river. They sent letters to the government, and laws got passed to stop all the pollution."
>
> "I agree with [Ricardo]. Marion went up and down the river getting people stirred up about the pollution. That's how the river got cleaned up."

As the students make inferences about the story, point them out (for example, "The story doesn't directly say that the Indians respected nature, but you figured it out from clues in the story").

5 ▶ Reflect on Giving Reasons for Opinions

Facilitate a brief discussion about how the students did using the prompt to give reasons for their opinions. Share your own observations and explain that you would like the students to continue to focus on giving reasons for their opinions throughout the week.

INDIVIDUALIZED DAILY READING

6 ▶ Think About Important Ideas

Remind the students that they have been thinking about important ideas in texts. Explain that you want them to use self-stick notes to mark at least one important idea in their reading today.

Distribute several self-stick notes to each student and have the students read independently for up to 30 minutes.

As the students read, circulate among them. Ask individual students questions such as:

Q *What is your book about?*

Q *Why do you think the idea you marked is important?*

Q *What other ideas might be important in this section?*

At the end of independent reading, have a few volunteers each share one important idea they found in their reading.

Day 2

Guided Strategy Practice

In this lesson, the students:

- *Make inferences* as they hear a nonfiction text
- *Think about what is important* in the text
- Use "Think, Pair, Write"
- Read independently for up to 30 minutes
- Reach agreement

Materials

- *A River Ran Wild* (pages 7–16)
- *Student Response Book* page 64
- Small self-stick notes for each student

1 Review *A River Ran Wild*

Show the cover of *A River Ran Wild* and ask:

Q *What do you remember about* A River Ran Wild?

Review that last week the students learned about distinguishing between important and supporting ideas to help them make sense of text. Remind them that because it's difficult to remember everything, good readers think about what is most important to understand or remember as they read.

Tell the students that today they will practice thinking about what's important as they hear the first part of *A River Ran Wild* again.

2 Reread Pages 7–8 and Model Thinking About What Is Important

Have the students turn to "Think, Pair, Write About *A River Ran Wild*" on *Student Response Book* page 64. Explain that you will reread the first part of the story aloud, stopping several times during the reading. The students will use "Think, Pair, Write" to think about what is important in the part they just heard, agree in pairs on one important idea, and individually record the important idea in their own *Student Response Books*. Tell the students that you will model this for the class at the first stop.

Read the first two pages of the story aloud twice. Stop after:

p. 8   "He named the river Nash-a-way—River with the
            Pebbled Bottom."

Model thinking quietly for a moment; then think aloud about what
seems important in the passage. (For example, you might say, "What
seems most important to understand and remember in this passage
is that long ago the river valley was home to many animals and that
native people settled along the river.")

Model writing a note about this. (For example, you might write,
"Long ago many animals lived in the river valley. Native people
settled along the river.") Ask the students to write the same note in
their *Student Response Books.*

3 ▶ **Read Pages 10–16 with "Think, Pair, Write"**

Ask the students to listen for what's important in the next passage.
Reread the last sentence on page 8 and continue reading. Stop after:

p. 10   "The river, land, and forest provided all they needed."

Ask:

Q *What seems most important to understand and remember in the
part I just read?*

 Give the students 5–10 seconds to think; then have them share
briefly in pairs. After a moment, ask the class to listen again for what
seems most important to understand or remember, and reread
page 10 aloud.

Ask partners to agree on one idea that seems the most important
in the passage, and then to individually record their idea on *Student
Response Book* page 64. Have a few volunteers share what they
wrote with the class. Facilitate a brief class discussion by asking:

Q *Why does that idea seem most important?*

Q *Do others agree that this idea seems most important? Why or
why not?*

Q *What other ideas seem most important? Why?*

Teacher Note ▶

If necessary, model again by
thinking aloud, recording your
thinking, and asking the students
to copy your note into their
own *Student Response Books*
(for example, "What seems most
important in this part of the story
is that native people respected
nature and killed only the animals
they needed to survive").

Reread the last sentence on page 10 and continue reading. Follow the same procedure at the following stops:

p. 16 "They called the land their own and told the Indians not to trespass."

p. 16 "Deer still came to drink from the river, and owls, raccoons, and beaver fed there."

Explain that in the next lesson the students will think more about what is important in *A River Ran Wild*.

 Reflect on Reaching Agreement

Have partners report briefly how they did today reaching agreement about important ideas. Point out that reaching agreement means partners need to keep talking until they agree. Sometimes partners have to convince each other of their thinking. This helps them learn to work together, and it also forces them to think more clearly about the book.

◀ **Teacher Note**

Important ideas in these passages include that settlers in the valley killed more animals than they needed, cut down forests, threatened the Indians' way of life, and later drove the Indians from the valley.

INDIVIDUALIZED DAILY READING

 Think About Important Ideas

Have the students continue to use self-stick notes to mark important ideas in their reading.

Have the students read independently for up to 30 minutes.

As the students read, circulate among them. Ask individual students questions such as:

Q *What is your book about?*

Q *Why do you think the idea you marked is important?*

Q *What other ideas might be important in this section?*

At the end of independent reading, have a few volunteers share one important idea they found in their reading.

Day 3

Materials

- *A River Ran Wild*
- *Student Response Book* pages 64–65
- Transparencies of the "Excerpt from *A River Ran Wild*" (BLM31–BLM32)
- Transparency pens in two colors
- *Student Response Book*, IDR Journal section

🌐 ELL Note

English Language Learners may benefit from extra support to make sense of the excerpt. Show and discuss the illustrations on pages 19–23 again; then read the excerpt aloud as the students follow along. Stop periodically to talk about what is happening. The students may benefit from an explanation of the following words and passages:

- "whose swiftly flowing current washed away the waste"
- "for many decades"

Guided Strategy Practice

In this lesson, the students:

- *Distinguish between important ideas and supporting ideas* in a story
- Read independently for up to 30 minutes
- Reach agreement

1 Review Important Ideas

Have the students turn to *Student Response Book* page 64. Remind them that in the previous lesson they heard you reread the first part of *A River Ran Wild* and used "Think, Pair, Write" to think about and record what is important in the story. Have them review their journal entries. Ask:

Q *What information in the first part of the story did we think was important to understand or remember?*

Remind the students that distinguishing between important ideas and supporting ideas (such as details, examples, and descriptions) helps them understand texts more deeply. Explain that today the students will think about what is important and what is supporting in another selection from *A River Ran Wild*.

2 Identify Important and Supporting Ideas in an Excerpt

Place the first transparency of the excerpt on the overhead projector, and have the students turn to *Student Response Book* page 65. Point out that the excerpt is from the part of the story that describes how the river became polluted. Read the excerpt aloud slowly and clearly as the students follow along.

Direct the students' attention to the first paragraph by darkening the rest of the excerpt with a sheet of paper on the overhead projector. Explain that today they will focus their discussion on just this paragraph, and they will work with the rest of the excerpt tomorrow.

Reread the paragraph aloud; then think aloud about what seems important in the paragraph. (For example, you might say, "One idea that seems important to understand and remember in this paragraph is that many new machines were invented. The reason I think this is that later we learn that machines polluted the river.") Underline the important idea on the transparency (for example, "Many new machines were invented").

Remind the students that supporting ideas are details, examples, and descriptions that tell more about the important ideas. First in pairs, and then as a class, have the students discuss:

Q *Which sentences in the paragraph are supporting ideas that tell more about the new machines?*

As the students identify supporting ideas, underline them on the transparency using a different colored pen.

> **Students might say:**
>
> "I think the sentences 'Some spun thread from wool and cotton. Others wove the thread into cloth. Some machines turned wood to pulp, and others made the pulp into paper' are supporting details. The reason I think this is that the sentences give examples of the kinds of machines that were invented."
>
> "I agree with [Cammy]. Those sentences give details that are not the most important things to remember."

▶ 3 Decide Whether an Idea Is Important or Supporting

Direct the students' attention to the last sentence in the paragraph: "Leftover pulp and dye and fiber was dumped into the Nashua River, whose swiftly flowing current washed away the waste."

Have the students use "Turn to Your Partner" to discuss:

Q *Is this sentence an important idea or a supporting idea? Why do you think so?*

Have one or two students share their thinking with the class. Remind the students to use the discussion prompts they have learned to connect their comments to those of others.

Students might say:

> "I think the sentence is an important idea. The reason I think this
> is that it tells how the machines began to pollute the river."

> "I agree with [Patrick]. The sentence says the machines dumped
> pulp and dye into the river, and that's what started the
> pollution. That's important to know."

Remind the students that good readers don't necessarily remember
everything they read, but they do remember what's important.
Distinguishing between important and supporting ideas helps
them identify what they want to remember.

Explain that in the next lesson they will think about what is
important and supporting in the rest of the excerpt.

Keep the transparency with the underlined sentences for Day 4.

INDIVIDUALIZED DAILY READING

▶4 **Have the Students Think About Important Ideas/
Document IDR Conferences**

Have the students continue to use self-stick notes to mark
important ideas in their reading.

Have the students read independently for up to 30 minutes.

Use the "IDR Conference Notes" record sheet to conduct and
document individual conferences.

At the end of independent reading, have volunteers share with the
class one important idea they found in their reading. Remind them
to ask clarifying questions and to use the prompt "The reason I think
this is _____" to support their thinking.

Ask and briefly discuss questions such as:

Q *What idea did you think was important?*

Q *Why do you think that is important?*

Day 4

Guided Strategy Practice

In this lesson, the students:

- *Distinguish between important ideas and supporting ideas* in a story
- Use "Think, Pair, Write"
- Read independently for up to 30 minutes
- Reach agreement

1 Review Important and Supporting Ideas

Have the students turn to *Student Response Book* page 65. Place the first transparency on the overhead projector. Remind the students that they discussed important and supporting ideas in the first paragraph of the excerpt together yesterday. Explain that today they will use "Think, Pair, Write" to think about what is important and supporting in the rest of the excerpt.

2 Identify Important and Supporting Ideas in the Rest of the Excerpt

As you read the rest of the excerpt aloud, have the students follow along and think about what is important and what is supporting.

At the end of the reading, remind the students that *A River Ran Wild* is essentially a story about what happens to a river over time. Ask them to keep this in mind as they think quietly about one important and one supporting idea in the excerpt (excluding the first paragraph). Then have partners discuss their thinking, agree on one important idea and one supporting idea in the excerpt, and individually underline the two ideas in their *Student Response Books.*

Materials

- *A River Ran Wild*
- *Student Response Book* page 65
- Transparencies of the "Excerpt from *A River Ran Wild*" (from Day 3)
- Transparency pens in two colors
- *Assessment Resource Book*
- *Student Response Book,* IDR Journal section
- Small self-stick notes for each student

> ## CLASS COMPREHENSION ASSESSMENT
>
> Circulate among the pairs and notice which sentences the students underline. Ask yourself:
>
> **Q** *Are the students making reasonable distinctions between important and supporting information?*
>
> **Q** *Are they supporting their thinking by referring to the story?*
>
> Record your observations on page 25 of the *Assessment Resource Book.*

3 ▶ Discuss Important and Supporting Ideas as a Class

After a few minutes, facilitate a class discussion. Ask:

Q *What sentence did you and your partner agree was an important idea? Explain your thinking.*

Q *What sentence did you and your partner agree was supporting? Explain your thinking.*

Q *Do you agree with [Chieko and John]? Why or why not?*

Students might say:

"My partner and I underlined 'Soon the Nashua's fish and wildlife grew sick from this pollution.' We think that is important because it's the start of the really bad pollution that killed animals."

"We underlined 'The Nashua was slowly dying.' It's an important idea because that's what this book is about—how pollution killed the river."

"My partner and I thought 'No one could see pebbles shining up through murky water' is a supporting idea. We think so because it's an example of how dirty the water was."

"We think 'Chemicals and plastic waste were also dumped into the river' is supporting because it's a detail."

As the students share, underline the important and supporting ideas on the transparency using two different colored pens.

Remind the students that the purpose of learning to identify important and supporting ideas in a text is to help them think about what's important to understand or remember in their own reading. Explain that in the coming weeks they will continue to think about important and supporting ideas in texts they hear and read independently.

4 ▶ Reflect on Reaching Agreement

Facilitate a brief discussion about how the students did reaching agreement during "Think, Pair, Write." Ask questions such as:

Q *How did you come to agreement today during "Think, Pair, Write"? If you didn't agree, how did you solve the problem?*

Q *How did giving reasons for your opinions help you reach agreement?*

INDIVIDUALIZED DAILY READING

5 ▶ Have the Students Write About an Important Idea in Their IDR Journals/Document IDR Conferences

Have the students continue to use self-stick notes to mark important ideas as they read.

Have the students read independently for up to 30 minutes.

Use the "IDR Conference Notes" record sheet to conduct and document individual conferences.

At the end of independent reading, have the students write in their IDR Journals about one important idea they marked in their reading and why they thought it was important. Have a few students share their writing with the class.

Teacher Note

In Unit 8, Week 3, the students focus on building summaries from important ideas in text. If you feel your students need more experience thinking about important ideas and distinguishing between important and supporting ideas before continuing, you may wish to repeat this week's activities with alternative books before going on to Week 3. Alternative titles are listed on this week's Overview page.

EXTENSION

Learn More About Protecting the Environment

You might read aloud other books with an environmental theme, giving the students additional practice thinking about important ideas. Stop occasionally during the reading to have the students discuss what is important to know and why. Here are some titles to consider: *Common Ground: The Water, Earth, and Air We Share* by Molly Bang; *The Drop in My Drink: The Story of Water on Our Planet* by Meredith Hooper; and *A North American Rain Forest Scrapbook* by Virginia Wright-Frierson.

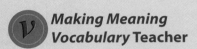

***Making Meaning
Vocabulary* Teacher**

Next week you will revisit
this week's reading to teach
Vocabulary Week 22.

Week 3

Overview

UNIT 8: DETERMINING IMPORTANT IDEAS AND SUMMARIZING

Fiction and Narrative Nonfiction

Harry Houdini: Master of Magic
by Robert Kraske
(Scholastic, 1989)

This is a biography of Harry Houdini, one of the greatest escape artists and magicians of all time.

ALTERNATIVE BOOKS

Mandela: From the Life of the South African Statesman
by Floyd Cooper

Langston Hughes: American Poet by Alice Walker

Comprehension Focus

- Students *think about important ideas and supporting ideas* in a text.

- Students use important ideas to build *summaries*.

- Students read independently.

Social Development Focus

- Students relate the value of respect to their behavior.

- Students develop the group skills of giving reasons for their opinions and discussing their opinions respectfully.

DO AHEAD

- Make a transparency of the "Summary of *A River Ran Wild*" (BLM33).

- Collect sample book and movie summaries, enough for one per pair of students (see Day 1, Step 4 and the Teacher Note on page 466).

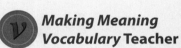

Making Meaning
***Vocabulary* Teacher**

If you are teaching Developmental Studies Center's *Making Meaning Vocabulary* program, teach Vocabulary Week 22 this week. For more information, see the *Making Meaning Vocabulary Teacher's Manual.*

Day 1

Materials

- *A River Ran Wild* (from Unit 8, Week 2)

- Transparency of the "Summary of *A River Ran Wild*" (BLM33)

- *Student Response Book* page 66

- Book and movie summaries (one summary per pair)

- (Optional) *Student Response Book* page 67

Strategy Lesson

In this lesson, the students:

- Hear, read, and discuss summaries

- Explore a summary

- Read independently for up to 30 minutes

- Give reasons for their opinions

About Summarizing

During the next three weeks, the focus of instruction is *summarizing*, a key strategy for helping readers understand and communicate what they read. The students continue to explore important ideas, a critical step in summarizing. Through teacher modeling, partner and class discussions, and guided practice, the students learn to put a text's important ideas together in a concise summary. The goal is for the students to be able to use summarization both orally and in writing to communicate with others about what they read.

1 ▶ Review Giving Reasons for Opinions

Ask partners to sit together. Remind the students that they learned the prompt "The reason I think this is _____" to give reasons for their opinions. Explain that you would like them to continue using the prompt in both partner and whole-class discussions this week.

Teacher Note ▶

If necessary, write the prompt where everyone can see it.

2 ▶ Review *A River Ran Wild*

Show *A River Ran Wild* and review that in the previous week the students heard the book read aloud and made inferences as they thought about the important and supporting ideas in it. Remind them that the book tells the story of the Nashua River, from the time before people lived near it to the present. Ask:

Q *What do you remember from the book about the Nashua River?*

Stimulate the students' recollection by reading each of the following sentences aloud and asking the students to remember what was happening in that part of the story. For each sentence, have a volunteer share what was happening:

p. 8 "He named the river Nash-a-way—River with the Pebbled Bottom."

p. 12 "…one day a pale-skinned trader came with a boatload full of treasures."

p. 18 "Many new machines were invented."

p. 22 "Each day as the mills dyed paper red, green, blue, and yellow, the Nashua ran whatever color the paper was dyed."

p. 26 "Marion traveled to each town along the Nashua. She spoke of the river's history and of her vision to restore it."

p. 31 "Once again the river runs wild through a towering forest greenway."

▶ 3 Read and Discuss a Summary of the Book

Place the transparency of the "Summary of *A River Ran Wild*" on the overhead projector. Explain that this is a summary of the book and that a summary is a brief description of what a text is about. Ask the students to follow along as you read the summary aloud.

After the reading, have the students turn to the "Summary of *A River Ran Wild*" on *Student Response Book* page 66. Point out that this is the summary you just read. Ask the students to read the summary again quietly to themselves.

After the reading, facilitate a whole-class discussion using the following questions. Remind the students to use "The reason I think this is _____" as they talk.

Q *What does this summary of the book do?*

Q *What kind of information is in the summary?*

◄ **Teacher Note**

Have students who are unable to read the summary on their own read it with a partner, or you might reread it aloud yourself as the students read along.

Students might say:

"The summary tells you what the book is about."

"It gives you the story, but in a shorter version."

"It has the main stuff about the river. The reason I think this is
that it doesn't tell everything—like how the river changed color
from the dye."

"I agree with [Anya]. The summary has the important ideas from
the book—like when the river got cleaned up and ran wild again."

Q *Why might you want to read a summary of a book?*

Students might say:

"You might want to know what the book is about before
you read it."

"From the summary, you can figure out if the book
sounds interesting."

4 ▶ Explore Other Summaries

Tell the students you collected summaries from various sources
for them to read today. Distribute the summaries, one to each pair.
Have each pair read their summary quietly to themselves, and
then discuss the following questions. Write the questions where
everyone can see them.

- What book or movie is your summary about?

- What did you learn about the book or movie from the summary?

When most pairs have finished, ask a few pairs to share with the
class what their summary is about and what they learned from the
summary. Follow up by asking:

Q *How might the summary be helpful to you or others who read it?*

Explain that *summarizing* means *using important information in a
text to say briefly what the text is about*. Readers summarize to help
them make sense of what they are reading and to remember the
important information. They also summarize to communicate to
others what a text is about.

Teacher Note ▶

You can find book summaries
on the back covers of
books as well as on Internet
bookseller websites. You
might also collect reviews that
summarize movies the students
might be familiar with.

If you do not have enough
summaries for all the pairs you can
have the students read "Summary
of *Letting Swift River Go*" on
Student Response Book page 67.

Explain that during the next few weeks the students will learn
how to summarize so they can write summaries of their own
independent reading books to share with the class.

 Reflect on Giving Reasons for Opinions

Facilitate a brief discussion about how the students did with using
the prompt to give reasons for their opinions.

INDIVIDUALIZED DAILY READING

 Self-monitor to Think About What Is Important

Remind the students that they have been thinking about important
ideas in texts. Explain that today you will stop them periodically
during IDR to have them think about how well they are recognizing
what is important in their reading to that point.

Have the students independently read books at appropriate levels
for up to 30 minutes. Stop them at 10-minute intervals and have
them think about the following questions:

Q *What seems important to understand in the reading so far?*

Q *What might the author want you to be thinking at this point?*

At the end of independent reading, have a few volunteers share
an important idea in their reading. Remind the students to use
evidence from the text to support their thinking.

Materials

• *Harry Houdini* (pages 7–16)

Read-aloud

In this lesson, the students:

• Hear and discuss a story
• *Make inferences*
• Read independently for up to 30 minutes
• Give reasons for their opinions

1 ▶ **Review Summaries and Summarizing**

Remind the students that in the previous lesson they heard a summary of *A River Ran Wild*. Review that a summary is a brief description of what a text is about. It includes important information or ideas from the text.

Explain that you will read part of a book aloud today, and in the next two days the class will build a summary of it together.

2 ▶ **Introduce *Harry Houdini: Master of Magic***

Show the cover of *Harry Houdini: Master of Magic* and read the name of the author aloud. Read the information on the back cover aloud, and ask:

Q *What do you think this book is going to be about?*

Q *What do you think an escape artist does?*

Explain that the book is a biography of Harry Houdini, a man who became world famous in the late 1800s and early 1900s for escaping from seemingly inescapable situations. Tell the students that you will read the beginning of the book today.

Read Aloud

Read pages 7–16, stopping as described below.

> **Suggested Vocabulary**
>
> **supernatural:** caused by powers outside of nature; magical (p. 8)
> **bluff:** trick (p. 13)
>
> **ELL Vocabulary**
>
> English Language Learners may benefit from discussing additional vocabulary, including:
>
> **safe:** locked box used to store valuable things (p. 7)
> **escape:** get out (p. 7)
> **trapeze:** high swing used in circuses (p. 11)

Stop after:

pp. 9–10 "He had been sitting behind the screen for almost a half hour while the audience's excitement grew."

 Have the students use "Turn to Your Partner" to discuss:

Q *What happened in the part of the story you just heard?*

Without sharing as a class, reread the last sentence before the stop and continue reading to the next stop. Stop after:

p. 11 "He had already learned the first rule of being a magician: Never tell how you do a trick!"

Have the students use "Turn to Your Partner" to discuss:

Q *What did you learn about Harry Houdini in this part of the story?*

Without sharing as a class, reread the last sentence and continue reading to the next stop. Repeat this procedure at the next two stops:

p. 13 "She hugged her hardworking son."

p. 16 "He was seventeen years old."

Finish today's reading with the above sentence on page 16.

4 ▶ **Discuss the Reading as a Class**

Facilitate a discussion of the story, using the following questions. Remind the students to use "The reason I think this is _____" and the other discussion prompts they have learned to add to one another's thinking.

Q *At the beginning of the passage, Harry was at the Euston Palace Theatre. Why was the audience at the theater so excited?*

Q *What word would you use to describe Harry when he was a boy? Why would you use that word? Why was Harry well suited to become a magician?*

> *Students might say:*
>
> "Harry was smart. He learned how to pick locks."
>
> "Harry was a showoff. He liked performing in front of people."
>
> "In addition to what [Stacy] said, he was hardworking. He worked hard to learn things, like how to pick locks."

As the students make inferences about the story, point them out (for example, "The book does not directly say Harry was smart, but you figured it out from clues such as how he learned to pick locks").

Explain that in the next lesson they will think about what information is important to know and remember in this story and prepare to write a summary of it.

INDIVIDUALIZED DAILY READING

5 ▶ **Self-monitor to Think About What Is Important**

Have the students independently read books at appropriate levels for up to 30 minutes. Continue to have the students think about what they are reading. Stop them at 10-minute intervals and have them think about the following questions:

Q *What seems important to understand in the reading so far?*

Q *What might the author want you to be thinking at this point?*

Teacher Note ▶

Be prepared to reread passages from the text to help the students recall what they heard.

As the students read, circulate among them and ask individuals to read a selection aloud to you and explain what they think is important so far.

At the end of independent reading, have a few volunteers share how they are doing at identifying important ideas as they read. Remind the students to use evidence from the text to support their thinking.

Day 3

Materials

- *Harry Houdini* (pages 7–16)
- Chart paper and a marker
- *Assessment Resource Book*
- Small self-stick notes for each student

Guided Strategy Practice

In this lesson, the students:

- *Distinguish between important ideas and supporting ideas in a text*
- Read independently for up to 30 minutes
- Give reasons for their opinions
- Discuss their opinions respectfully

 Review Important and Supporting Ideas

Remind the students that in the past few weeks they have been thinking about the important and supporting ideas in books such as *Letting Swift River Go* and *A River Ran Wild*. Review that *determining important ideas* is a comprehension strategy that can help them identify what is essential to know and remember in a text.

Explain that identifying important ideas is also necessary for summarizing because a summary is made up of the important information in the text. Tell the students that today they will think about what is important in the passage they heard yesterday from *Harry Houdini*. This will prepare them to write a summary of it as a class tomorrow.

 Reread the Passage

Explain that as you reread the section from *Harry Houdini* you will stop several times. At each stop, the students will think quietly about what is important in the part of the story they just heard. They will then share their thinking in pairs.

Reread pages 7–16, stopping at the following points to have the students talk about their ideas.

Stop after:

p. 8   "'Then,' Houdini said, shaking hands with the last man, 'let me enter the safe. Lock the door behind me!'"

Ask:

Q   *What is most important to understand or remember about what you've heard so far?*

 Have the students use "Think, Pair, Share" to discuss their ideas. Then have a couple of volunteers share their ideas with the class. Record the ideas on a chart entitled "Important Ideas in *Harry Houdini*."

> **Students might say:**
>
> "Houdini is getting into a safe that is locked in front of an audience. He's going to try to get out."
>
> "He could die if he doesn't get out."

 Follow this procedure at the next five stops, recording a couple of ideas on the chart at each stop.

pp. 9–10   "He had been sitting behind the screen for almost a half hour while the audience's excitement grew."

p. 10   "As they grew up, Ehrich and his brothers had to earn money for the family by shining shoes and selling newspapers."

p. 12   "He can pick any lock in the place!"

p. 14   "Ehrich never thought about making a living doing tricks."

p. 16   "He was seventeen years old."

Teacher Note

If the students have difficulty identifying important ideas in the passages, you may want to teach this lesson over two days. Follow the procedure you used in Days 2 and 3 of Week 2, in which the students hear the passage, discuss important ideas in pairs, hear the passage again, and record their ideas.

Teacher Note

Some important ideas are:

- Houdini is getting into a safe in front of an audience. He's going to try to get out.
- The audience thinks he's dead.
- He escapes, but he is sitting behind the screen.
- His real name was Ehrich Weiss.
- His family came to America from Hungary.
- His family was poor.
- He performed tricks for his friends.
- He earned a few dollars doing magic shows in clubs.
- He read a book about a French magician and changed his name to Houdini.
- He decided to make magic his life's work.

> ## CLASS COMPREHENSION ASSESSMENT
>
> Circulate as partners talk. Ask yourself:
>
> **Q** *Are the students able to identify important information in the text?*
>
> **Q** *Are they referring to the text to support their thinking?*
>
> Record your observations on page 26 of the *Assessment Resource Book*.

 3 ## Discuss Important Ideas as a Class

Facilitate a discussion using the following questions. Remind the students to give reasons for their opinions.

Q *Are there any important ideas that we need to add to the chart?*

Q *Are there any ideas on the chart that you think are supporting ideas? Why do you think that?*

Students might say:

"I think the idea that he earned money doing tricks is a supporting idea. I don't think we need to remember that."

"I agree with [Min Soo]. The important idea is that he was doing magic when he was young. The information about where he did it is a detail."

"I think it's important that he stole cakes from the cupboard. It shows he could pick locks."

"I disagree with [Pam]. The important idea is that he was learning how to pick locks."

Make adjustments to the chart as needed during this discussion, adding important ideas and crossing out supporting information. If the students have difficulty distinguishing between what is important and what is supporting, you might think aloud to model your own thinking and revise the chart as needed.

Explain that in the next lesson the class will use the ideas on the chart to write a summary of the passage.

Reflect on Discussing Opinions Respectfully

Point out that it is normal for people to have different opinions about what is important and what is supporting in a text. Remind the students of any disagreements during today's whole-class discussion. Ask:

Q *When someone disagrees with you, how do you like them to tell you that?*

Q *If they don't tell you in that way, how might you feel? Why?*

Q *How can we make sure that we can disagree respectfully during our discussions?*

Tell the students that they will continue to discuss their opinions in the coming weeks and that you would like them to focus on doing so respectfully.

Save the "Important Ideas in *Harry Houdini*" chart for Day 4.

INDIVIDUALIZED DAILY READING

5 ▸ Discuss Important and Supporting Ideas/Document IDR Conferences

Remind the students that they have been thinking about both important and supporting ideas in texts. Explain that you want them to use self-stick notes to mark one important idea and one supporting idea in their reading today.

Have the students read independently for up to 30 minutes. Use the "IDR Conference Notes" record sheet to conduct and document individual conferences.

At the end of independent reading, have volunteers share the important and supporting ideas they marked. Remind them to ask clarifying questions and to use the prompt "The reason I think this is _____" to support their thinking.

Conduct a whole-class discussion by asking and briefly discussing questions such as:

Q *What passage did you mark as important?*

Q *How did you know that idea was important?*

Q *What passage did you mark as supporting? How does this passage support the important ideas in your reading?*

Day 4

Guided Strategy Practice

In this lesson, the students:

- *Build a summary* as a class
- Read independently for up to 30 minutes
- Give reasons for their opinions

1 ▶ **Review Important Ideas and Summarizing**

Direct the students' attention to the "Important Ideas in *Harry Houdini*" chart and remind them that in the previous lesson they made a list of the important ideas in the story. Review that knowing what is important in a text is necessary for summarizing it, and that *summarizing* is a powerful strategy for remembering important information and communicating it to others.

Explain that today the class will use the ideas on the chart to write a summary of the passage from *Harry Houdini*. Remind them that they will be writing summaries of their own books in the next couple of weeks.

2 ▶ **Review the "Summary of *A River Ran Wild*"**

Put the transparency of the "Summary of *A River Ran Wild*" on the overhead projector, and have the students turn to *Student Response Book* page 66, where the summary is reproduced. Explain that this summary, which they read earlier in the week, can serve as a model for the summary they will write today.

Ask the students to reread the summary quietly to themselves (or follow along as you read it aloud again); then have the students use "Think, Pair, Share" to discuss:

Q *What do you notice in the summary of* A River Ran Wild *that might serve as a model when we summarize the passage from* Harry Houdini?

Materials

- *Harry Houdini* (pages 7–16)
- "Important Ideas in *Harry Houdini*" chart (from Day 3)
- Transparency of the "Summary of *A River Ran Wild*" (BLM33)
- *Student Response Book* page 66
- Chart paper or a blank transparency and a marker
- "Reading Comprehension Strategies" chart
- Small self-stick notes for each student
- *Student Response Book*, IDR Journal section

Important Ideas in Harry Houdini

- Houdini is getting into a safe in front of an audience. He's going to try to get out.

Students might say:

"The first sentence just tells you what it's about."

"It doesn't say everything that's in the book. The reason I think
this is that lots of supporting details are left out."

"It's not too long."

If the students have difficulty answering this question, suggest some
ideas like those in the "Students might say" note. Point out that the
summary begins with a general statement of what the book is about
and continues with important events or ideas from the book.

 ## Model Starting the Summary of *Harry Houdini*

On a blank transparency or a sheet of chart paper, write the title
"Summary of the Passage from *Harry Houdini.*" Explain that you will
begin the summary and the class will write the rest of it together.

Tell the students that you want to begin the summary with a
general statement of what the book is about. Ask:

Q *In a sentence, what is the passage we read from* Harry
Houdini *about?*

Students might say:

"It's about a famous magician and escape artist when he
was a kid."

"It's about how Harry Houdini started getting into magic
and things when he was still young."

Using the students' suggestions, model writing an opening
sentence about the book (for example, "This passage is about the
famous magician and escape artist Harry Houdini and how he got
started in magic as a kid"). If the students cannot come up with a
general opening sentence, provide one yourself.

Explain that the rest of the summary will be made up of ideas that are listed on the "Important Ideas in *Harry Houdini*" chart. Model selecting information for the second sentence by thinking aloud. (For example, you might say, "Since this story starts by describing Houdini as an adult, and then moves to his childhood, it makes sense to tell how it happened in that order. The first thing Houdini does in the book is attempt an escape from a safe in front of a live audience. I'll use that information for the second sentence of the summary.")

Model writing the second sentence of the summary (for example, "It begins with a story of how, as an adult, Houdini escaped from a locked safe in front of a live audience").

Follow this procedure to provide the third sentence of the summary.

 4 Complete the Summary as a Class

Referring to the "Important Ideas in *Harry Houdini*" chart, elicit suggestions for what to add to the summary by asking:

Q   *What information do you think should come next in the summary? Why do you think that?*

Use the students' suggestions to add sentences to the chart. If possible, model combining two or three pieces of information on the chart into a single sentence. Point out that combining information in this way helps to keep the summary brief. (For example, "He read a book about a French magician and changed his name to Houdini" and "He decided to make magic his life's work" can be combined into the sentence "After reading about the French magician Robert-Houdin, Ehrich changed his name to Houdini and decided to make magic his life's work.")

Continue to add sentences, shaping and combining the students' ideas as necessary to keep the summary clear and concise. You may need to model the use of words such as *then, next,* and *after that* to connect sentences and show the sequence of events.

◀ **Teacher Note**

If the students are unable to suggest sentences, continue to model by thinking aloud and adding your own sentences to the chart.

The completed summary might look like this:

Summary of the Passage from <u>Harry Houdini</u>

This passage is about the famous magician and escape artist Harry Houdini and how he got started in magic when he was a kid. It begins with a story of how, as an adult, Houdini escaped from a locked safe in front of a live audience. Houdini's real name was Ehrich Weiss, and his family came to America from Hungary when he was a child. The family was poor, and Ehrich and his brother had to earn money to live. Ehrich performed tricks for his friends, sometimes even earning a few dollars at the neighborhood club. After reading about the French magician Robert-Houdin, Ehrich changed his name to Houdini and decided to make magic his life's work.

When the summary is finished, reread it aloud and ask:

Q *Do you think someone who hasn't read the passage from* Harry Houdini *could get a good idea of what it is about from reading this summary? If not, what can we add?*

Save this summary for use in Weeks 4 and 5.

5 ▶ Add to the "Reading Comprehension Strategies" Chart

Direct the students' attention to the "Reading Comprehension Strategies" chart and add *summarizing* to it. Review that summarizing is using important information in a text to say briefly what the text is about. Readers summarize to help them make sense of important information in a text and also to communicate to others what a text is about.

Tell the students that during the next couple of weeks they will practice summarizing, with the goal of writing a summary of their own book to share with their classmates.

Reading Comprehension Strategies

- recognizing text features

---

6 Reflect on Today's Partner and Class Conversations

Facilitate a brief discussion about today's conversations and how the students did giving reasons for their opinions and discussing their opinions respectfully. Report any examples you noticed of students disagreeing respectfully and giving reasons for their opinions.

INDIVIDUALIZED DAILY READING

7 Write About Important and Supporting Ideas in Their IDR Journals/Document IDR Conferences

Have the students continue to use self-stick notes to mark one important idea and one supporting idea in their reading.

Have the students read independently for up to 30 minutes.

Use the "IDR Conference Notes" record sheet to conduct and document individual conferences.

At the end of independent reading, have the students write in their IDR Journals about the important and supporting ideas they marked in their reading and why they thought the ideas were important or supporting.

EXTENSION

Learn More About Harry Houdini

If the students are interested, you may want to read the rest of *Harry Houdini: Master of Magic* aloud. Alternatively, you can make the book available for them to read independently. Students who want to know more about Houdini might search for websites about him or look for other books in the library.

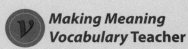

***Making Meaning Vocabulary* Teacher**

Next week you will revisit this week's reading to teach Vocabulary Week 23.

Week 4

Overview

UNIT 8: DETERMINING IMPORTANT IDEAS AND SUMMARIZING

Fiction and Narrative Nonfiction

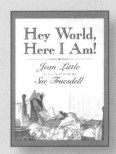

"Mrs. Buell"
in ***Hey World, Here I Am!****
by Jean Little, illustrated by Sue Truesdell
(HarperTrophy, 1990)

Kate doesn't think much about grouchy Mrs. Buell until the old woman disappears from her life.

*This book is also used in Unit 9, Week 1.

ALTERNATIVE BOOKS

"Ana" in ***Seedfolks*** by Paul Fleischman
The Cello of Mr. O by Jane Cutler

Comprehension Focus

- Students *think about important ideas and supporting ideas* in a text.

- Students use important ideas to *summarize*.

- Students read independently.

Social Development Focus

- Students relate the value of respect to their behavior.

- Students develop the group skills of giving reasons for their opinions and discussing their opinions respectfully.

DO AHEAD

- Make transparencies of "Mrs. Buell" (BLM34–BLM39).

- Prepare charts for taking notes about important ideas (see Day 2, Step 4 on page 490 and Day 3, Step 4 on page 495).

Making Meaning Vocabulary Teacher

If you are teaching Developmental Studies Center's *Making Meaning Vocabulary* program, teach Vocabulary Week 23 this week. For more information, see the *Making Meaning Vocabulary Teacher's Manual.*

Day 1

Materials

- "Mrs. Buell" in *Hey World, Here I Am!* (pages 42–47)
- Small self-stick notes for each student

 Note

Summarize the story for your English Language Learners prior to today's read-aloud.

Read-aloud

In this lesson, the students:

- *Think about important ideas* in a text
- Read independently for up to 30 minutes
- Give reasons for their opinions
- Discuss their opinions respectfully

1 ▸ Review the Social Focus and Summarizing

Ask partners to sit together. Remind the students that they have been focusing on giving reasons for their opinions and on discussing their opinions respectfully. Explain that you would like them to continue to practice these skills in the coming week.

Explain that this week the students will continue to learn about using important ideas to summarize the text. Remind them that *summarizing* is an important strategy to know because it helps readers understand and communicate to others what a text is about.

2 ▸ Introduce "Mrs. Buell"

Tell the students that today you will read aloud from the book *Hey World, Here I Am!* Show the cover of the book, and read the names of the author and illustrator aloud. Explain that the book is a collection of stories, poems, and other writing by a fictional teenager named Kate Bloomfield. Today you will read a story called "Mrs. Buell," in which Kate tells about a woman who owns a neighborhood store.

3 ▸ Read "Mrs. Buell" Aloud

Ask the students to listen for important ideas as you read. Tell them that you will stop several times and have partners talk about what seems important about the part they just heard.

Read the story aloud, stopping as described below.

Suggested Vocabulary

intent on: focused on (p. 43)

slunk out: sneaked away quietly (p. 44)

gawking: staring stupidly (p. 45)

ELL Vocabulary

English Language Learners may benefit from discussing additional
vocabulary, including:

run-down: in poor condition (p. 42)

corner store: small neighborhood store (p. 42)

licorice, jawbreakers: kinds of candy (p. 42)

grouch: person who is in a bad mood (p. 42)

Stop after:

p. 43   "She was always the same except that once."

 Have the students use "Think, Pair, Share" to discuss:

Q   *What's most important to understand or remember about the part
you just heard?*

Without sharing as a class, reread the last sentence and continue
reading to the next stop. Repeat this procedure at the following stops:

p. 44   "I didn't go near the store for weeks."

p. 46   "'I said we're shut. If you don't want anything, beat it,' she
told me."

Continue reading to the end of the story.

4 ▸ **Discuss the Story as a Class**

Facilitate a discussion of the story, using the following questions.
Remind the students to use "The reason I think this is _____"
and the other discussion prompts they have learned to add to one
another's thinking.

Q   *What are some of the important ideas you heard in this reading?
Why does that idea seem important?*

Students might say:

"Mrs. Buell is grouchy and mean to the kids. They're all kind of afraid of her."

"I agree with [Denise]. The part where Mrs. Buell puts a bandage on Kate's knee is important, too. It shows that Mrs. Buell has this nice side that Kate didn't know about."

"Kate feels bad when Mrs. Buell dies. The reason I think this is that she says she has a hole in her life."

"To add to what [LaVaughn] said, Kate wishes she had been nicer to Mrs. Buell because in the story Kate wonders why she didn't smile back at Mrs. Buell."

Q *How did Kate's feelings toward Mrs. Buell change during the story? Why did her feelings change?*

Reread the last paragraph on page 46.

Q *What do you think Kate means by "I knew, for the first time, that nothing was safe—not even the everyday, taken-for-granted background of my being"? Explain your thinking.*

Explain that in the next lesson the students will think again about important ideas in this story and use those important ideas to create a summary.

INDIVIDUALIZED DAILY READING

 Discuss Important and Supporting Ideas

Remind the students that they have been thinking about both important and supporting ideas in texts. Explain that you want them to use self-stick notes to mark one important idea and one supporting idea in their reading today.

Have the students read independently for up to 30 minutes. As they read, circulate among them. Ask individual students questions such as:

Q *What is your book about?*

Q *Why do you think this passage is important?*

Q *How does the passage you marked support the important ideas in your reading?*

Q *Why do you think this passage is supporting?*

At the end of independent reading, have volunteers share the important and supporting ideas they marked and the reasons for their thinking.

Day 2

Materials

- *Student Response Book* pages 68–71
- Transparencies of sections 1–3 of "Mrs. Buell" (BLM34–BLM36)
- Chart for thinking about important ideas, prepared ahead (see Step 4)

Guided Strategy Practice

In this lesson, the students:

- *Think about important ideas* in a text
- Read independently for up to 30 minutes
- Give reasons for their opinions
- Discuss their opinions respectfully

1 ▶ Review Important Ideas and Summarizing

Review that *determining important ideas* helps readers better understand what they read and remember the essential ideas in a text. Remind the students that summaries are made up of important information and that summarizing helps readers understand a text and communicate to other readers what it is about.

Explain that this week they will use important ideas in "Mrs. Buell" to practice writing a summary of the story together. This week's activities will prepare them to write summaries of their own books for their classmates.

2 ▶ Model Taking Notes and Underlining Important Ideas in Section 1

Place the transparency of section 1 of "Mrs. Buell" on the overhead projector and explain that this is the beginning of the story they heard yesterday.

As the students follow along, read the section aloud. Then think aloud about what the section is about. On the transparency, model writing a brief note about this in the margin and underlining sentences that seem the most important in the section. (For example, you might say, "What's important in this section is Kate's description of Buells and Mrs. Buell. She says Buells is the run-down neighborhood store and that Mrs. Buell, the owner, is run-down, too, and grouchy. I'll underline the sentences that talk about that directly." In the margin, write "Mrs. Buell is the run-down, grouchy owner of a run-down, not very clean corner store" and underline "It's a run-down, not very clean corner store" and "Mrs. Buell is run-down too, and a grouch.")

Ask:

Q *What are some of the sentences in this section that support the important ideas I underlined? How do they support the idea?*

Students might say:

"'She only has three flavors and the cones taste stale.' That sentence might be a supporting idea. It's an example of the run-down store."

"In addition to what [Stan] said, I think the part about licorice and bubble gum and jawbreakers and things is supporting."

3 Practice Taking Notes and Underlining Important Ideas in Section 2

Explain that the story, divided into six sections, is reproduced on *Student Response Book* pages 68–71. Direct the students to the first section, and have them write in their own margin the note you modeled and underline the sentences you underlined.

Explain that you would like them to read the second section in pairs and discuss what seems most important in this section.

After partners talk for several minutes, bring their attention back to the whole class. Place the transparency of section 2 of the story on the overhead projector. Ask:

Q *What is this section about? What seems most important in this section?*

Q *Which sentences give you the most important information?*

Students might say:

"In this section, Kate falls in the store. Mrs. Buell helps her."

"I agree with [Connor]. I think 'I tripped going in, and fell and scraped my knee' and 'she took a bit of rag out of her sweater pocket, bent down, and wiped the smear of blood off my knee' are important sentences."

◀ **Teacher Note**

Copying your work in the first and second sections gives the students a record of your modeled thinking as they take notes and underline important ideas in the rest of the excerpt.

As the students respond, jot notes in the margin of the transparency and underline sentences. If the students have difficulty identifying the most important ideas in the section, model again by thinking aloud, writing a note in the margin, and underlining important sentences, such as those listed in the "Students might say" note.

Have the students copy your notes and underlines in their own *Student Response Books.*

4 ▶ Have Partners Take Notes and Underline Important Ideas in Section 3

Explain the following directions, which you have charted and posted where everyone can see them:

1. Read section 3 with your partner.

2. Discuss what it is about.

3. Write notes in the margin that tell what this section is about.

4. Underline sentences that seem most important.

 Circulate as the pairs work and notice whether they are able to identify important ideas and take notes about them. If the students are having difficulty, support them by asking questions such as:

Q *What happens in this section? Tell me in your own words.*

Q *What does Mrs. Buell do in this passage?*

Q *How does Kate feel in this passage? What sentences tell you how she feels?*

If you notice many students struggling with identifying the important ideas or taking notes about them, bring the class together and go through this section in the more directed way you did for the first two sections.

Teacher Note

Keep in mind that identifying and taking notes about important ideas can be challenging. It can be difficult for students to sort out major ideas from supporting details, especially in very concise texts. Students will benefit from repeated experiences hearing and thinking about important and supporting ideas.

Discuss Important Ideas in Section 3 as a Class

Place the transparency of section 3 of the story on the overhead projector. Facilitate a discussion about the section using the following questions. As the students report their thinking, jot notes and underline sentences on the transparency. Remind the students to give reasons for their opinions.

Q *What do you and your partner think this section is about? What sentences did you underline that talk about that directly? What notes did you write?*

Q *Why do you think that idea is important?*

Q *Do you agree or disagree with [Tamika and Lily]? Why?*

 ## Reflect on Discussing Opinions Respectfully

Facilitate a brief discussion about how the students interacted by asking:

Q *Did people disagree with you today? If so, did they disagree in a way that felt comfortable for you? Why or why not?*

Q *What might we want to do differently tomorrow so we know we are discussing our opinions respectfully?*

Explain that in the next lesson, the students will take notes and underline important sentences in the rest of the story.

Save your marked transparencies of "Mrs. Buell" for Days 3 and 4.

INDIVIDUALIZED DAILY READING

 ## Practice Orally Summarizing Reading

Have the students read independently for up to 30 minutes.

 At the end of independent reading, explain that you would like the students to think about a brief summary of the book they are reading by reflecting on some of the important ideas they have found. Have the students share their thinking, first in pairs, and then as a class. Ask:

Q *If you were to tell someone in a few sentences what your book is about, what would you say?*

Day 3

Guided Strategy Practice

In this lesson, the students:

- *Think about important ideas* in a text
- Read independently for up to 30 minutes
- Give reasons for their opinions
- Discuss their opinions respectfully

Materials

- Transparencies of "Mrs. Buell" (BLM34–BLM39)
- *Student Response Book* pages 68–71
- Chart for thinking about important ideas, prepared ahead (see Step 4)

1 **Review Important Ideas in the First Part of "Mrs. Buell"**

Show the transparencies of the first three sections of "Mrs. Buell" and review the notes you wrote and the sentences you underlined yesterday. Remind the students that they thought about the most important ideas in these three sections of the story.

Have the students use the same process they used yesterday to identify important ideas in the rest of the story. This will prepare them to summarize the story tomorrow.

2 **Model Taking Notes and Underlining Important Ideas in Section 4**

Place the transparency of section 4 of "Mrs. Buell" on the overhead projector.

As the students follow along, read aloud to the end of the section. Then think aloud about what the section is about. On the transparency, model writing a brief note about this in the margin and underlining sentences that seem the most important in the section. (For example, you might say, "What seems important in this section is that Kate and the other kids didn't really think about Mrs. Buell, until one day she wasn't there. I'll underline the sentences that talk about that." In the margin, write "Kate never thought about Mrs. Buell, until one day when she wasn't there" and underline "I didn't once wonder about her life" and "Then I stopped at Buells one afternoon and she wasn't there.")

Ask:

Q *What are some of the sentences in this section that support the important ideas I underlined? How do they support the idea?*

Students might say:

"'We didn't like her or hate her.' That sentence might be a supporting idea. It's an example of how they didn't think about her."

"In addition to what [Stan] said, I think the part about the man and woman behind the counter is supporting."

Direct the students to section 4 on *Student Response Book* page 69, and have them write in their own margin the notes you modeled and underline the sentences you underlined.

▶ **3** **Practice Taking Notes and Underlining Important Ideas in Section 5**

 Explain that you would like the students to read section 5 in pairs and discuss what seems most important in this section.

After partners talk for several minutes, bring their attention back to the whole class. Place the transparency of section 5 of the story on the overhead projector. Ask:

Q *What is this section about? What seems most important in this section?*

Q *Which sentences give you the most important information?*

Students might say:

"In this section, Kate finds out that Mrs. Buell is dead."

"I agree with [Connor]. I think 'She's dead. She won't bother you any longer' are important sentences."

As the students respond, jot notes in the margin of the transparency and underline sentences. If the students have difficulty identifying the most important ideas in the section, model again by thinking aloud, writing a note in the margin, and underlining important sentences.

Have each student copy your notes and underlines into her own *Student Response Book*.

Have Partners Take Notes and Underline Important Ideas in Section 6

Explain the following directions, which you have written on a chart and posted where everyone can see them:

1. Read section 6 with your partner.

2. Discuss what it is about.

3. Write notes in the margin that tell what this section is about.

4. Underline sentences that seem most important.

Circulate as pairs work and notice whether they are able to identify important ideas and take notes about them. If the students are having difficulty, support them by asking questions such as:

Q *What happens in this section? Tell me in your own words.*

Q *How does Kate feel about Mrs. Buell's death? What sentences tell you how she feels?*

If you notice many students struggling with identifying the important ideas or taking notes about them, bring the class together and go through the section in the more directed way you did in Step 3 of this lesson.

Discuss Important Ideas in Section 6 as a Class

Facilitate a discussion about the last section of the story using the following questions. As the students report their thinking, jot notes and underline sentences on the transparency. Remind the students to give reasons for their opinions.

Q *What do you and your partner think this section is about? What sentences did you underline that talk about that directly? What notes did you write?*

Q *Why do you think that idea is important?*

Q *Do you agree or disagree with [Barb and Christopher]? Why?*

Explain that in the next lesson, the students will use their notes and underlined passages to write a summary of the story together.

Save your marked transparencies of "Mrs. Buell" for Day 4.

INDIVIDUALIZED DAILY READING

 ### Document IDR Conferences/Have the Students Practice Orally Summarizing Reading

Have the students read independently for up to 30 minutes.

Use the "IDR Conference Notes" record sheet to conduct and document individual conferences.

 At the end of independent reading, ask each student to summarize his reading for his partner by telling his partner in a few sentences what he read. Have a few volunteers share with the class.

Day 4

Guided Strategy Practice

In this lesson, the students:

- *Build a summary* as a class
- Read independently for up to 30 minutes
- Give reasons for their opinions
- Discuss their opinions respectfully

1 ▎ Review Important Ideas and Summarizing

Have partners sit together. Explain that today they will use their notes and the important ideas they underlined in "Mrs. Buell" to write a summary of the story.

Have the students open to *Student Response Book* pages 68–71 and review their notes and the sentences they underlined.

2 ▎ Model Writing the First Few Sentences of the Summary

On a piece of chart paper, write the title "Summary of 'Mrs. Buell.'" Explain that you will help the class start the summary, and then partners will work together to continue writing it.

Review that a summary should give readers a good idea of what a piece of text is about. Refer to the summary of the passage in *Harry Houdini* and remind the students that in a summary, a general statement about the topic of the text is followed by important ideas in the piece.

Materials

- *Student Response Book* pages 68–71
- Chart paper and a marker
- "Summary of the Passage from *Harry Houdini*" chart (from Week 3)
- Transparencies of "Mrs. Buell," with marks from Days 2 and 3 (BLM34–BLM39)
- Paper and a pencil for each student
- *Assessment Resource Book*
- *Student Response Book,* IDR Journal section

Teacher Note

This lesson may take longer than one class period.

Ask:

Q *How might you say in one or two sentences what "Mrs. Buell" is about?*

Have a few volunteers share their thinking with the class. Then ask the students to listen and watch as you think aloud about what the story is about and write an opening sentence on the chart (for example, "In this story, a girl named Kate tells about Mrs. Buell, an old woman who owns a store in Kate's neighborhood").

Place the transparency of the first section of "Mrs. Buell" on the overhead projector. Read aloud the note(s) you wrote and the sentences you underlined. Think aloud about how you might summarize the section; then add a few sentences to the summary on the chart (for example, "The store is run-down and dirty, and Mrs. Buell is a grouch").

Ask the students to copy onto their own paper the sentences you wrote on the chart.

 3 **Practice Adding to the Summary Together**

 Direct the students to the second section of the story on *Student Response Book* page 68. Have them reread their notes and the sentences they underlined; then have them use "Turn to Your Partner" to discuss how they might summarize this section.

After a minute or two, bring the students' attention back to the whole class. Ask one or two volunteers for sentences to summarize this section. Help them by asking questions such as:

Q *How can we describe in one or two sentences what happened the day Kate fell?*

Q *What is one sentence we can write that captures both [Quinn's] and [Luis's] ideas?*

Students might say:

"My partner and I think you can add the sentences 'One day Kate
skins her knee in the store. Mrs. Buell is nice to her for the first
time. She scoops Kate up and puts a bandage on her knee.'"

"I think we should add that 'Mrs. Buell has kind hands.'"

"I disagree with [Lila]. I think that is a detail about Mrs. Buell."

As the students respond, add to the summary on the chart. If the
students have difficulty generating sentences that summarize
this section, model again by thinking aloud and adding your own
sentences, like those in the "Students might say" note.

Again, have the students copy your sentences onto their own paper.

 ## Have Partners Write the Rest of the Summary

Explain that you would like partners to work together to write
the rest of the summary, looking at one section at a time while
reviewing their notes and underlined sentences.

Circulate and support the students by asking them questions like
those in Step 3 of this lesson. If you notice many students having
difficulty, bring the class together and summarize the remaining
section of the story together in the more directed way you did
earlier in the lesson.

CLASS COMPREHENSION
ASSESSMENT

Circulate as partners write their summaries. Ask yourself:

Q *Are the students able to identify important ideas in
each section?*

Q *Can they summarize the information in a few sentences?*

Record your observations on page 27 of the *Assessment
Resource Book*.

A completed summary might look like this:

Summary of "Mrs. Buell"

In this story, a girl named Kate tells about Mrs. Buell, an old woman who owns a store in Kate's neighborhood. The store is run-down and dirty, and Mrs. Buell is a grouch. One day Kate falls and skins her knee in the store. Mrs. Buell picks Kate up and puts a bandage on her knee. It's the first time she's ever been nice to Kate. Kate never thanks Mrs. Buell, though, because she starts being her mean old self again. Later, Kate finds out that Mrs. Buell has died. Kate is sorry she never bothered to get to know the old woman. She is also upset because she realizes that nothing in her life is permanent—not even grouchy old Mrs. Buell.

---

5 ▶ Discuss Summaries as a Class

Facilitate a discussion using the following questions. Remind the students to give reasons for their opinions.

Q *What did you and your partner include in your summary? How does that capture what's important in the story?*

Have a few volunteers read their summary aloud and ask the class:

Q *Do you agree that [Alex] captured the important ideas of the story in [his] summary? Why or why not?*

Q *What did you include in your summary that is [similar to/different from] what [Alex] included in [his] summary?*

Explain that in the coming weeks the students will use what they have learned about summarizing to write a summary of their own book.

Teacher Note ▶

This lesson's extension gives the students more support in thinking about what a summary is and what is important to include in a summary.

Reflect on Discussing Opinions Respectfully

Facilitate a brief discussion of how the students did giving reasons for their opinions and discussing their opinions respectfully.

Collect the students' summaries and save them for Week 5.

INDIVIDUALIZED DAILY READING

 Document IDR Conferences/Have the Students Summarize Their Reading in Their IDR Journals

Have the students read independently for up to 30 minutes.

Use the "IDR Conference Notes" record sheet to conduct and document individual conferences.

At the end of independent reading, ask each student to verbally summarize her reading for her partner. Then have each student write a brief summary of her reading in her IDR Journal.

Have several volunteers read their summaries to the whole class. Facilitate a discussion using questions such as:

Q *Based on the summary [Matthew] just gave, what was [his] reading about?*

Q *Can you get an idea of what [Ananda's] book is about from the summary [she] gave? Why or why not?*

Q *What questions do you want to ask [Jonah] about the book [he] summarized?*

EXTENSION

Analyze Summaries

Make a copy of each student's summary, obscuring the students' names. Place the students in groups of four and randomly distribute the summaries, four to each group. Have each group read the summaries and discuss:

Q *Which summaries give a good idea of what this story excerpt is about? Why do you think so?*

Have a whole-class discussion to share what the groups discussed. Groups may want to read aloud summaries they agreed gave them a good idea of the story. (Be sure to facilitate this activity in such a way as to keep the authors of the summaries anonymous.)

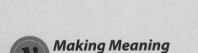

***Making Meaning®
Vocabulary* Teacher**

Next week you will revisit this week's reading to teach Vocabulary Week 24.

Week 5
Overview

UNIT 8: DETERMINING IMPORTANT IDEAS AND SUMMARIZING
Fiction and Narrative Nonfiction

Comprehension Focus

• Students *think about important and supporting ideas* in a text.

• Students use important ideas to *summarize*.

• Students read independently.

Social Development Focus

• Students take responsibility for their learning and behavior.

• Students develop the group skills of supporting one another's independent work and giving feedback in a caring way.

• Students have a class meeting to discuss working independently.

DO AHEAD

• Collect short stories, articles, picture books, and other short pieces of writing at various reading levels (see Day 1, Step 2 on page 504).

• Prepare a chart for independent reading (see Day 1, Step 3 on page 505).

• Make copies of the Unit 8 Parent Letter (BLM17) to send home with the students on the last day of the unit.

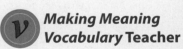

Making Meaning Vocabulary Teacher

If you are teaching Developmental Studies Center's *Making Meaning Vocabulary* program, teach Vocabulary Week 24 this week. For more information, see the *Making Meaning Vocabulary Teacher's Manual.*

Independent Strategy Practice

In this lesson, the students:

- *Think about important ideas* in a text read independently
- Support one another's independent work

Materials

- "Summary of the Passage from *Harry Houdini*" chart (from Week 3)
- Students' summaries of "Mrs. Buell" (from Week 4)
- Short texts at appropriate levels (see Step 2)
- Chart for independent reading, prepared ahead (see Step 3)
- Small self-stick notes for each student
- Paper and a pencil for each student

Teacher Note ▶

Post the charted summary of the passage from *Harry Houdini* where everyone can see it. Also, hand out the students' summaries of "Mrs. Buell" and encourage the students to refer to these as they write their own summaries this week.

1 ▶ Review Identifying Important Ideas and Summarizing

Review that over the past weeks the students watched you model identifying important ideas and writing a summary of *Harry Houdini*. They also identified important ideas and wrote a summary of the story "Mrs. Buell" together. Tell them that this week they will identify important ideas and write summaries of their own independent reading books to share with their classmates next week.

Explain that today the students will select their texts and read them, marking important ideas they want to include in their summaries. They will write their summaries tomorrow.

2 ▶ Select Texts to Read Independently and Summarize

Explain that the students should select a whole, short piece of text to read and summarize. Direct their attention to the short texts you collected (short stories, picture books, and articles from magazines and newspapers) and invite them to choose a text from this collection or choose a short piece of their own. Students reading chapter books may choose to read and summarize a whole chapter. Encourage the students to choose a text that they would be interested in summarizing for their classmates.

Give the students time to select their short text.

▶3 Prepare to Read Independently and Identify Important Ideas

Explain the following directions, which you have written and posted where everyone can see them:

1. *Read your text through once independently.*

2. *Read your text again, using self-stick notes to mark important ideas for your summary.*

3. *Talk with your partner about the important ideas that you might want to include in your summary tomorrow.*

Remind the students to give reasons for their opinions when talking in pairs and to discuss their opinions in a respectful way.

▶4 Read Independently and Identify Important Ideas

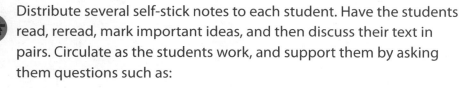
Distribute several self-stick notes to each student. Have the students read, reread, mark important ideas, and then discuss their text in pairs. Circulate as the students work, and support them by asking them questions such as:

Q *What are some important ideas you marked that you want to include in your summary?*

Q *Why do those ideas seem important?*

▶5 Discuss as a Whole Class

When most students have finished, facilitate a whole-class discussion using the following questions. Remind the students that when they share, they should briefly tell what their text is about. Ask:

Q *What is one important idea that you want to make sure to include in your summary tomorrow? Why does that idea seem important?*

Q *Was it hard or easy to identify important ideas in your text? Explain your thinking.*

FACILITATION TIP

Reflect on your experience over the past four weeks with **responding neutrally** with interest during class discussions. Does this practice feel natural to you? Are you integrating it into class discussions throughout the school day? What effect is it having on the students? We encourage you to continue to use this practice and reflect on students' responses as you facilitate class discussions in the future.

Reflect on Supporting One Another's Independent Work

Point out that the students had to work independently today and that they will work independently again tomorrow. Ask:

Q *How did you do with working independently today?*

Q *How did your classmates help or hinder your independent work?*

Q *What might we want to work on tomorrow to help one another work better independently?*

Ask the students to put their text, with self-stick notes in place, in a safe location until tomorrow's lesson.

Day 2

Independent Strategy Practice

In this lesson, the students:

- *Think about important ideas* in a text read independently
- *Build a summary* of their own text
- Support one another's independent work

▶1 Review Supporting One Another's Independent Work

Explain that today the students will each write a summary of the short text they selected and read yesterday. Remind them that they will be working independently and that you would like them to focus on taking responsibility for their own independent work and on helping others to work independently. Ask:

Q *What will you do today to help your partner and others around you work independently?*

Tell the students that you will check in to see how they did at the end of the lesson.

▶2 Write Opening Sentences for Summaries

Have the students spend a moment reviewing the important ideas they marked in their text yesterday. Then remind them that summaries usually begin with a general sentence about what the text is about and continue with the important ideas. Direct their attention to the opening sentence of the charted summary of the passage from *Harry Houdini*, as well as that of their summaries of "Mrs. Buell." Have the students think quietly about this question:

Q *How might you say in one sentence what your text is about?*

After a moment, have the students share in pairs. Bring their attention back to you and ask them to each write an opening sentence for their summary on a sheet of paper.

Materials

- Students' marked short texts from Day 1
- "Summary of the Passage from *Harry Houdini*" chart (from Week 3)
- Paper and a pencil for each student

Teacher Note

This lesson may take longer than one class period.

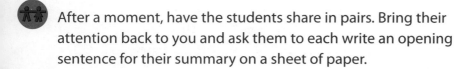

Ask a few volunteers to read their opening sentence aloud to the class. Point out that they might want to come back and revise their opening sentence once they have started writing their summary. Encourage them to do so if necessary.

3 ▶ Write Summaries

Ask the students to identify the first important idea they want to write about in their summary and begin writing. Remind them that they will share their summary with the class, so the summary must give a good idea of what the text is about.

Circulate as the students write their summaries, and support them by having students read aloud some important ideas they marked. Ask:

Q *How might you communicate those ideas briefly in your own words?*

During the writing, you might stop the class periodically and have a few students read what they have written so far to provide examples for those who are having trouble getting started.

4 ▶ Reflect on Writing Summaries and Working Together

When most students have finished writing, bring them together for a brief discussion. Explain that tomorrow they will have a chance to revise (or finish, if necessary) their summary. Use "Turn to Your Partner" as needed during this discussion to increase accountability and to encourage participation.

Ask:

Q *Do you think your summary in its current form would give another reader a good idea of what your text is about? Why or why not?*

Q *What might you want to add, or how else might you want to revise your summary tomorrow?*

Q *What did you do today to help your partner and others around you work independently?*

Collect the students' summaries and save them for Day 3.

Day 3

Independent Strategy Practice

In this lesson, the students:

- Give each other feedback about their summaries
- Revise their summaries
- Give feedback in a caring way

1 ▶ Get Ready to Give Feedback in a Caring Way

Explain that today each student will read the summary he wrote aloud to his partner. Partners will give each other feedback to help them revise or add to their summaries, if necessary. Ask:

Q *If your partner has a suggestion for how to make your summary stronger, how do you want your partner to give you that feedback?*

Q *What are some words we can use to give each other feedback in a caring way?*

As the students suggest ideas, record these on a sheet of chart paper entitled "Words to Use When Giving Feedback." If the students do not generate any ideas, offer some like those suggested in the "Students might say" note.

> *Students might say:*
>
> "I'm confused about this part. What are you trying to say?"
>
> "This part is really clear, but I'm not sure I understand this part."
>
> "I wonder if this part would be clearer if you said…"
>
> "You might consider adding…"
>
> "Have you thought about…?"

Encourage the students to use some of the ideas on the chart today to give feedback.

Materials

- Chart paper and a marker
- Students' marked short texts from Day 1
- Students' summaries from Day 2
- *Assessment Resource Book*

2 Discuss Summaries in Pairs and Revise as Needed

Distribute the students' summaries and have partners read their
summaries to each other and discuss the following questions. Write
the questions where everyone can see them:

- Does this summary begin with a general sentence describing
  what this text is about?

- Does this summary give some important ideas in the text?

- What do you understand about the text from this summary?

CLASS COMPREHENSION ASSESSMENT

Circulate as partners share and discuss their summaries, and
ask yourself:

Q *Do the students' summaries successfully communicate
what their texts are about?*

Q *Is there evidence in the partners' feedback that they
understand something about the texts being summarized?*

Q *Are the students revising or adding to their summaries
based on the feedback?*

Record your observations on page 28 of the *Assessment
Resource Book.*

When most partners have had a chance to talk, briefly interrupt the
students and ask them to revise or add to their summaries based on
the feedback they received.

3 Discuss Giving Feedback on Summaries as a Class

When partners have discussed their summaries and made any
necessary revisions, bring their attention back to the whole class
and ask:

Q *What did your partner say about your summary that was helpful?*

Q *Did you revise your summary based on what your partner said? How?*

Q *How did you and your partner give each other feedback in a caring way? How did that help your work?*

Explain that the students will have an opportunity in the coming week to share their summaries with the whole class. Collect the students' summaries and save them for Unit 9.

Teacher Note

Next week, the students will add a paragraph of opinion to the summary they write today. A student whose summary does not communicate what a text is about may have difficulty adding an opinion paragraph to it. If necessary, give feedback on the summaries and have the students write second drafts based on your feedback before beginning Unit 9.

Day 4

Materials

- Space for the class to sit in a circle
- "Class Meeting Ground Rules" chart
- Chart paper and a marker
- *Student Response Book,* IDR Journal section
- *Assessment Resource Book*
- Unit 8 Parent Letter (BLM17)

Class Meeting Ground Rules

- one person talks at a time
- listen to one another

Class Meeting

In this lesson, the students:

- Have a class meeting to discuss how they are working independently and supporting one another's independent work
- Read independently for up to 30 minutes
- Take responsibility for themselves

1 Gather for a Class Meeting

Tell the students that today they will have a class meeting. Before the class meeting, make sure the "Class Meeting Ground Rules" chart is posted where everyone can see it. Review the procedure for coming to a class meeting, and remind the students that they have been working towards becoming a caring and safe community of readers.

Have partners sit together and ask them to make sure they can see each member of the class.

2 Introduce and Discuss the Topic

Review the "Class Meeting Ground Rules." Explain that during today's class meeting the students will talk about how they have been working independently and supporting one another's independent work. Ask:

Q *How have you been doing working independently?*

Q *What helps or hinders your ability to work independently?*

Q *Why is it important that we support one another's ability to work independently in our class?*

Students might say:

"I can concentrate better when it's quiet and I don't hear other people talking."

"If everyone else is working independently, it helps me to work independently, too."

"It's important to support each other because we want to help each other learn, not bother each other."

3 ▶ Discuss Ways to Support One Another

Have the students use "Think, Pair, Share" to think about and discuss:

Q *What are some ways that we can try to support one another when we work independently?*

Students might say:

"We can agree to work quietly during independent work time."

"I think we can support one another by not banging our desks or sharpening our pencils while people are trying to read or write."

"In addition what [Xavier] said, I think we can support our partner by getting everything we need before the work starts so we don't have to get up and distract people."

Have a few pairs share their ideas with the whole class and write their responses on a sheet of chart paper.

Review the suggestions on the chart and ask:

Q *Is there anything on this list that you can't agree to try in the coming days?*

Make adjustments to the list only if the students give reasonable explanations for why certain solutions are unfeasible. Explain that you would like the students to use the suggestions on the chart in the coming days.

4 ▶ Adjourn the Meeting

Briefly discuss how the students felt they did following the ground rules during the class meeting. Review the procedure for returning to their desks, and then adjourn the meeting.

Teacher Note

This is the last week in Unit 8. You will reassign partners for Unit 9.

Display the chart where everyone can see it. Hold the students accountable by checking in periodically in the coming days to see how they are doing with supporting one another's independent work.

INDIVIDUALIZED DAILY READING

5 ▶ **Document IDR Conferences/Have the Students Summarize Their Reading in Their IDR Journals**

Have the students read independently for up to 30 minutes.

Use the "IDR Conference Notes" record sheet to conduct and document individual conferences.

At the end of independent reading, ask each student to verbally summarize his reading for his partner. Then have each student write a brief summary of his reading in his IDR Journal.

Have several volunteers read their summary to the whole class. Facilitate a discussion using questions such as:

Q *Based on the summary [Marcus] just gave, what was [his] reading about?*

Q *Can you get an idea of what [Anita's] book is about from the summary [she] gave? Why or why not?*

Q *What questions do you want to ask [Jermaine] about the book [he] summarized?*

INDIVIDUAL COMPREHENSION ASSESSMENT

Before continuing with Unit 9, take this opportunity to assess individual students' progress in determining important ideas and summarizing to make sense of what they read. Please refer to pages 46–47 in the *Assessment Resource Book* for instructions.

Parent Letter

Send home with each student the Parent Letter for this unit (see "Do Ahead," page 503). Periodically, have a few students share with the class what they are reading at home.

Unit 9

Synthesizing

FICTION AND EXPOSITORY NONFICTION

During this unit, the students synthesize by making judgments and forming opinions about text, using evidence from the text to support their conclusions. During IDR, the students practice verbally summarizing their reading, and they make judgments and form opinions about their independent reading. They also read magazine and newspaper articles and discuss points of view. Socially, the students continue to relate the values of respect and responsibility to their behavior. They develop the group skills of giving and receiving feedback, expressing their true opinions, giving reasons for their opinions, and discussing their opinions respectfully.

Week 1   "Mrs. Buell" in *Hey World, Here I Am!* by Jean Little
"Zoo" by Edward D. Hoch

Week 2   "12 seconds from death" in *True Stories of Heroes* by Paul Dowswell

Week 3   "Is Dodge Ball Too Dangerous?" by Dina Maasarani
"Turn It Off!" by Kathryn R. Hoffman

Week 4   Review of *The Legend of Sleepy Hollow* by Jennifer B. (age 12)
Review of *The Ballad of Lucy Whipple*

Week 1

Overview

UNIT 9: SYNTHESIZING
Fiction and Expository Nonfiction

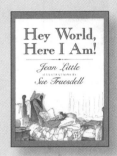

"Mrs. Buell"
in *Hey World, Here I Am!**
by Jean Little, illustrated by Sue Truesdell
(HarperTrophy, 1990)

Kate doesn't think much about grouchy Mrs. Buell, until the old woman disappears from her life.

*This book was also used in Unit 8, Week 4.

Short Story

"Zoo"
by Edward D. Hoch

Earthlings shudder with horror as they file by the alien creatures in Professor Hugo's Interplanetary Zoo—unaware of what the creatures are thinking about them.

ALTERNATIVE STORIES

"Vanishing Cream" in *The Daydreamer* by Ian McEwan

Birthday Surprises edited by Johanna Hurwitz

Comprehension Focus

- Students *synthesize* by *making judgments* and *forming opinions* about a text, using evidence from the text to support their conclusions.

- Students read independently.

Social Development Focus

- Students relate the values of respect and responsibility to their behavior.

- Students develop the group skills of giving reasons for their opinions and discussing their opinions respectfully.

DO AHEAD

- Prior to Day 1, decide how you will randomly assign partners to work together during the unit.

- Make a transparency of the "Review of 'Mrs. Buell'" (BLM40).

- Collect reviews of books and movies (see Day 1, Step 4, on page 523).

- Prepare a chart for exploring reviews (see Day 1, Step 4, on page 523).

- Make a transparency of the "Review of 'Zoo'" (BLM41).

- Prepare a chart for discussing opinions (see Day 3, Step 3, on page 530).

- Prepare a chart with directions for writing a review (see Day 4, Step 3, on page 538).

Day 1

Materials

- "Mrs. Buell" in *Hey World, Here I Am!* (from Unit 8, Week 4)
- Transparency of the "Review of 'Mrs. Buell'" (BLM40)
- *Student Response Book* page 72
- Reviews you collect (one review per pair of students)
- Chart for exploring reviews, prepared ahead
- (Optional) *Student Response Book* page 73
- "Self-monitoring Questions" chart

Being a Writer™ **Teacher**

You can either have the students work with their *Being a Writer* partner or assign them a different partner for the *Making Meaning* lessons.

Strategy Lesson

In this lesson, the students:

- Begin working with new partners
- Learn what a review is
- Hear, read, and discuss reviews
- Read independently for up to 30 minutes
- Give reasons for their opinions
- Discuss their opinions respectfully

About Synthesizing

Synthesizing is a complex strategy that requires readers to integrate new information and ideas with existing knowledge to produce new understanding. In this unit, the students explore the aspect of synthesizing that has to do with making judgments and forming opinions about text. The students learn to expand a summary of a text into a review that gives their opinion. They will also write book reviews to share with classmates. As with all the strategies, the goal is for the students to learn to form opinions and make judgments as they read on their own.

▶ 1 Pair Students and Discuss Sharing Opinions Respectfully

Randomly assign partners and have them sit together. Remind the students that as they talked in pairs and as a class in recent weeks they used the prompt "The reason I think this is _____" to give reasons for their opinions. Explain that you would like them to continue using the prompt in partner and whole-class discussions this week. Ask:

Q *Sometimes you may disagree with what your partner or another classmate says in a discussion. Why is it important to be respectful when you discuss your opinions?*

Q *How can you disagree respectfully?*

Students might say:

"You can give your own opinion without making fun of what the other person said."

"You can disagree without shouting or being sarcastic."

"You can say something like 'I have a different opinion.'"

◀ **Teacher Note**

During this unit's lessons, observe the students as they interact with one another and take note of responsible behavior as they share opinions. You will share your observations throughout the unit.

Review "Mrs. Buell"

Show the cover of *Hey World, Here I Am!* and remind the students that they heard the story "Mrs. Buell" in a previous lesson and wrote a summary of it together. Remind them that in the story, Kate, the narrator, tells about a neighborhood woman named Mrs. Buell. Ask:

Q *What do you remember about the story?*

Have one or two volunteers briefly tell what they remember.

If necessary, stimulate the students' recollection of the story by reading each of the following sentences aloud and asking the students to remember what was happening in that part of the story. For each sentence, have a volunteer share what was happening:

p. 42 "For years and years, for what seems like forever, I've gone to BUELLS when I had a dime to spare."

p. 43 "She was always the same except that once. I tripped going in, and fell and scraped my knee."

pp. 43–44 "I waited for her to look at me again so that I could thank her."

p. 44 "Then I stopped at BUELLS one afternoon and she wasn't there."

p. 46 "But, to be honest, something else bothered me even more. Her going had left a hole in my life."

3 ▶ **Read and Discuss a Review of "Mrs. Buell"**

Place the transparency of the "Review of 'Mrs. Buell'" on the overhead projector. Point out that this is a review of the story and explain that a review is a piece of writing that gives an opinion about a story, book, movie, work of art, or performance. Explain that a review of a book or story usually contains a summary of the text, along with the reviewer's opinions about it.

Ask the students to follow along as you read the review aloud.

After reading it aloud, have the students turn to the "Review of 'Mrs. Buell'" on *Student Response Book* page 72. Point out that this is the review you just read. Ask the students to read the review again quietly to themselves.

After the reading, facilitate a whole-class discussion using the following questions. Remind the students to use "The reason I think this is _____" as they talk.

Q *What part of this review summarizes the story? What part gives the reviewer's opinion? Explain your thinking.*

Students might say:

"The first paragraph is the summary. The reason I think this is that it's where the reviewer tells about the story."

"The last paragraph gives the opinion. The reason I think that is because it starts out with 'I would recommend this story.' That means the reviewer liked it and thought other people should read it."

Q *Why might you want to read a review of a story or book?*

Students might say:

"I would read a review to find out what a book is about—to see if I want to read it."

"I would read it to find out if someone else liked the book. If the reviewer really didn't like the book, I might not want to read it."

Teacher Note ▶

Have students who are unable to read the review on their own read it with a partner, or you might reread it aloud yourself as the students follow along.

4 ▶ Explore Other Reviews

Distribute the reviews you collected, one to each pair. Have partners read their review quietly to themselves and then discuss the following three questions, which you have written on a chart and posted where everyone can see them:

- *What book or movie is the review about?*

- *What did you learn about the book or movie from the review?*

- *What parts of the review express the reviewer's opinion?*

When most pairs have finished, ask a few pairs to share with the class what their review is about and what they learned from the review. Follow up by asking:

Q *How might the review be helpful to you or others who read it?*

Remind the students that in the previous week they wrote summaries of the books they were reading independently, and that summarizing is a way to communicate what a book is about. Explain that it is also important for readers to form opinions about what they read and to communicate those opinions to others. Explain that during the next couple of weeks they will learn how to expand their summaries into reviews by including their own thoughts and opinions.

5 ▶ Reflect on Discussing Opinions

Facilitate a brief discussion about how the students did giving reasons for their opinions and discussing their opinions respectfully.

Teacher Note

In this part of the lesson, you may be able to use some of the summaries you collected for Unit 8, Week 3, if they include the writers' opinions. You can find other book, movie, and music reviews for children on Internet sites. You might also videotape movie reviews on television to show to the class.

If you show a videotaped movie review, have the students watch the video as a class. Then have partners discuss what they saw and heard, using the charted questions.

If you do not have enough reviews for each pair, you can have the students read the "Review of *A Picture Book of Jesse Owens*" on *Student Response Book* page 73.

INDIVIDUALIZED DAILY READING

 Review and Discuss Self-monitoring

Direct the students' attention to the "Self-monitoring Questions" chart and remind them that a technique they learned this year is to stop and think about what they are reading and to ask themselves questions to help them track their understanding. Tell them that they will practice this self-monitoring technique today during independent reading.

Have the students read independently for up to 30 minutes. Stop them at 10-minute intervals and have them monitor their comprehension by thinking about the charted questions.

At the end of independent reading, facilitate a whole-class discussion about how self-monitoring helps them track their understanding.

Discuss questions such as:

Q *How does stopping and checking your understanding help you?*

Q *What are some things you do when you do not understand?*

Self-monitoring Questions

- What is happening in my story right now?

- Does the reading make sense?

Day 2

Read-aloud

In this lesson, the students:

- Hear and discuss a science fiction story
- Read independently for up to 30 minutes
- Give reasons for their opinions
- Discuss their opinions respectfully

▶ 1 Discuss the Importance of Forming Opinions While Reading

Remind the students that in the previous lesson they heard a review of "Mrs. Buell." Remind them that a review gives a summary of a text and the reviewer's opinion about it. Explain that this week the students will learn to write a book review. Ask:

Q *Why is it important to form opinions and make judgments as you read?*

If the students have difficulty answering this question, you might point out that not everything in print is clearly written, interesting, or true. Explain that readers need to form opinions and make judgments as they read by asking questions such as: Is this text well written? Do I believe what the text is saying? Do I agree with it? What is the author's point of view or bias? Do I want to read more texts like this?

▶ 2 Introduce "Zoo"

Explain that today you will read a science fiction story called "Zoo" by Edward D. Hoch. Ask:

Q *What do you think you know about science fiction? What science fiction have you read or seen?*

Materials

- "Zoo" (see pages 533–535)

ELL Note

English Language Learners may benefit from previewing the story prior to the lesson.

Students might say:

"I think science fiction usually takes place in the future."

"Sometimes it's about martians or aliens from outer space."

"I agree with [Mina]. The *Star Wars* movies are science fiction."

If necessary, explain that science fiction stories are often about life in the future and feature amazing inventions and scientific developments, such as space travel and robots. Explain that in "Zoo" the students will hear about an incredible zoo of the future.

3 ▶ Read "Zoo" Aloud

Read the story aloud, stopping as described below.

Suggested Vocabulary

interplanetary: between planets (p. 533)
high-pitched tongue: high or squeaky voice (p. 533)

ELL Vocabulary

English Language Learners may benefit from discussing additional vocabulary, including:

annual: once a year (p. 533)
filed: walked by in a line (p. 533)
horrified: filled with horror, or great fear (p. 533)
fascinated: very interested in (p. 533)
mate: partner (p. 534)
offspring: young of an animal or human (p. 534)

Stop after:

> **p. 533** "This year, as the great round ship settled slowly to earth in the huge tri-city parking area just outside of Chicago, they watched with awe as the sides slowly slid up to reveal the familiar barred cages." (Note that this stop is mid-paragraph.)

Teacher Note ▶

You may want to read the beginning of the story (to the first stop) twice to help the students follow what is happening.

 Have the students use "Turn to Your Partner" to discuss:

Q *What happened in the part of the story you just heard? What do you think will happen next?*

Without sharing as a class, reread the last sentence before the stop and continue reading to next stop. Repeat the procedure at the following stops:

p. 534 "'This is certainly worth a dollar,' one man remarked, hurrying away. 'I'm going home to get the wife.'"

p. 534 "Professor Hugo was there to say a few parting words, and then they scurried away in a hundred different directions, seeking their homes among the rocks."

Reread the last sentence before the stop and continue reading to the end of the story.

4 ▶ Discuss the Story as a Class

Facilitate a discussion of the story using the following questions. Remind the students to use "The reason I think this is _____" and discussion prompts to add to one another's thinking.

Q *What is this story about?*

Q *What is interesting or unexpected about this story?*

Students might say:

"I didn't expect the horse-spider people to be intelligent, like humans. The reason I think this is because the creatures were more like animals than people."

"I agree with [Tuan]. In addition, I was surprised to find out that the horse-spider people paid to travel to Earth."

"I think it is interesting that the creatures thought the cages had bars to protect them. The reason I think this is because the humans were thinking just the opposite—that the bars protected them from the creatures."

Q *Would you recommend this story to someone else? Give reasons for your opinion.*

Q *Are you interested in reading more science fiction stories? Why or why not?*

Explain that in the next lesson the students will revisit their opinions about the story and write a review of it together.

FACILITATION TIP

During this unit, we invite you to continue to practice **responding neutrally** with interest during class discussions. This week, continue to respond neutrally by refraining from overtly praising or criticizing the students' responses. Try responding neutrally by nodding, asking them to say more about their thinking, or asking other students to respond.

◄ **Teacher Note**

This question helps the students begin to form opinions about the story and think about the reasons for their opinions. They will explore their opinions in more depth in the next lesson.

INDIVIDUALIZED DAILY READING

 Document IDR Conferences/Have the Students Use Important Ideas to Summarize Verbally

Remind the students that they have been using important ideas in texts to help them summarize what they have read. Explain that you would like them to think about the important ideas in their reading and be ready to share a summary of what they read today with their partner.

Have the students read independently for up to 30 minutes.

Use the "IDR Conference Notes" record sheet to conduct and document individual conferences.

 At the end of independent reading, have each student verbally summarize her reading for her partner by telling her partner in a few sentences what she read. Have a few volunteers share with the class. As the students share with the class, ask questions such as:

Q *What are the important ideas in your summary?*

Q *Would you recommend this book to someone? Why? Why not?*

EXTENSION

Read More Science Fiction Stories

Read other science fiction stories and have the students discuss their opinions about them.

Day 3

Guided Strategy Practice

In this lesson, the students:

- *Form opinions* about a text
- Learn to write a review
- Read independently for up to 30 minutes
- Give reasons for their opinions
- Discuss their opinions respectfully

▶ 1 Review "Zoo"

Have partners sit together. Remind the students that in the previous lesson they heard the story "Zoo." Ask:

Q *What happened in the story?*

Q *After hearing it once, did you think you would recommend this story to someone else? Why or why not?*

Explain that the class will write a review of "Zoo" together. Remind them that they will use what they learn today to write a review of their own book tomorrow.

▶ 2 Reread "Zoo"

Have the students turn to *Student Response Book* pages 74–76 and explain that this is a copy of the story. Explain that you will reread the story aloud and that you would like them to follow along in their *Student Response Books*. Tell them that during the reading they should think again about whether or not they would recommend the story to another reader, and why. After the reading they will talk about their opinions in pairs.

Read the story aloud, slowly and clearly.

Materials

- "Zoo" (see pages 533–535)
- *Student Response Book* pages 74–76
- Chart with two questions, prepared ahead (see Step 3)
- Transparency of the "Review of 'Zoo'" (BLM41)

◀ **Teacher Note**

Keep this discussion brief. The purpose is to help the students remember the story and their initial opinions of it. They will have an opportunity later in the lesson to discuss their opinions in more depth.

Discuss the Story

 Have partners discuss the following questions, which you have written where everyone can see them:

- *Would you recommend this story? Why or why not?*

- *Did your opinion of the story change during the second reading? Why or why not?*

Circulate as partners talk and notice whether the students are expressing opinions and supporting their opinions by referring to the story. If the students are having difficulty forming or expressing an opinion, ask questions such as:

Q *Were you interested in what was happening in the story? Why or why not?*

Q *Was there anything surprising or unexpected in the story? Why was it surprising or unexpected?*

Q *How did you feel as you listened to the story? Why did you feel that way?*

When most pairs have finished, ask a few volunteers to share their ideas with the class.

4 **Read a Summary of "Zoo" and Model Writing an Opinion**

Remind the students that a review includes both a summary and an opinion. Ask:

Q *How might you summarize "Zoo"?*

Place the transparency of the "Review of 'Zoo'" on the overhead projector. Tell the students that this is one way the story might be summarized.

ELL Note

Consider having your English Language Learners think about questions such as these during their partner conversations.

Read the summary aloud. Point out that the summary does not give away the ending of the story and that this is typical of reviews. (Giving away the surprise could spoil the story for other readers.) Ask:

Q *What might someone who recommends the story say about it? What might someone who doesn't recommend the story say about it?*

Have a few volunteers share their thinking; then ask them to listen and watch as you add an opinion to the summary. Begin by thinking aloud about your opinion. (For example, you might say, "I would recommend this story to others. The zoo of the future seemed very real to me. I liked the way the author described the horse-spider people. I could visualize how they ran up the cage walls and squeaked in high-pitched tones. It was very creepy. I also like the surprise ending.")

Model adding a paragraph of opinion to the summary on the transparency. Begin the paragraph "I recommend this book because…." (For example, you might write, "I recommend this book because the author creates a world of the future that seems very real. The horse-spider creatures were very creepy, running up the cage walls and squeaking. The ending was unexpected and really made me think.")

Point out that a review always gives evidence from the text to support the opinions. Remind the students that forming opinions and making judgments helps readers think and communicate more meaningfully about text.

5 ▶ Reflect on Discussing Opinions Respectfully

Without giving names, share some of your observations of respectful ways the students shared their opinions. Ask:

Q *What went well when we shared opinions today? What problems did we have? What can we do to avoid the problems the next time we share opinions?*

Explain that in the next lesson the students will add their opinions to the summaries they wrote last week.

Save the completed transparency of the "Review of 'Zoo'" for Day 4.

Teacher Note

You might also want to model adding a paragraph that expresses the opposite opinion. (For example, you might write, "I would not recommend 'Zoo' because the world of the future seemed unbelievable. Although aliens in science fiction can be very real and scary, the creatures in 'Zoo' did not seem entirely real. The author tries to surprise us at the end, but I think most readers will be able to predict what happens.")

Point out to the students that a respectful tone is important when writing both negative and positive reviews.

Teacher Note

On Day 4, the students add opinion paragraphs to their summaries from Unit 8, Week 5 to create reviews. If you feel they need more modeling of how to write their opinions, you may want to repeat Days 2 and 3 of this week with an alternative book before continuing with Day 4. Alternative titles are listed on this week's Overview page.

INDIVIDUALIZED DAILY READING

 ## Document IDR Conferences/Have the Students Use Important Ideas to Summarize Verbally

Have the students read independently for up to 30 minutes. Continue to have the students think about important ideas in their reading and be ready to summarize for a partner.

Use the "IDR Conference Notes" record sheet to conduct and document individual conferences.

 At the end of independent reading, have the students verbally summarize their reading in pairs by telling in a few sentences what they read. Have a few volunteers share with the class. As the students share with the class, ask questions such as:

Q *What are the important ideas in your summary?*

Q *Would you recommend this book to someone? Why or why not?*

EXTENSION

Draw Mental Images from "Zoo"

Have the students reread the description of the horse-spider people, visualize the creatures, and draw their mental images of them. The students might be interested in sharing and comparing their visualizations.

Zoo

by Edward D. Hoch

The children were always good during the month of August, especially when it began to get near the twenty-third. It was on this day that Professor Hugo's Interplanetary Zoo settled down for its annual six-hour visit to the Chicago area.

Before daybreak the crowds would form, long lines of children and adults both, each one clutching his or her dollar, and waiting with wonderment to see what race of strange creatures the Professor had brought this year.

In the past they had sometimes been treated to three-legged creatures from Venus, or tall, thin men from Mars, or even snakelike horrors from somewhere more distant. This year, as the great round ship settled slowly to earth in the huge tri-city parking area just outside of Chicago, they watched with awe as the sides slowly slid up to reveal the familiar barred cages. In them were some wild breed of nightmare—small, horselike animals that moved with quick, jerking motions and constantly chattered in a high-pitched tongue. The citizens of Earth clustered around as Professor Hugo's crew quickly collected the waiting dollars, and soon the good Professor himself made an appearance, wearing his many-colored rainbow cape and top hat. "Peoples of Earth," he called into his microphone.

The crowd's noise died down as he continued. "Peoples of Earth, this year you see a real treat for your single dollar—the little-known horse-spider people of Kaan—brought to you across a million miles of space at great expense. Gather around, study them, listen to them, tell your friends about them. But hurry! My ship can remain here only six hours!"

And the crowds slowly filed by, at once horrified and fascinated by these strange creatures that looked like horses but ran up the walls

continues

Zoo

continued

of their cages like spiders. "This is certainly worth a dollar," one man remarked, hurrying away. "I'm going home to get the wife."

All day long it went like that, until ten thousand people had filed by the barred cages set into the side of the spaceship. Then, as the six-hour limit ran out, Professor Hugo once more took microphone in hand. "We must go now, but we will return next year on this date. And if you enjoyed our zoo this year, phone your friends in other cities about it. We will land in New York tomorrow, and next week on to London, Paris, Rome, Hong Kong, and Tokyo. Then on to other worlds!"

He waved farewell to them, and as the ship rose from the ground the Earth peoples agreed that this had been the very best Zoo yet....

- - - - - - - - - -

Some two months and three planets later, the silver ship of Professor Hugo settled at last onto the familiar jagged rocks of Kaan, and the queer horse-spider creatures filed quickly out of their cages. Professor Hugo was there to say a few parting words, and then they scurried away in a hundred different directions, seeking their homes among the rocks.

In one, the she-creature was happy to see the return of her mate and offspring. She babbled a greeting in the strange tongue and hurried to embrace them. "It was a long time you were gone! Was it good?"

And the he-creature nodded. "The little one enjoyed it especially. We visited eight worlds and saw many things."

continues

Zoo

continued

The little one ran up the wall of the cave. "On the place called Earth it was the best. The creatures there wear garments over their skins, and they walk on two legs."

"But isn't it dangerous?" asked the she-creature.

"No," her mate answered. "There are bars to protect us from them. We remain right in the ship. Next time you must come with us. It is well worth the nineteen commocs it costs."

And the little one nodded. "It was the very best Zoo ever...."

Day 4

Materials

- Completed transparency of the "Review of 'Zoo'" (from Day 3)

- Students' summaries of their own books (from Unit 8, Week 5)

- Chart paper and a marker

- Chart with directions for writing a review, prepared ahead

- (Optional) *Student Response Book* pages 72–73

- *Assessment Resource Book*

- "Reading Comprehension Strategies" chart

- *Student Response Book,* IDR Journal section

Teacher Note

This lesson may take longer than one class period.

Guided Strategy Practice

In this lesson, the students:

- *Form opinions* about a text read independently

- Add an opinion paragraph to a summary

- Read independently for up to 30 minutes

- Give reasons for their opinions

- Discuss their opinions respectfully

▶1 Review Forming Opinions and Writing Reviews

Show the completed transparency of the "Review of 'Zoo'" on the overhead projector. Review that the students heard the story and watched you model writing a review of it. Remind them that a review contains a summary and the reviewer's opinion, and that forming opinions can help readers bring their own thinking to a text and communicate more meaningfully about it.

Remind them that in the previous week they each wrote a summary of a text they read independently. Tell them that today they will expand their summary into a review by adding a paragraph of opinion to it. They will then share their reviews with one another.

▶2 Discuss Factors to Consider When Forming an Opinion

Explain that readers usually consider many factors when forming an opinion about a text. Ask:

Q *What helps you decide whether or not you like a fiction story?*

Q *What helps you decide whether or not you like a nonfiction text?*

Students might say:

"For me to like a story, it has to have a lot of action. I get bored if it's just description."

"I like books that tell me lots of facts about things I'm interested in. Like wild animals."

"I like stories with good characters—I like reading about girls like me."

"I like nonfiction books that have pictures and that explain things clearly, so I don't get confused."

Use the students' ideas to start a chart entitled "Factors to Consider When Forming an Opinion." If the students have difficulty generating ideas, suggest some yourself such as those listed on the sample chart below:

Factors to Consider When Forming an Opinion

<u>About Fiction</u>

- Does the story make me want to keep reading? Why?

- What is interesting about the characters and the conflicts they face?

- Does the story have action? Suspense? Humor? Mystery? How?

- What is unexpected in the plot?

- What is interesting about the setting?

- How does the story make me feel?

<u>About Nonfiction</u>

- Does the book make me want to keep reading? Why?

- What's interesting about the topic?

- Does the book answer some of my questions about this topic? How?

- Does it make me curious to know more? What?

- How is the information presented? Clearly? In a confusing way?

ELL Note

You may want to model this activity for your English Language Learners.

Ask the students to keep some of these factors in mind as they think about their own text and why they would or would not recommend it to other readers.

 Think About and Discuss Opinions

Distribute the students' summaries and explain the following directions, which you have written on a chart and posted where everyone can see them:

- Reread your summary.

- Think quietly about whether or not you would recommend the book to another reader, and why.

- Talk with your partner about what you want to say in your opinion paragraph.

- Add an opinion paragraph to your summary. Begin the paragraph with "I recommend this book because…" or "I don't recommend this book because…."

Remind the students to give reasons for their opinions when talking in pairs and to discuss their opinions respectfully.

4 Write Opinion Paragraphs

Have the students add opinion paragraphs to their summaries. Keep the transparency of the "Review of 'Zoo'" on the overhead projector as a model for the students to use as they write their paragraphs. For additional models, have them refer to the "Review of 'Mrs. Buell'" and the "Review of *A Picture Book of Jesse Owens*" on *Student Response Book* pages 72 and 73.

> ### CLASS COMPREHENSION ASSESSMENT
>
> Circulate as the students write their paragraphs of opinion. Ask yourself:
>
> **Q** *Can the students express an opinion about their reading?*
>
> **Q** *Can they use information from the book to support their opinion?*
>
> Record your observations on page 29 of the *Assessment Resource Book*.

◀ **Teacher Note**

As you observe, look for a few effective reviews to use as examples in the whole-class discussion.

5 Analyze and Revise Reviews

When most students are finished, call on a few students who wrote effective reviews and have them read their reviews aloud. Ask:

Q *Does this review give you a good idea of what this text is about? How?*

Q *Does this review use evidence from the text to explain why [Heidi] recommends the book? How?*

After the students hear these examples, ask them to each reread their own review and revise it as needed. Remind them that their review should communicate what the text is about and give reasons why they recommend or do not recommend the book.

◀ **Teacher Note**

If the students are having difficulty writing effective reviews, you may want to collect their reviews at this point and read them. Give each student individual feedback and have them write second drafts incorporating your feedback before going on to Step 6 of this lesson.

6 Share Reviews as a Class

Give every student an opportunity to read his complete review aloud to the class. This may happen over several days. After each student shares, facilitate a discussion about the text and summary using the following questions. During the discussions, remind the students to express their opinions respectfully. Ask:

Q *What questions do you want to ask [Jerome] about [his] book or review?*

Q *Based on [Jerome's] review, do you think you would like to read the book? Why or why not?*

Q *Has anyone else read [Jerome's] book? If so, do you share [his] opinion? Why or why not?*

7 **Add to the "Reading Comprehension Strategies" Chart**

Explain that when readers form opinions and make judgments about texts, they are bringing their own thinking to the text. Point out that *making judgments* and *forming opinions* are important reading comprehension strategies and add the strategies to the chart. Remind the students that making judgments and forming opinions helps readers think more deeply and critically about texts and communicate more meaningfully about them. Explain that in the coming weeks they will continue to practice these strategies.

Keep the "Factors to Consider When Forming an Opinion" chart for Week 2.

Reading Comprehension Strategies

- recognizing text features

INDIVIDUALIZED DAILY READING

8 **Write a Review of Their Reading in Their IDR Journals**

Continue to have the students think about important ideas in their reading and be ready to summarize for a partner.

Have the students read independently for up to 30 minutes.

As the students read, circulate among them. Ask individual students questions such as:

Q *What is your reading about?*

Q *What are the important ideas in your summary?*

Q *What do you think of this book? Would you recommend it to someone? Why or why not?*

At the end of independent reading, have the students verbally summarize their reading and review what they read in pairs. Then have the students write a brief summary and review of their reading in their IDR Journals. Remind the students to think about the ideas on the "Factors to Consider When Forming an Opinion" chart as they write their review.

EXTENSION

Create a Class Book of Reviews

Have the students revise and edit their reviews as needed and create final drafts. Collect these in a class book entitled "Reviews of Books You May Want to Read." You might want to copy the book for each student to take home.

Teacher Note

Being a Writer, a writing curriculum from Developmental Studies Center, provides lessons that will help your students write in a variety of genres.

 Making Meaning Vocabulary Teacher

Next week you will revisit this week's reading to teach Vocabulary Week 25.

Week 2 Overview

UNIT 9: SYNTHESIZING
Fiction and Expository Nonfiction

"12 seconds from death"
in ***True Stories of Heroes*** by Paul Dowswell
(Usborne, 2002)

Three skydivers make a parachute jump that almost ends in disaster.

ALTERNATIVE BOOKS

"The Bully" in ***The Daydreamer*** by Ian McEwan

The Ghost Dance by Alice McLerran

Comprehension Focus

• Students *synthesize* by *making judgments* and *forming opinions* about a text, using evidence from the text to support their conclusions.

• Students read independently.

Social Development Focus

• Students relate the values of respect and responsibility to their behavior.

• Students develop the group skills of discussing their opinions respectfully and expressing their true opinions.

• Students have a class meeting to discuss the importance of expressing their true opinions.

DO AHEAD

• Prepare a chart with questions about "12 seconds from death" (see Day 2, Step 2, on page 549).

• Prepare a chart with questions about independent reading text (see Day 3, Step 3, on pages 552–553).

• Prepare to model recording opinions and evidence (see Day 3, Step 4, on page 553).

• Make a transparency of "Double-entry Journal: My Opinions About _____" (BLM42).

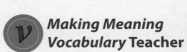

***Making Meaning
Vocabulary* Teacher**

If you are teaching Developmental Studies Center's *Making Meaning Vocabulary* program, teach Vocabulary Week 25 this week. For more information, see the *Making Meaning Vocabulary Teacher's Manual.*

Day 1

Materials

- "12 seconds from death"

Read-aloud

In this lesson, the students:

- Hear, read, and discuss a nonfiction text
- Read independently for up to 30 minutes
- Discuss their opinions respectfully

▶1 Introduce the Week

Remind the students that in the previous week they read the story "Zoo," by Edward D. Hoch, watched you model writing a review of the story, and wrote reviews of stories they read independently. In their reviews, they summarized their texts and then said if they would recommend the text and why. Explain that this week they will continue to focus on expressing opinions about their reading and think about ways to express their opinions in greater depth.

 Note

English Language Learners may benefit from previewing the text. In addition, consider showing your students photos of skydivers.

▶2 Introduce "12 seconds from death"

Show the cover of *True Stories of Heroes* and explain that the book is a collection of true stories about real-life heroes. Tell the students that today you will read an action/adventure story called "12 seconds from death." The story is about three skydivers who make a parachute jump that almost ends in disaster. Explain that skydivers are people who jump from airplanes for sport, using parachutes to slow their landing to Earth. Ask and briefly discuss as a class:

Q *What do you know about the sport of skydiving?*

Introduce the skydivers in the story by writing each man's name and a brief description on the board:

Richard Maynard - man making his first jump

Mike Smith - instructor strapped to Richard

Ronnie O'Brien - instructor paid to videotape Richard's jump

3 Read "12 seconds from death" Aloud

Read the story aloud, stopping as described below. Read the first two paragraphs (to the first stop) twice. Explain that you are rereading the beginning of the story because it contains important information about the skydivers.

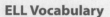

Suggested Vocabulary

substantial: large (p. 22)

plummet: fall rapidly (p. 22)

commissioned: paid (p. 22)

290kmph: 290 kilometers per hour (p. 22)

spread-eagled posture: with arms and legs spread wide (p. 23)

veteran: experienced person (p. 23)

lurch: roll away suddenly (p. 23)

adrenaline: chemical produced by the body in times of fear or excitement (p. 25)

ELL Vocabulary

English Language Learners may benefit from discussing additional vocabulary, including:

videotape: use a camera to record pictures and sounds on tape to be played back later (p. 22)

consciousness: being in a normal waking state, able to think and feel (p. 23)

descent: fall (p. 23)

Stop after:

> **p. 22** "Expecting this experience (known as a 'tandem jump') to be the thrill of a lifetime, Maynard had also commissioned instructor Ronnie O'Brien, to videotape him."

Have the students use "Turn to Your Partner" to discuss:

Q *What did you find out about the skydivers in the first part of the story?*

Without sharing as a class, reread the last sentence before the stop and continue reading to the next stop.

> **p. 23** "If O'Brien could not help them, they both faced certain death."

Have the students use "Turn to Your Partner" to discuss:

Q *What happened in the part of the story you just heard? What do you think might happen next?*

Without sharing as a class, reread the last sentence before the stop and continue reading to the next stop. Repeat this procedure at the following stop.

> **p. 23**   "The ground was a mere 20 seconds away and O'Brien knew he had only one more chance to save their lives."

Continue reading to the end of the story. Show the illustration and read the accompanying captions on page 24 to help the students understand the story.

4 ▸ Discuss the Story as a Class

Facilitate a discussion of the story using the following questions. Remind the students to use "The reason I think this is _____" and other prompts to add to one another's thinking.

Q *What are the important events in this story?*

Q *What parts of the story were especially interesting or exciting?*

> ### Teacher Note ▶
>
> This question helps the students begin to form opinions about the story and think about the reasons for them. They will explore their opinions in more depth in the next lesson.

Students might say:

"I thought it was exciting how O'Brien saved the other skydivers just in time."

"I agree with [Roland]. I also thought it was interesting how O'Brien caught up to the other two skydivers. I think he changed his posture to fly faster through the air."

"I thought it was interesting that Maynard didn't even know he was in trouble."

Q *Would you recommend this story, or stories like it, to someone else? Give reasons for your opinion.*

Explain that in the next lesson they will revisit their opinions.

INDIVIDUALIZED DAILY READING

 Document IDR Conferences/Have the Students Use Important Ideas to Summarize Verbally

Have the students think about the important ideas in their reading. Explain that at the end of IDR partners will share a summary of what they read today.

Have the students read independently for up to 30 minutes.

Use the "IDR Conference Notes" record sheet to conduct and document individual conferences.

 At the end of independent reading, have each student verbally summarize her reading for her partner by telling her partner in a few sentences what she read. Remind the students to ask clarifying questions.

After partners have shared, have a few volunteers share with the class. As the students share with the class, ask questions such as:

Q *What are the important ideas in your summary?*

Q *Would you recommend this book to someone? Why or why not?*

Day 2

Materials

- "12 seconds from death"
- "Factors to Consider When Forming an Opinion" chart (from Week 1, Day 4)
- Chart with questions about "12 seconds from death," prepared ahead
- *Student Response Book* pages 77–80

Guided Strategy Practice

In this lesson, the students:

- *Form opinions* about a nonfiction text
- Find evidence in the text that supports their opinions
- Read independently for up to 30 minutes
- Discuss their opinions respectfully

1 ▶ ## Review "12 seconds from death"

Help the students remember "12 seconds from death" by reading each of the following sentences aloud and asking the students to recall what was happening in that part of the story. For each sentence, have a volunteer share what was happening.

Teacher Note ▶

If necessary, show the illustrations on page 24 ("How it all happened") again to help the students recall the sequence of events.

> **p. 22** "He had paid a substantial fee to plummet from 3,600m (12,000ft), strapped to Mike Smith, a skilled parachute instructor."

> **p. 22** "O'Brien leaped backwards from the plane to film Maynard and Smith's exit."

> **p. 23** "It pulled tight, strangling him, and he quickly lost consciousness."

> **p. 25** "With barely 12 seconds before they hit the ground, O'Brien found the handle…."

> **p. 25** "He released his own parachute when he was safely out of the way, a few seconds before he himself would have hit the ground."

> **p. 25** "…he had had no idea that anything out of the ordinary had happened."

Teacher Note ▶

Keep this discussion brief. The purpose is to help the students remember the story and their initial opinions of it. They will have an opportunity later in the lesson to discuss their opinions in more depth.

Ask:

Q *After hearing the story once yesterday, did you think you would recommend this story to someone else? Why or why not?*

Discuss Opinions of the Story

Remind the students that they have been focusing on forming opinions about their reading, specifically, whether they would recommend a text to someone else, and why. Remind them that readers usually consider many factors when forming an opinion, and use the "Factors to Consider When Forming an Opinion" chart to review the factors you discussed previously.

Direct the students' attention to the following questions, which you have written on a chart and posted where everyone can see them:

- *Did the story "12 seconds from death" hold your interest? Why?*

- *Were the people or events described in the story interesting? Why?*

- *How did you feel as you listened to the story? Why did you feel that way?*

 Ask the students to use "Think, Pair, Share" to think about and discuss these questions with a partner.

After partners have had a chance to talk, have the students turn to *Student Response Book* page 77 and write some of their opinions about the story.

 ## Reread the Story Aloud

Have the students turn to *Student Response Book* pages 78–80 and reread the story in pairs or quietly to themselves. Ask them to think about the opinions they wrote, look for evidence that supports their opinions, and underline the evidence. After the reading, partners will talk about their opinions and what they underlined.

Point out that the students' opinions may change as they reread the story. If this happens, they can revise or add to the opinions and underline evidence in the story that supports their new opinions.

> ### Factors to Consider When Forming an Opinion
>
> - Does the story make me want to keep reading?

Discuss Opinions as a Class

Facilitate a discussion using the following questions.

Q *What is your opinion about the story? What did you underline in the story that supports your opinion? How does that support your opinion?*

Q *Did your opinion of the story change? Why or why not?*

Students might say:

"I think the story has suspense because you don't know if O'Brien is going to save the two skydivers. I underlined 'He had to judge his descent very carefully. If he overshot, he would have little chance of saving the two men' because that shows how dangerous the situation was."

"I disagree with [Caleb] because you know from the start that the three skydivers are going to make it. In the first paragraph, I underlined 'three skydivers were about to make a parachute jump they would never forget.'"

"I liked the story because I learned about skydiving, like what a tandem jump is and how a skydiver uses his position to fly faster or slower."

5 **Reflect on Discussing Opinions Respectfully**

Without giving names, share some of your observations of respectful ways the students shared their opinions. Ask:

Q *How did you and your partner do sharing your opinions today? What problems did you have? How can you avoid those problems the next time you share opinions?*

Explain that tomorrow the students will practice forming and discussing opinions about their own independent reading books.

INDIVIDUALIZED DAILY READING

 Document IDR Conferences/Have the Students Use Important Ideas to Summarize Verbally

Continue to have the students think about the important ideas in their reading and be ready to share a summary of what they read in pairs.

Have the students read independently for up to 30 minutes.

Use the "IDR Conference Notes" record sheet to conduct and document individual conferences.

 At the end of independent reading, have each student verbally summarize his reading for his partner by telling his partner in a few sentences what he read. Remind the students to ask clarifying questions when necessary.

After partners have shared, have a few volunteers share with the class. As the students share with the class, ask questions such as:

Q *What are the important ideas in your summary?*

Q *Would you recommend this book to someone? Why or why not?*

EXTENSION

Read Other Stories from *True Stories of Heroes*

If the students enjoy true action/adventure stories, you might read more from *True Stories of Heroes* aloud. After reading a story, encourage the students to express their opinions about the story and support the opinions with evidence.

Day 3

Materials

- Narrative texts at appropriate levels for independent reading
- "Factors to Consider When Forming an Opinion" chart
- Small self-stick note for each student
- Chart with questions about independent reading texts, prepared ahead
- *Student Response Book* page 81
- Book for modeling recording opinions and evidence (see Step 4)
- Transparency of "Double-entry Journal: My Opinions About _____" (BLM42)
- *Assessment Resource Book*

Independent Strategy Practice

In this lesson, the students:

- *Form opinions* about a text they read independently
- Find evidence in the text that supports their opinions
- Use a double-entry journal to record their opinions
- Read independently for up to 30 minutes
- Discuss their opinions respectfully

1 Review Forming Opinions

Review that in the past two weeks the students have heard and read stories, formed opinions about them using factors such as those on the "Factors to Consider When Forming an Opinion" chart, and looked for evidence to support their opinions. Remind them that good readers think about their personal response to text. Explain that today they will practice forming opinions about the books they are reading independently.

2 Read Independently Without Stopping

Ask the students to use a self-stick note to mark the place they begin reading today, and have them read independently for 10 minutes. Ask them to be aware of whether or not the text is holding their interest and why.

3 Record Opinions in a Double-entry Journal

After 10 minutes, stop the students. Ask each student to think about the following questions, which you have written where everyone can see them. Read each question aloud; then pause to give the students time to think before you read the next question.

- Is the story you are reading holding your interest? Why?

- Are the people/characters interesting? Why?

- How does the story make you feel? Why?

- Would you recommend this story to someone else? Why?

Have the students open to *Student Response Book* page 81, "Double-entry Journal: My Opinions About _____." Ask them to write the title of their book on the line at the top of the journal. Then have them write a few of their opinions in the left-hand column of the journal.

◀ **Teacher Note**

You introduced the double-entry journal in Unit 5, Week 2. If necessary, review how to use the journal.

 4 Model Using the Double-entry Journal

Explain that the students will reread the section of text, beginning at the self-stick note, and look for evidence that supports their opinions. When they find evidence, they will write the evidence in the right-hand column of the journal.

Model the procedure by thinking aloud about your own book and recording an opinion and evidence on the transparency of the "Double-entry Journal: My Opinions About _____." (For example, you might say, "I read the story, 'Mrs. Buell,' again. I think the character of Mrs. Buell is very believable—I can almost see her. Some evidence of this is in this description: 'In winter she wore the same sweater every day, a man's gray one, too big, with the sleeves pushed up. They kept slipping down and she'd shove them back a million times a day.'")

5 Reread Independently and Record Evidence

Have the students reread and record evidence for their opinions in the right-hand column of their journal.

Remind the students that as they reread, their opinions may change. If that happens, they can revise or add to the opinions and look for evidence to support the new opinions.

If the students have difficulty forming opinions or finding evidence for them, support them by asking questions such as:

Q   *What happened in the part of the story you read today? Did it hold your interest? Why or why not?*

 Note

This might be especially helpful for your English Language Learners.

Q *What did the people/characters do or say that surprised or interested you? Read that part aloud.*

Q *How did you feel as you read the selection? What made you feel that way? Read that part aloud.*

▶ **6** ▶ **Discuss Opinions in Pairs and as a Class**

When most students are finished, have them use "Turn to Your Partner" to discuss their opinions and the supporting evidence.

> **CLASS COMPREHENSION ASSESSMENT**
>
> Circulate as partners talk and ask yourself:
>
> **Q** *Can the students express an opinion about their reading?*
>
> **Q** *Can they support their opinion with evidence from their text?*
>
> Record your observations on page 30 of the *Assessment Resource Book*.

Have a few students share a journal entry with the class. Remind each student to tell the name of her book and briefly what it is about before sharing her opinion and the evidence she found. After each student shares, elicit questions from the class and allow the student who shared to respond.

Remind the students that the reason they are learning to form and discuss opinions about their reading is to help them bring their own thinking to a text and to get better at communicating about that text. Encourage them to continue to practice forming and communicating opinions as they read on their own.

Day 4

Class Meeting

In this lesson, the students:

- Have a class meeting to discuss the importance of expressing their true opinions
- Read independently for up to 30 minutes
- Discuss their opinions respectfully

1 Gather for a Class Meeting

Before the class meeting, make sure the "Class Meeting Ground Rules" chart is posted where everyone can see it. Review the procedure for coming to a class meeting and remind the students that they have been working toward creating a caring and safe learning community.

Have partners sit together and ask them to make sure they can see all their classmates.

2 Discuss the Importance of Expressing True Opinions

Review the ground rules. Explain that during today's class meeting, the students will talk about the importance of expressing one's true opinions in class and how to make the classroom environment feel like a safe place to do that.

Remind the students that they have been focusing in the past weeks on forming and discussing opinions about their reading. Explain that it is normal for people to have differences of opinion when discussing books. However, sometimes it can be challenging to express one's true opinion, especially if it seems that most other people have a different opinion. Ask:

Q   *What can be challenging about expressing your true opinions in a group?*

Materials

- Space for the class to sit in a circle
- "Class Meeting Ground Rules" chart
- Chart paper and a marker
- "Factors to Consider When Forming an Opinion" chart
- *Student Response Book,* IDR Journal section

Class Meeting Ground Rules

- one person talks at a time
- listen to one another

Teacher Note

Use "Turn to Your Partner" as needed during this discussion to increase participation, especially if you are hearing from only a few students. You can also use "Turn to Your Partner" if many students want to speak at the same time.

Q *I've noticed that sometimes students change their opinion to what others are thinking, rather than sticking with their own opinion. Why do you think they might do this?*

Q *Why is it helpful for a group to hear opinions that are not the ones of the majority?*

Students might say:

"Sometimes I get embarrassed when people don't agree with me. It makes me feel like I don't know what's going on."

"I agree with [Mohammed]. One time I voted to hear a book that no one else liked. I got embarrassed, so I changed my vote."

"Just because not everyone thinks the way you do doesn't mean you're wrong."

"In addition to what [Devon] said, I think that sometimes one person's way of looking at something can make everyone else think about something in a new way."

If the students have difficulty answering these questions, prompt them using examples like those in the "Students might say" note. You might also provide examples of famous people who helped change things for the better by expressing opinions that were different from those of the majority (for example, Martin Luther King Jr., Rosa Parks, Susan B. Anthony, and César Chávez).

▶ **3 Discuss Solutions**

State your expectation that the students will be responsible for both expressing their true opinions and doing their part to create a safe atmosphere for discussing opinions in the class.

 Have the students use "Think, Pair, Share" to think about and discuss:

Q *If you express an opinion that others disagree with, how would you like them to tell you? Why would that help?*

Q *What can we do to create an environment where everyone feels safe expressing their true opinions?*

Students might say:

"When someone says something we disagree with, we should think about it for a moment before saying anything."

"We can ask the person why she feels that way. She might make us change our minds."

"We can say, 'It's neat that you have a different idea than I do.'"

Have a few pairs share their ideas with the whole class; write their responses on chart paper. If necessary, suggest some solutions like those in the "Students might say" note to stimulate their thinking.

Review the suggestions on the chart and ask:

Q *Is there anything on this list that you can't agree to try in the coming days?*

Make adjustments to the list only if the students give reasonable explanations for why certain solutions are unfeasible. Explain that you would like the students to use the suggestions on the chart in the coming days and that you will be checking in with them to see how they are doing.

 Reflect on the Class Meeting

Facilitate a brief discussion about how the students felt they did following the ground rules during the class meeting. Review the procedure for returning to their desks, and adjourn the meeting.

Display the chart where everyone can see it. Hold the students accountable by checking in periodically in the coming days to see how they are doing expressing their true opinions and making the class a safe place to do so.

INDIVIDUALIZED DAILY READING

 Write a Review of Their Reading in Their IDR Journals

Have the students read independently for up to 30 minutes.

As the students read, circulate among them. Ask individual students questions such as:

Q *What is your reading about?*

Q *What do you think of this book? Would you recommend it to someone? Why? Why not?*

At the end of independent reading, draw the students, attention to the "Factors to Consider When Forming an Opinion" chart and have the students write a brief summary and review of their reading in their IDR Journals. Have several volunteers share their writing with the class. Discuss questions such as:

Q *Based on [Farhad's] summary and review, would you be interested in reading this book? Why? Why not?*

Q *What questions do you want to ask [Charlene] about [her] book?*

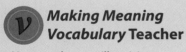

Making Meaning
Vocabulary **Teacher**

Next week you will revisit this week's reading to teach Vocabulary Week 26.

Week 3

Overview

UNIT 9: SYNTHESIZING
Fiction and Expository Nonfiction

"Is Dodge Ball Too Dangerous?"
by Dina Maasarani, from *TIME For Kids*
(timeforkids.com, May 15, 2001)

"Turn It Off!"
by Kathryn R. Hoffman, from *TIME For Kids*
(timeforkids.com, April 12, 2002)

ALTERNATIVE RESOURCES

PBS NewsHour Extra, www.pbs.org/newshour/extra/speakout/

CNN Student News, www.cnn.com/studentnews

Comprehension Focus

- Students *synthesize* by *making judgments* and *forming opinions* about a text, using evidence from the text to support their conclusions.

- Students read independently.

Social Development Focus

- Students relate the values of respect and responsibility to their behavior.

- Students develop the group skills of expressing their true opinions and discussing their opinions respectfully.

DO AHEAD

- Collect newspapers and magazines at a variety of reading levels for IDR.

- Prepare a chart for discussing the article "Is Dodge Ball Too Dangerous?" (see Day 2, Step 2, on page 566).

- Prepare a chart for discussing the article "Turn It Off!" (see Day 4, Step 2, on page 575).

Making Meaning Vocabulary Teacher

If you are teaching Developmental Studies Center's *Making Meaning Vocabulary* program, teach Vocabulary Week 26 this week. For more information, see the *Making Meaning Vocabulary Teacher's Manual.*

Day 1

Materials

- "Is Dodge Ball Too Dangerous?" (see pages 570–571)

- Magazine and newspaper articles for IDR

ELL Note

English Language Learners may benefit from previewing the article prior to the lesson.

Read-aloud

In this lesson, the students:

- Hear, read, and discuss a news article
- Read independently for up to 30 minutes
- Express their true opinions
- Give reasons for their opinions

 Discuss Expressing Opinions

Have partners sit together. Remind them that in the past two weeks they have been thinking about and discussing their opinions and judgments about texts. Tell them that they will continue this focus this week and ask:

Q *How have we been doing discussing our opinions in a respectful way?*

Q *What do you want to remember from our last class meeting about making our class a safe place for everyone to express their true opinions?*

Encourage the students to focus on being open to one another's thinking and to continue to focus on giving reasons for their opinions.

 Introduce "Is Dodge Ball Too Dangerous?"

Explain that this week, the students will hear and read news articles written for young readers. Remind the students that they read and discussed articles in previous units. Review that news articles can provide good opportunities for readers to form their own opinions because they often include different points of view, or opinions, on a topic.

Explain that the article you will read aloud today is called "Is Dodge Ball Too Dangerous?" The article, from May 15, 2001, appears on the

TIME For Kids website. (*TIME For Kids* is a news magazine for young readers.) Ask:

Q *What do you know about the game dodge ball?*

Q *From the title, what do you think this article might be about?*

Q *What points of view (opinions) do you think might appear in the article?*

 Read "Is Dodge Ball Too Dangerous?" Aloud

Read the article aloud, stopping as described below.

Suggested Vocabulary

banning: not allowing (p. 570)

critics: people who express opinions (in this case negative ones) publicly (p. 570)

a whole gamut of sports: a variety of sports (p. 571)

ELL Vocabulary

English Language Learners may benefit from discussing additional vocabulary, including:

eliminated: removed from competition (p. 570)

defenders: people who agree with something (p. 571)

debating: discussing different points of view (p. 571)

deflated ball: ball with the air taken out (p. 571)

Stop after:

p. 570 "'If a boy doesn't throw hard and make a hit, the other boys call him a girl,' says Lilla Atherton, a fifth grader in Fairfax County, Virginia, where the game has been banned."

Ask:

Q *What point of view have you heard so far, and what supports that point of view?*

 Have the students use "Turn to Your Partner" to discuss the question.

Without sharing as a class, reread the last sentence and continue reading to the next stop:

p. 571 "'If we are going to ban dodge ball for aggressiveness, we would have to look at a whole gamut of sports,' she says."

 Once again, ask and have the students discuss in pairs:

Q *What point of view is expressed in this part of the article, and what supports that point of view?*

Reread the last sentence and continue reading to the end of the article.

▶ **Discuss the Article as a Class**

Facilitate a discussion of the article using the following questions. Be ready to reread from the article to help the students recall what they heard.

Q *What is this article about?*

Q *What were some of the reasons people gave for wanting to ban dodge ball at school?*

Q *What were some of the reasons people gave for wanting to keep dodge ball as a school game?*

Students might say:

"The people who were against it said it's dangerous for kids to throw a ball at a 'human target.'"

"In addition to what [Masa] said, I also heard that they thought it wasn't a good form of exercise."

"The people who were for it said that most balls are soft and kids are not allowed to throw the ball at another kid's head."

Q *What do you think about Lilla Atherton's comment, "If a boy doesn't throw hard and make a hit, the other boys call him a girl"? What does this comment assume about girls? Do you agree with this assumption? Why or why not?*

Explain that in the next lesson you will reread the article and the students will discuss their own opinions about whether or not dodge ball is too dangerous.

INDIVIDUALIZED DAILY READING

 Review Previewing a Text Before Reading

. Remind the students that readers often preview newspaper or magazine articles before they read. They think about the title and subtitles and wonder what the article might be about. Explain that sometimes newspaper or magazine headlines are written to grab your attention and make you curious. At other times the headline is more straightforward and tells exactly what the article is about.

Have the students read magazine or newspaper articles independently for up to 30 minutes. Ask them to take a few minutes before reading an article to preview the headlines and any subtitles or photos.

As the students read, circulate among them. Ask individual students questions such as:

Q *After reading the title and subtitle, what do you think this article is about?*

Q *Does the headline grab your attention? Why or why not?*

At the end of independent reading, discuss questions such as:

Q *What do you think about your article's headline? Is it straightforward or not? Explain.*

Q *What was your article about?*

Day 2

Materials

- "Is Dodge Ball Too Dangerous?" (see pages 570–571)
- *Student Response Book* pages 82–83
- Chart for discussing the article "Is Dodge Ball Too Dangerous?" prepared ahead
- *Assessment Resource Book*
- Magazine and newspaper articles for IDR

Teacher Note ▶

Keep this discussion brief. The purpose is to help the students remember the article. They will have an opportunity later in the lesson to discuss their opinions in more depth.

Strategy Lesson

In this lesson, the students:

- Consider pros and cons and *form opinions*
- Read independently for up to 30 minutes
- Express their true opinions
- Give reasons for their opinions
- Discuss their opinions respectfully

▌1 Review "Is Dodge Ball Too Dangerous?"

Remind the students that in the previous lesson they heard "Is Dodge Ball Too Dangerous?"—an article that gives two points of view. Ask:

Q *What are the points of view expressed in the article?*

▌2 Reread and Discuss the Article

Have the students turn to *Student Response Book* pages 82–83 and explain that this is a copy of the article. Explain that you will reread the article aloud and ask them to follow along in their *Student Response Books*. Tell them that during the reading they should form an opinion about dodge ball as a school game and look for evidence in the text to support their opinion.

Read the article aloud slowly and clearly.

After the reading, ask the students to quietly consider the following questions, which you have written where everyone can see them:

- *What is your opinion about dodge ball as a school game?*
- *What evidence in the article supports your opinion?*
- *Did your opinion change during the second reading? Why or why not?*

Without discussing the questions, have the students read the article again in pairs or quietly to themselves. As they read, they should underline sentences that support their opinion about dodge ball as a school game and take notes in the margins of the article.

 When most students have finished, have them use "Turn to Your Partner" to discuss the questions on the chart.

CLASS COMPREHENSION ASSESSMENT

Circulate as partners talk. Ask yourself:

Q   *Are the students expressing their opinions about dodge ball?*

Q   *Are they supporting their opinions by referring to the article?*

Record your observations on page 31 of the *Assessment Resource Book*.

 Discuss Opinions as a Class

When most pairs have finished, facilitate a discussion using the questions that follow. Remind the students to be respectful of one another's opinions and to use the discussion prompts they have learned.

Q   *The title of the article asks, "Is dodge ball too dangerous?" What is your opinion? Explain your thinking.*

Q   *Why do you disagree with the other opinion expressed in the article?*

Q   *Do you agree or disagree with [Chantel]? Why?*

Point out that while many news articles, like this one, express different points of view about a topic, some articles are written from a single point of view.

Ask:

Q *Why is it important for readers to be thinking about what the writer's point of view, or opinion, might be?*

> **Students might say:**
>
> "You might read an article and think everything is true, when you're just reading someone's opinion. Someone else might say something different about the same situation."
>
> "It's important to decide if you agree or disagree."

If the students have difficulty answering this question, suggest some responses, such as those listed in the "Students might say" note.

4 ▶ Reflect on Expressing True Opinions

Facilitate a brief discussion about how the students interacted. Ask:

Q *How did you do expressing your true opinions today, rather than going with what others were thinking? How was that responsible?*

Q *What did you do today to make the class a safe place for others to express their true opinions?*

Explain that in the next lesson the students will read and discuss an article written from a single point of view.

INDIVIDUALIZED DAILY READING

5 ▶ Discuss Points of View

Ask the students to be aware of opinions or points of view expressed in the articles they read and think about whether or not they agree with those points of view.

Have the students read magazine or newspaper articles independently for up to 30 minutes.

As the students read, circulate among them. Ask individual students questions such as:

Q *What points of view are expressed in your article? What did you read that makes you think so?*

Q *Do you agree or disagree with that point of view? Why?*

Q *Would you recommend the article to others to read? Explain.*

Q *Does the headline reflect the author's point of view? Explain.*

At the end of independent reading, give the students time to share what they read as a class.

by **Dina Maasarani**

from *TIME For Kids* (timeforkids.com, May 15, 2001)

Is Dodge Ball Too Dangerous?
Many schools are banning a gym game
they say is too violent

Is dodge ball on the verge of being tossed out? Dodge ball, one of the most popular games in gym class, is now also being called one of the most dangerous. More and more schools are banning dodge ball, a game in which kids throw balls at other kids who have to avoid—or dodge—them. Now, the game itself is having to dodge some pretty serious criticism.

Why Ban Dodge Ball?

What's all the fuss about a game that's been played across the country for decades? School districts in states such as Texas, Virginia, Maine and Massachusetts have banned it because many educators and parents say dodge ball is a violent and aggressive game. They say a game where there is a "human target" makes it more likely for kids to get hurt.

Neil Williams, an Eastern Connecticut State University physical education professor, has created a Physical Education Hall of Shame. He considers dodge ball (also known as bombardment, burning ball, killer ball, prison ball, and ball chaser) the most shameful school sport on his list. "It allows the stronger kids to pick on and target the weaker kids," Williams says. Critics also complain the game is not a good form of exercise because it requires kids who are eliminated (or hit by the ball) to sit on the sidelines while others get to keep playing. "If a boy doesn't throw hard and make a hit, the other boys call him a girl," says Lilla Atherton, a fifth grader in Fairfax County, Virginia, where the game has been banned.

continues

Is Dodge Ball Too Dangerous?

continued

Dodge Ball Defenders

Fans of the classic game say it's simple and fun and helps kids
improve their reflexes and hand-eye coordination. Dodge ball
supporters also say injuries are rare because most gym teachers do
not allow students to aim for the head and because most balls are
made from foam or other soft materials. Martha Kupferschmidt, an
official at the Murray school district in Utah, wonders why dodge
ball is being singled out when other sports like football, kickball
and wrestling are also aggressive. "If we are going to ban dodge
ball for aggressiveness, we would have to look at a whole gamut of
sports," she says.

While some adults are debating whether kids should be
playing dodge ball, others are starting to play the game themselves.
The first-ever world dodge ball indoor championship for adults was
held in Schaumburg, Illinois in January. "Dodge Ball Day 2001" is
scheduled for July 28, also in Illinois.

Changing the Rules of the Game

Some school districts that do not want to ban dodge ball have
instead decided to change the rules to make it less violent. In
several districts, kids who are hit with the ball get to re-enter the
game so there are no hurt feelings. In other schools, kids aim at a
deflated ball instead of other kids.

Day 3

Materials

- "Turn It Off!"
  (see pages 578–579)

- Magazines and newspaper articles for IDR

Read-aloud

In this lesson, the students:

- Hear, read, and discuss a news article
- Read independently for up to 30 minutes
- Express their true opinions
- Give reasons for their opinions

 Discuss Forming Opinions About Articles with a Single Point of View

Review that the students read "Is Dodge Ball Too Dangerous?"— a news article that presents two different points of view. After reading the article, they thought about and discussed their own point of view. Remind them that some articles express different points of view about a topic, and other articles are written from only one point of view. It is up to the reader to recognize the point of view and decide whether he agrees.

Explain that today, the students will read and discuss an article written from a single point of view. Stress that it is important for readers to think critically and form opinions about what they are reading, because this helps them better understand and respond to the reading.

 Introduce "Turn It Off!"

Explain that today you will read an article entitled "Turn It Off!" This article, from April 12, 2002, also appears on the *TIME For Kids* website. Read the subtitle aloud: "Next week, millions of people will go TV-free. How about you?" Ask:

Q *From the title, what do you think this article might be about?*

Q *What point of view about TV do you think might appear in the article? Why?*

Read "Turn It Off!" Aloud

Read the article aloud, stopping as described below.

> **Suggested Vocabulary**
>
> **annual event:** something that happens once a year (p. 578)
> **journal:** magazine (p. 578)
>
> **ELL Vocabulary**
>
> English Language Learners may benefit from discussing additional vocabulary, including:
>
> **promoted:** made people aware of (p. 578)
> **overwhelming:** having a strong effect (p. 578)

Read the title and subtitle, then continue reading aloud, stopping after:

> **p. 578** "This year, there will be participants in every state and more than 12 countries."

 Have the students use "Turn to Your Partner" to discuss:

Q *What did you learn in the part of the article you just heard?*

Without sharing as a class, reread the last sentence and continue reading. Follow the same procedure at the remaining stops:

> **p. 579** "'Almost anything uses more energy than watching TV,' says Dr. William H. Dietz of the U.S. Centers for Disease Control and Prevention in Atlanta, Georgia."

> **p. 579** "Says TV-Turnoff veteran Carly Cara, 11, of Niles, Illinois: 'You're doing so many fun things that before you know it, it's over!'"

 Discuss the Article as a Class

Facilitate a discussion of the article using the following questions. Be ready to reread passages to help the students recall what they heard.

Q *What is this article about?*

Q *What is the point of view about TV represented in the article? What did you hear in the article that makes you think so?*

Q *What might an article written from the opposite point of view (in favor of television viewing) say?*

Students might say:

"The article talks about how TV viewing leads to unhealthy habits. The reason I think this is that it talked about how kids are shown a lot of junk food commercials, and they think this leads to them being overweight and unhealthy."

"In addition to what [Rafael] said, the article talked about how TV makes kids violent."

"An article written from the opposite point of view might say that watching TV is good for you because you can learn a lot of things from shows about nature and news."

Explain that in the next lesson you will reread the article and the students will decide whether they agree or disagree with the point of view expressed in it.

INDIVIDUALIZED DAILY READING

 5 ▶ **Discuss Points of View/Document IDR Conferences**

Ask the students to be aware of opinions or points of view expressed in the articles they read and whether or not they agree with those points of view.

Have the students read magazine or newspaper articles independently for up to 30 minutes.

Use the "IDR Conference Notes" record sheet to conduct and document individual conferences.

At the end of independent reading, give the students time to share what they read as a class. Probe the students' thinking by asking questions such as:

Q *What points of view are expressed in your article? What did you read that makes you think so?*

Q *Do you agree or disagree with that point of view? Why?*

Q *Would you recommend the article to others to read? Explain.*

Day 4

Guided Strategy Practice

In this lesson, the students:

- Consider pros and cons and *form opinions*
- Read independently for up to 30 minutes
- Express their true opinions
- Give reasons for their opinions
- Discuss their opinions respectfully

1 Review "Turn It Off!"

Remind the students that in the previous lesson they heard the article "Turn It Off!" about TV-Turnoff Week. Ask:

Q *What was the point of view about TV expressed in the article?*

2 Reread and Discuss the Article

Have the students turn to *Student Response Book* pages 84–86 and explain that this is a copy of the article. Explain that you will reread the article aloud and that you would like them to follow along in the *Student Response Book.* Tell them that during the reading, they should think about whether they agree or disagree with the point of view in the article and why.

Reread the article aloud.

After the reading, ask the students to quietly consider the following questions, which you have written where everyone can see them:

- *Do you agree or disagree with the point of view expressed in the article?*

- *What part of the article supports your opinion, or what part makes you disagree? Why?*

- *Did your opinion change during the second reading? Why or why not?*

Materials

- "Turn It Off!"

- *Student Response Book* pages 84–86

- Chart for discussing the article "Turn It Off!" prepared ahead

- Magazine and newspaper articles for IDR

- *Student Response Book,* IDR Journal section

Without discussing the questions, have the students read the article again in pairs or quietly to themselves. If they agree with the point of view in the article, they should underline sentences that support their opinion and take notes in the margins of the article. If they disagree, they should underline the sentences that make them disagree and write notes in the margin.

 When most students have finished, use "Turn to Your Partner" to have them discuss the questions on the chart.

Teacher Note

Circulate as partners talk. Notice whether the students are expressing opinions and supporting their opinions by referring to the article. If the students are having difficulty expressing opinions, ask questions such as:

Q *According to the article, what are some of "TV's Many Turnoffs"?*

Q *Do you agree or disagree with this view of watching TV? Why?*

3 ▶ **Discuss Opinions as a Class**

When most pairs have finished, facilitate a discussion using the questions that follow. Remind the students to be respectful of one another's opinions and to use the discussion prompts they have learned. Ask:

Q *Do you agree or disagree with the article's point of view about watching TV? Why?*

Q *What did you read in the article or think about that supports your opinion?*

Remind the students that it is important for readers to think critically and form opinions about what they are reading, as this helps them better understand and respond to the reading. Tell them that they will have more opportunities in the coming weeks to form opinions and make judgments about their reading.

4 ▶ **Reflect on Expressing Opinions Truthfully and Respectfully**

Facilitate a brief discussion about how the students did this week expressing their true opinions, giving reasons for their opinions, and discussing their opinions respectfully. Share examples of these behaviors that you observed over the course of the week, and give the students an opportunity to share examples they observed.

INDIVIDUALIZED DAILY READING

 5 ▶ **Write About an Article in Their IDR Journals**

Ask the students to pay attention to the opinions or points of view expressed in the articles they read and think about whether they agree with them. They will write about one of the articles in their IDR Journals.

Have the students read magazine or newspaper articles independently for up to 30 minutes.

As the students read, circulate among them. Ask individual students questions such as:

Q *What points of view are expressed in your article? What did you read that makes you think so?*

Q *Do you agree or disagree with that point of view? Why?*

Q *Would you recommend the article to others to read? Explain.*

At the end of independent reading, have each student use her IDR Journal to write a brief summary of an article and say whether she agrees with the point of view expressed in it. Have several volunteers share their writing with the class.

EXTENSION

Read and Discuss More Articles

Have the students read and discuss other articles and editorials you have collected from sources such as: www.timeforkids.com, www.pbs.org/newshour/extra, and www.askforkids.com.

If you locate editorials written from opposing points of view, you might have half the class read one point of view and the other half read the second point of view. Then you can organize a class debate based on the opinions in the editorials.

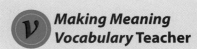

***Making Meaning
Vocabulary* Teacher**

Next week you will revisit this week's reading to teach Vocabulary Week 27.

by Kathryn R. Hoffman

from *TIME For Kids* (timeforkids.com, April 12, 2002)

Turn It Off!

**Next week, millions of people
will go TV-free. How about you?**

On April 22, millions of TVs around the world will go blank. But instead of fiddling with the remote or calling the cable company, avid TV watchers everywhere will take drastic action. Entire families will go outside to ride bikes; groups of friends will play games. Will you join in—or will you just sit there and watch?

April 22–28 is TV-Turnoff Week. TV-Turnoff Network, a nonprofit organization, has promoted the annual event since 1995. In the beginning, only a few thousand people took part. This year, there will be participants in every state and more than 12 countries.

TV's Many Turnoffs

Each year, kids in the U.S. spend more time glued to the tube than doing anything else—except for sleeping! People have worried about the effects of TV ever since the 1940s, when television became popular. Over the years, health care groups like the American Academy of Pediatrics and the American Medical Association have voiced their concern. They point to studies that link excessive TV viewing to such problems as bad eating habits, lack of exercise, obesity and violent behavior.

Two weeks ago, a new study published in the journal *Science* gave fresh evidence of a connection between TV viewing and violence. Psychologist Jeffrey G. Johnson and his research team followed children in 707 families for 17 years. The researchers found that kids who watched more than one hour of TV a day were more likely than other kids to take part in aggressive and violent behavior as they grew older. Says Johnson, the link between TV, with all its violent shows, and aggressive behavior "has gotten to the point where it's overwhelming."

continues

Turn It Off!

continued

Others worry about the impact of commercials on kids. One study found that during four hours of Saturday-morning cartoons, TV networks ran 202 ads for junk foods. The steady stream of reminders to buy sugary soda, cereal and candy are one reason that more than one in eight American kids is overweight. Long hours sitting in front of the tube are another reason. "Almost anything uses more energy than watching TV," says Dr. William H. Dietz of the U.S. Centers for Disease Control and Prevention in Atlanta, Georgia.

Enjoying Life, Unplugged

TV-Turnoff Network wants to encourage life outside the box. "We're not anti-TV," says the group's director, Frank Vespe. The goal is to help kids tune into real life so that "they won't have time for TV."

But this is an adult speaking. Is it really possible to live without popular TV shows? Sarah Foote, of Burke, Virginia, says she made it through TV-Turnoff Week last year—and enjoyed herself! After a few days, says Sarah, 10, "I thought, 'Why did I ever need TV?'" Her brother Nathaniel, 8, agrees: "There are about 8,000 other things you can do."

Still, some kids can't picture life without TV. Christian Cardenas, 10, of New York City, doesn't plan on tuning out. "It entertains you on rainy days," he says.

Could you go without TV for a whole week? Says TV-Turnoff veteran Carly Cara, 11, of Niles, Illinois: "You're doing so many fun things that before you know it, it's over!"

Week 4

Overview

UNIT 9: SYNTHESIZING
Fiction and Expository Nonfiction

Review of *The Legend of Sleepy Hollow*
by Jennifer B. (age 12),
from *Spaghetti Book Club*
(spaghettibookclub.org, school year 1999–2000)

Review of *The Ballad of Lucy Whipple*

ALTERNATIVE RESOURCES

KidsBookshelf, www.kidsbookshelf.com

Spaghetti Book Club, www.spaghettibookclub.org

Comprehension Focus

• Students *synthesize* by *making judgments* and *forming opinions* about text, using evidence from the text to support their conclusions.

• Students read independently.

Social Development Focus

• Students relate the values of respect and responsibility to their behavior.

• Students develop the group skills of discussing opinions respectfully and giving and receiving feedback.

DO AHEAD

• Prior to Day 2, have each student select a book to recommend to classmates for summer reading (see the "Teacher Note" on page 586).

• Prepare to model gathering information for a book review (see Day 2, Step 2, on page 591).

• Make transparencies of the "Review of *The Legend of Sleepy Hollow*" (BLM43–BLM44).

• Make a transparency of "Things to Include in My Book Review" (BLM45).

• Prepare a chart for giving feedback about reviews (see Day 4, Step 2, on page 597).

• Prepare to read a passage aloud (see Day 4, Step 3, on page 598).

• Make copies of the Unit 9 Parent Letter (BLM18) to send home with the students on the last day of the unit.

Making Meaning Vocabulary Teacher

If you are teaching Developmental Studies Center's *Making Meaning Vocabulary* program, teach Vocabulary Week 27 this week. For more information, see the *Making Meaning Vocabulary Teacher's Manual*.

Read-aloud

In this lesson, the students:

* Hear, read, and discuss two book reviews
* Discuss summary and opinion in a book review
* Begin their summer reading list
* Read independently for up to 30 minutes
* Give reasons for their opinions

Materials

* Review of *The Legend of Sleepy Hollow* (see page 588)
* Review of *The Ballad of Lucy Whipple* (see page 589)
* *Student Response Book* pages 87–88
* Transparencies of the "Review of *The Legend of Sleepy Hollow*" (BLM43–BLM44)
* "Reading Comprehension Strategies" chart
* Small self-stick notes for each student

Teacher Note

This lesson might take more than one class period.

▶1 Review the Focus for the Week

Have partners sit together. Remind them that in the past three weeks they have been thinking about forming opinions and making judgments about texts. Tell them that in the coming weeks they will continue this focus by reviewing and recommending books for summer reading. They will hear their classmates present reviews of favorite books and decide whether they want to read those books this summer.

▶2 Introduce the Summer Reading List

Have the students turn to *Student Response Book* page 87, "Summer Reading List." Explain that as they hear book reviews in the coming days they will list the books they might be interested in reading this summer. Point out that the page has space for the book title and author and a few words to remind them what the book is about.

Explain that today you will read two book reviews aloud. The students will discuss the reviews, then decide whether they want to add the books to their summer reading list.

▶ ### 3 Read the Review of *The Legend of Sleepy Hollow* Aloud

Tell the students that the first book review is about *The Legend of Sleepy Hollow,* by Washington Irving. The review was written by Jennifer B. (age 12) for the website spaghettibookclub.org.

ELL Vocabulary

English Language Learners may benefit from discussing the following vocabulary:

legend: story handed down from earlier times (p. 588)
headless: missing a head (p. 588)

Read the review without stopping. Then explain that you will read the review a second time and that the students should determine whether there is enough information to help them decide whether they want to read the book. Read the review a second time. When you are finished, facilitate a discussion by asking:

Q *Based on the review, what is this book about? What makes you say that?*

Q *Is there enough information about the book for you to decide whether or not to read it? Why or why not?*

Q *Do you want to read this book over the summer? Why?*

Students might say:

"This sounds like a story about a ghost who cuts off people's heads because he's missing his own head. The reviewer says this at the beginning of the review."

"In addition to what [Lupe] said, I think the book reviewer liked this book because she said it's a scary and funny old story."

"I think there's enough information in the review because I know some details about what it's about, like how Ichabod meets the headless horseman on the bridge."

At the end of the discussion, invite interested students to add *The Legend of Sleepy Hollow* to their summer reading list. Write the title and author on the board for the students to copy.

◀ **Teacher Note**

The two book reviews in this lesson are examples of effective and less effective reviews. The first review provides a sufficient summary of the story, an interesting presentation ("Did Ichabod ever escape?"), and reasons that support the recommendation. The second review provides less information and a less compelling argument for the recommendation. Discussing and comparing the two reviews will help to prepare the students to write more effective reviews of their own books.

Explain that you will read a second review aloud, and ask them to consider again whether they want to read the book and whether there is enough information in the review to help them decide.

 Read the Review of *The Ballad of Lucy Whipple* Aloud

Tell the students that the second review is of a book called *The Ballad of Lucy Whipple,* by Karen Cushman.

Follow the same procedure you used with the first review by reading the review aloud, prompting the students to listen to determine whether there is enough information in the review, and then rereading the review. Facilitate a discussion by asking:

Q *Based on the review, what is this book about? What makes you say that?*

Q *Is there enough information about the book for you to decide whether or not to read it? Why or why not?*

Q *Do you want to read this book over the summer? Why?*

Students might say:

"The book is about a girl who moves to California, but she doesn't like it."

"I don't think there's enough information to decide. Maybe the book is interesting, but you can't tell from the review."

Explain that this review is a good example of why readers need to make judgments and ask questions as they read. While the review might make *The Ballad of Lucy Whipple* sound uninteresting, the book itself is a Newbery Award–winning adventure in which the main character, a girl with the unlikely name of California Morning Whipple, moves to a California mining camp with her family during the Gold Rush. She hates living in the camp and decides to change her name to Lucy because "I cannot hate California and be California." Lucy's personality and exaggerations (for example, she says she lives in a space so small "I can lie in bed and stir the beans on the stove without getting up") make her a very amusing character.

After providing this additional information about *The Ballad of Lucy Whipple,* invite the students to add it to their reading list, if they wish. Write the title and author on the board so interested students can copy them.

▶ 5 Analyze the Review of *The Legend of Sleepy Hollow*

Have the students turn to *Student Response Book* page 88, "Review of *The Legend of Sleepy Hollow.*" Explain that this is the first review you read aloud. Ask them to reread the review with a partner or to themselves, and then talk in pairs about which parts summarize the book and which parts give the reviewer's opinion.

Have the students underline the sentences that summarize and circle the sentences that give opinion. Write the following directions on the board:

- Underline sentences that summarize (tell what it's about).

- Circle sentences that give the reviewer's opinion.

As partners work, circulate among them. If you notice students having difficulty recognizing summary and opinion, support them by asking them questions such as:

Q *What is this book about? What part of the review tells you that?*

Q *Does the reviewer like the book? Why? What part of the review tells you that?*

▶ 6 Discuss the Review as a Whole Class

When most students are finished, place the transparency of the "Review of *The Legend of Sleepy Hollow*" on the overhead projector, and facilitate a brief discussion. Ask:

Q *What parts of the review did you underline? How does that part tell what the book is about, rather than the reviewer's opinion?*

Q *What did you circle? How does that part give the reviewer's opinion?*

ELL Note

If necessary, reread the review aloud and have the students follow along.

FACILITATION TIP

Reflect on your experience over the past weeks with **responding neutrally** with interest during class discussions. Does this practice feel natural to you? Are you integrating it into class discussions throughout the school day? What effect is it having on the students? We encourage you to continue to try this practice and reflect on students' responses as you facilitate class discussions in the future.

As the students identify summary and opinion, underline or circle those parts on the transparency.

Point out that the purpose of this activity is to help the students recognize facts about a book and opinions about it. In their reviews, they will need to include both factual information (a summary) and their own opinion about the book.

Teacher Note

Prior to Day 2, have each student select a favorite book to recommend to classmates for summer reading. These should be books they have already read, and may be from home or from the classroom, school, or public library (see Day 2, Step 1, on page 590).

▶ 7 **Reflect on Sharing Opinions**

Have the students briefly discuss how they did voicing their own opinions and respecting the opinions of others.

INDIVIDUALIZED DAILY READING

▶ 8 **Review the "Reading Comprehension Strategies" Chart**

Direct the students' attention to the "Reading Comprehension Strategies" chart. Ask them to notice which strategies they use during their reading today. Have them use self-stick notes to mark any place in their book where they use a strategy.

Reading Comprehension Strategies

- *recognizing text features*

Have the students read independently for up to 30 minutes.

As the students read, circulate among them. Ask individual students questions such as:

Q *What is your book about? What is an important idea or message in your reading?*

Q *What strategies have you used? How did they help you understand what you were reading?*

 At the end of independent reading, have partners each share a passage they marked and the strategy they used to make sense of it.

EXTENSION

Explore Websites with Book Reviews Written by Young People

Have the students visit websites that give book reviews by young people, for example, www.spaghettibookclub.org or www.worldreading.org. If you prefer, you can choose several book reviews from these sites yourself and make them available to the students.

by Jennifer B. (age 12)

from *Spaghetti Book Club*
(spaghettibookclub.org, school year 1999–2000)

The Legend of Sleepy Hollow
by Washington Irving

Ichabod Crane has just arrived to Sleepy Hollow and has met a lot of people. Those people have told Ichabod the legend of Sleepy Hollow.

This legend is about a headless horseman who goes around cutting other people's heads in search of his own. This legend scared Ichabod every time it was told. Ichabod Crane had fallen in love with Katrina, a very rich girl, a couple of weeks after he arrived to Sleepy Hollow. One day Ichabod was invited to Katrina's party, and before the party was over a woman started to say the legend of Sleepy Hollow and at the end she said the only way you can escape the headless horseman is by crossing the bridge. That night Ichabod and his horse ran as fast as they could to reach their house. Finally he was up to the bridge that meant that he was near his house. Then something got in his way, it was the headless horseman. Did Ichabod ever escape?

I think that this book was very interesting because it was a legend about a headless horseman that lost his head in a war and since then has been looking for it by cutting other people's heads off. I recommend this book to people who like scary legends that took place a long time ago.

This story reminds me of 'Bloody Mary' because they are both scary and they are both legends. What makes this story more scary is that it has been told for more than 100 years and it has been told by people who are already dead.

The Ballad of Lucy Whipple
by Karen Cushman

In this story a girl named Lucy moves to California with her parents but she doesn't like it there.

I liked this book because Lucy says funny things. She reminds me of my friend May, except May doesn't want to change her name.

I learned a lot about California from a long time ago. I recommend this book to people who want to know more about Lucy Whipple's trip to California.

Day 2

Materials

- Book to model gathering information for a book review (see Step 2)

- Transparency of "Things to Include in My Book Review" (BLM45)

- Students' books to recommend for summer reading (see the "Teacher Note" on page 586)

- Small self-stick notes for each student

- *Student Response Book* page 89

Guided Strategy Practice

In this lesson, the students:

- Gather information for their book reviews
- Read independently for up to 30 minutes
- Give reasons for their opinions

 Prepare to Write Reviews

Remind the students that they heard and read examples of effective and less effective book reviews yesterday. Also remind them that they each selected a favorite book to recommend to their classmates for their summer reading.

Explain that this week they will each write a review of their selected book to share with their classmates next week. In addition, they will each select a passage from their book to read aloud when they present their review to the class.

Remind the students that book reviews consist of both summary and opinion, and ask:

Q *What information might be important to include in the summary of your book? Why?*

Q *What might be important to include when you give your opinion about the book?*

Explain that each student will gather information for his book review today and write the book review tomorrow.

 Model Gathering Information for a Review

Ask the students to watch as you model gathering information for your book review. Show the cover of your book and read the title and names of the author and illustrator.

Show the transparency of "Things to Include in My Book Review" on the overhead projector, scan your book, and model writing your notes on the transparency and marking with self-stick notes places you might want to read aloud.

As you model, think aloud about the notes you take and the places you mark, for example:

* *"The book I am going to review is* Shiloh, *by Phyllis Reynolds Taylor. It's the story of an eleven-year-old boy named Marty, who finds a beagle that has been abused by its owner."* (Write notes: Marty, 11 years old, finds a beagle abused by its owner.)

* *"Marty's parents tell him he must return the dog, but he decides he will do anything to save it."* (Write notes: Marty's parents say to return the dog. Marty decides to save it.)

* *"My favorite part of the book is when Marty's parents find out that he's been hiding the dog. I want to include something about that in my book review."* (Write notes: Favorite part: Marty's parents find out he's been hiding the dog.)

* *"I might read that part aloud because it's very dramatic. You hold your breath and wonder what his parents will do."* (Mark the page with a self-stick note.)

* *"Or I might read aloud the passage where Marty first finds the dog because it shows how compassionate Marty is."* (Mark the page with a self-stick note.)

Tell the students that if they are reviewing a longer book, they may want to scan the table of contents to help them remember what's important in it. Have them turn to *Student Response Book* page 89, "Things to Include in My Book Review," and begin gathering information for their review and marking interesting passages with self-stick notes.

▶3 Gather Information About Books

As the students scan, take notes, and mark their books, circulate among them and support them by asking questions such as:

Q *What is your book about? Write some notes to help you remember what you just said.*

Teacher Note

These are some things to consider when modeling how to gather book information:

* Summarize the book in your think-aloud.
* Take brief notes to include in the written summary.
* Think aloud and take notes about your favorite parts.
* Mark possible passages to read aloud that are dramatic, suspenseful, or revealing of character. Tell the students why you are marking the passages.

Q *What might you say about your book that would intrigue your classmates? Write some notes.*

Q *What are some of your favorite parts of this book? Why do you like them? Find those parts and mark them with a self-stick note.*

Q *What parts might you want to read aloud? Why? Mark them with a self-stick note.*

Remind the students that they will use their notes to write their book review tomorrow.

INDIVIDUALIZED DAILY READING

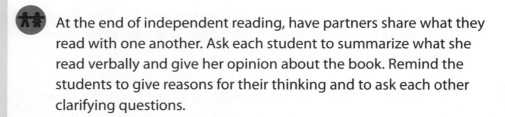

4 ▶ Document IDR Conferences/Have the Students Form Opinions About Their Reading

Have the students read independently for up to 30 minutes.

Use the "IDR Conference Notes" record sheet to conduct and document individual conferences.

At the end of independent reading, have partners share what they read with one another. Ask each student to summarize what she read verbally and give her opinion about the book. Remind the students to give reasons for their thinking and to ask each other clarifying questions.

After partners have shared, facilitate a whole-class discussion. Ask questions such as:

Q *Do you think you would like to read your partner's book? Why? Why not?*

Q *What interests you about your partner's book?*

Day 3

Guided Strategy Practice

In this lesson, the students:

- Write a book review
- Read independently for up to 30 minutes
- Give reasons for their opinions

▶ 1 Review Information to Include in Book Reviews

Review that yesterday the students scanned their chosen books, took notes, and marked passages in preparation for writing book reviews today. Have them quietly review their notes on *Student Response Book* page 89 and the marked passages in their books to see if they have enough information to write a review.

Remind the students that reviews include both summary and opinion; the opinions in their review will be about why they are recommending the book to the class.

Explain that students who feel they need to collect more information for their review will have time for this before they start to write.

▶ 2 Model Writing a Review from Notes

Show your completed transparency of "Things to Include in My Book Review" and ask the students to watch as you model using your notes and marked text to write a review.

Write your review on a sheet of chart paper. Refer to your notes and think aloud about how you will use the notes to write the review. (For example, you might say, "I know that my review needs to start with a general statement about what the book is about. My notes from yesterday say, 'Marty, 11 years old, finds a beagle abused by its owner.' I think I'll write, 'This story is about an eleven-year-old boy named Marty, who finds a beagle that he believes is being abused by its owner.'")

Materials

- Book used to model gathering information for a book review (from Day 2)
- Students' books to recommend for summer reading
- *Student Response Book* page 89
- Transparency of "Things to Include in My Book Review" (BLM45)
- Chart paper and a marker
- Paper and a pencil for each student

Teacher Note

This lesson may take longer than one class period.

Teacher Note ▶

These are some things to consider as you model writing your review:

- Begin with a general statement that says what the book is about.
- Summarize, using interesting details from the book.
- Say why you recommend the book.
- Emphasize writing in a way that intrigues the reader (e.g., writing about exciting parts, not giving too much information).

Continue to think aloud and write until you have completed the review. Here is an example of a review for *Shiloh*:

---

*Review of Shiloh by Phyllis Reynolds Naylor
Reviewed by Ms. Tanaka*

This story is about an eleven-year-old boy named Marty, who finds a beagle that he believes is being abused by its owner. The dog follows him home, and Marty names him Shiloh. Marty's parents tell him he must return the dog to its owner, but Marty will do anything to save Shiloh. He decides to hide it. He secretly feeds and takes care of the dog, until one day his parents find out! You won't believe what happens next.

I recommend this story because Marty is such a great character. He will do anything to protect Shiloh, even if it means getting into trouble himself. You won't want to stop reading until the very end, when you find out whether Marty is able to save Shiloh or not.

---

3 ▶ Write Reviews

Have the students write their reviews, following your example. Remind them that they are writing the review to recommend the book to their classmates. Write the following reminders on the board:

- Start by saying what the book is about.

- Add interesting details.

- Say why you recommend the book.

As the students write, circulate and support them by asking questions such as:

Q *What is your book about? Write that down as your opening sentence.*

Q *What notes did you take about your book? How might you use those notes to write a sentence?*

Q *What parts did you mark in your book? What might you want to say about those parts in your review?*

Q *Why are you recommending this book? What examples of that are there in the book? Write that down.*

It may take more than one class period for the students to finish writing their reviews. You might ask students who finish early to illustrate a favorite scene from their book to share with the class later.

Save the book review you wrote today for Day 4.

INDIVIDUALIZED DAILY READING

4 ▶ Document IDR Conferences/Have the Students Form Opinions About Their Reading

Have the students read independently for up to 30 minutes.

Use the "IDR Conference Notes" record sheet to conduct and document individual conferences.

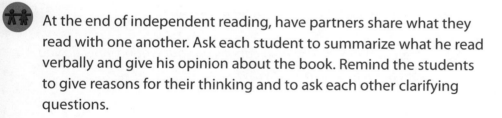 At the end of independent reading, have partners share what they read with one another. Ask each student to summarize what he read verbally and give his opinion about the book. Remind the students to give reasons for their thinking and to ask each other clarifying questions.

After partners have shared, facilitate a whole-class discussion. Ask questions such as:

Q *Do you think you would like to read your partner's book? Why or why not?*

Q *What interests you about your partner's book?*

Day 4

Materials

- Chart for giving feedback, prepared ahead
- Book used to model writing a book review (from Days 2 and 3)
- Book review you modeled writing (from Day 3)
- Students' books to recommend for summer reading
- *Assessment Resource Book*
- *Student Response Book,* IDR Journal section
- Unit 9 Parent Letter (BLM18)

Guided Strategy Practice

In this lesson, the students:

- *Make judgments* about book reviews
- Select a passage from their book and practice reading it aloud
- Read independently for up to 30 minutes
- Give and receive feedback

1 ▶ Prepare to Give Feedback About Reviews

Have partners sit together. Explain that today partners will read their book reviews and give each other feedback about them. The feedback will be about whether the review communicates what the book is about and why it is being recommended. Then they will add to or revise their review based on the feedback.

Explain that the purpose of giving feedback is to help them make their reviews as clear and complete as possible. Ask:

Q *When someone gives you feedback on your writing, how do you want them to talk to you? Why?*

> **Students might say:**
>
> "I like people to tell me what they think is good first, then what I need to change. It helps me feel like the whole thing isn't all that bad."
>
> "I like it better when someone says, 'Another way you could say this is…' rather than 'What you wrote doesn't make any sense.'"

 Have partners briefly tell each other how they would like to receive feedback. Encourage them to keep these things in mind as they work together.

2 Give Feedback About Reviews

Explain that each student will read her review to her partner. Then the listening partner will answer the following three questions for the reviewing partner. The reviewing partner will then add to or revise the review, based on the feedback.

Display the questions you have written where everyone can see them and have the partners begin:

- Does this review tell you what this book is about?

- Does this review give reasons for the recommendation?

- Is there enough information to help you decide whether you want to read the book or not? If not, what more is needed?

> **CLASS COMPREHENSION ASSESSMENT**
>
> Circulate as partners read their reviews and give each other feedback, and ask yourself:
>
> **Q** *Are the students able to communicate what their books are about?*
>
> **Q** *Do they support their recommendation by giving examples from the text?*
>
> **Q** *Are they able to give and receive feedback in a helpful way?*
>
> Record your observations on page 32 of the *Assessment Resource Book*.

When partners are finished giving each other feedback and revising their reviews, bring their attention back to the whole class and ask:

Q *What feedback did your partner give you that was helpful? How was it helpful?*

Q *Was your partner able to give you feedback in the way that you requested at the beginning of the lesson? Give us an example.*

Collect the students' book reviews and save them for Unit 10.

◀

Teacher Note

You might want to have the students edit their reviews and create final drafts. If so, give them time to do this before beginning Unit 10.

3▶ Model Reading a Passage Aloud

Teacher Note ▶

Choose a passage to read aloud
that you feel will be intriguing
to the students. This may be
a passage that is suspenseful,
descriptive, or dramatic. The
passage should take several
minutes to read aloud.

Briefly revisit the book review you wrote yesterday; then ask the
students to listen as you read a passage aloud from the book you
reviewed. (For example, if you use *Shiloh,* you might want to read
the passage in which Marty first spots the dog, on pages 13–16.)

After reading the passage, ask:

Q *How does hearing a passage help you get a sense of what this
book is about?*

Q *Now that you've read a review of this book and heard a passage
read aloud, would you want to read this book over the summer?*

Write the title and author of your book on the board so interested
students can copy the information onto their summer reading list.

Tell the students that they will now spend some time selecting their
passage and practicing reading it aloud. Remind them that they
marked some interesting places in their book on Day 2 and that they
might want to read a passage from one of these places aloud. Ask:

Q *What kind of passage might be good to read aloud with your
review? Why?*

> **Students might say:**
>
> "You might want to pick a passage with something exciting
>   happening in it. It would really make people want to read
>   the book."
>
> "I agree with [Amanda], but I don't want to read too much so it
>   gives everything away."
>
> "Maybe a part that lets us know the main character a little would
>   be good."

If the students have difficulty answering this question, suggest
some ideas such as those in the "Students might say" note.

Choose Passages and Practice Reading Aloud

Have each student choose a passage from his own book, and then practice reading it aloud quietly. Tell the students that the purpose for practicing is to make sure that they can read smoothly in front of the class. Encourage them to practice reading their passage slowly and clearly.

Remind the students that they will share their book reviews and passages with their classmates next week, and they will also hear many book recommendations for their summer reading list.

INDIVIDUALIZED DAILY READING

 Write an Opinion About Their Reading in Their IDR Journals/Document IDR Conferences

Ask the students to be aware of opinions they are forming as they read and what evidence they are using to form the opinions. Explain that at the end of independent reading, they will write about their opinions in their IDR Journals.

Have the students read independently for up to 30 minutes.

Use the "IDR Conference Notes" record sheet to conduct and document individual conferences.

At the end of independent reading, have the students write an opinion about their reading in their IDR Journals. Then, have several volunteers share their writing with the class. Facilitate the discussion by asking questions such as:

Q *After hearing [Franco's] opinion about the book, are you interested in reading it? Why or why not?*

Q *What questions do you have for [Marianna] about [her] book?*

Q *Have you read [Clayton's] book? If so, do you agree or disagree with [Clayton's] review? Explain.*

Teacher Note

This is the last week of Unit 9. You will assign new partners for Unit 10.

INDIVIDUAL COMPREHENSION ASSESSMENT

Before continuing with Unit 10, take this opportunity to assess individual students' progress in synthesizing by making judgments and forming opinions to understand text. Please refer to pages 48–49 in the *Assessment Resource Book* for instructions.

EXTENSION

Create a Class Book of Reviews

If the students have revised their reviews and created final drafts, you might want to collect them in a class book. Do this after they have shared their reviews with the class during Unit 10. Then gather the reviews in a class book entitled "Class Recommendations for Summer Reading," and copy the book for individual students to take with them at the end of the school year.

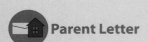

Parent Letter

Send home with each student the Parent Letter for this unit (see "Do Ahead," page 581). Periodically, have a few students share with the class what they are reading at home.

Unit 10

Revisiting the Reading Life

During this unit, the students synthesize by making judgments and forming opinions about text, using evidence from the text to support their conclusions. They continue to develop the group skills of giving reasons for their opinions and discussing their opinions respectfully. During IDR, the students continue to practice self-monitoring and reflect on the reading strategies they use that help them understand what they are reading. They have a class meeting to discuss their growth as readers and as members of a classroom community.

Week 1   Student-selected book

Week 1

Overview

UNIT 10: REVISITING THE READING LIFE

Comprehension Focus

- Students *use important ideas* to *build summaries*.

- Students *synthesize* by *making judgments* and *forming opinions* about text, using evidence from the text to support their conclusions.

- Students reflect on their growth as readers over the year.

- Students read independently.

Social Development Focus

- Students analyze the effect of their behavior on others and on the group work.

- Students develop the group skills of giving reasons for their opinions and discussing their opinions respectfully.

- Students reflect on their growth as members of a classroom community.

- Students have a class meeting to discuss how they have grown as readers and as members of a classroom community.

DO AHEAD

- Prior to Day 1, decide how you will randomly assign partners to work together during the unit.

- Prior to Day 1, collect five read-aloud books that your students might enjoy hearing (see Day 1, Step 2, and the "Teacher Note" on pages 604–605).

- Make copies of the Unit 10 Parent Letter (BLM19) to send home with the students on the last day of the unit.

Day 1

Materials

- Five read-aloud books, selected ahead
- Scratch paper and pencil for each student
- *Student Response Book* page 87
- "Reading Comprehension Strategies" chart
- "Self-monitoring Questions" chart

Being a Writer™ **Teacher**

You can either have the students work with their *Being a Writer* partner or assign them a different partner for the *Making Meaning* lessons.

Teacher Note

The five read-aloud books you collect could include *Making Meaning* books that the students liked when you read them earlier this year, other popular books you have read aloud, books on the *Making Meaning* alternative book lists, or books the students have not heard before.

Read-aloud

In this lesson, the students:

- Begin working with new partners
- Make choices about books they want to hear read aloud
- Reflect on the comprehension strategies they are using
- Read independently for up to 30 minutes

▶1 Pair Students and Get Ready to Work Together

Randomly assign partners and have them sit together. Tell them that during this last week of the *Making Meaning* program they will review the comprehension strategies they have learned, think about how they have grown as readers and as a community, share their favorite books, and plan their summer reading.

Tell the students that at the end of the week they will also be asked to discuss some things they really enjoyed about working with a partner this year. Encourage them to focus during the coming week on enjoying their partner work and using the skills they have learned to help them in their work together.

▶2 Choose from Five Read-aloud Books

Write the titles of the five read-aloud books you selected on the board. Show the students the books, and explain that this week the class will choose one of these books to hear read aloud. Tell them that you selected books you thought they would enjoy hearing (or hearing again). Give a brief synopsis of each book that is new to the students, and if necessary, briefly review the books from earlier in the year.

Explain that you would like the students to choose the three books they are most interested in hearing and to write these three titles on a sheet of scratch paper. The title with the most votes is the one you will read aloud today. Before voting, ask:

Q *What factors might you consider when deciding which three books to choose?*

Q *Why is it important to make your choices based on what you are really interested in hearing, rather than on what other people are choosing?*

Have the students write their three book choices, and gather the votes. Have the students turn to their "Summer Reading List" on *Student Response Book* page 87, and add the titles of any of these five books that they might want to read or reread this summer. While they are doing this, tally the votes.

3 Review the "Reading Comprehension Strategies" Chart

Tell the class which book was chosen for today's read-aloud. Refer to the "Reading Comprehension Strategies" chart and review that the students learned and practiced each of these strategies this year. Review that the goal of learning comprehension strategies is to help them actively think about what they are reading in order to make sense of it. Ask:

Q *Which strategies do you find yourself using regularly? How do those strategies help you make sense of what you're reading?*

Q *When might it make sense to use [making inferences]? How might this strategy help you read?*

Remind the students to think about the comprehension strategies they are using as they listen to today's read-aloud, and explain that you will ask them to discuss their thinking after the reading.

Teacher Note

If the students finish writing before you are done tallying the votes, ask them to scan through their *Student Response Books* and talk in pairs about the work they did this year.

If partners need help focusing on their *Student Response Book* work, pose a question for them to think about, such as:

Q *What is one piece of work in your* Student Response Book *that represents some of your best thinking?*

Q *What is one piece of work that was most interesting or enjoyable for you?*

Reading Comprehension Strategies

- recognizing text features

Introduce the Book and Read Aloud

Introduce the book by reading the information on the cover and providing any necessary background information.

Read the book aloud, showing the illustrations. You might stop periodically to have partners discuss what they have heard so far.

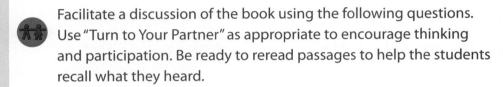 **Discuss the Reading as a Class**

Facilitate a discussion of the book using the following questions. Use "Turn to Your Partner" as appropriate to encourage thinking and participation. Be ready to reread passages to help the students recall what they heard.

Q *What is this story about?*

Q *What do you want to add to the summary [Lawrence] just gave?*

Q *What comprehension strategy or strategies did you use as you listened to this story? How did that help you?*

6 ▶ **Reflect on Working Together**

Facilitate a brief discussion about how the students interacted.

INDIVIDUALIZED DAILY READING

7 ▶ **Review and Discuss Self-monitoring**

Direct the students' attention to the "Self-monitoring Questions" chart and remind the students that a comprehension technique they learned this year is to stop and think about what they are reading and ask themselves questions to help them track their understanding. Tell them that they will practice this self-monitoring technique today during independent reading.

Teacher Note

On Day 2, the students will begin sharing the book recommendations they wrote in Unit 9. They will continue to share in subsequent lessons. Before teaching Day 2, make sure each student has had time to finish writing his recommendation and has identified a book passage to read aloud.

Self-monitoring Questions

- *What is happening in my story right now?*

- *Does the reading make sense?*

Have the students read independently for up to 30 minutes. Stop them at 10-minute intervals and have them monitor their comprehension by thinking about the charted questions.

At the end of independent reading, facilitate a whole-class discussion about how self-monitoring helps the students track their understanding.

Discuss questions such as:

Q   *How does stopping to check your understanding help you?*

Q   *What are some things you do when you do not understand?*

EXTENSION

Introduce the Second-choice Book and Read Aloud

Tell the students that you will read them their second-choice book. Refer to the "Reading Comprehension Strategies" chart and remind the students to think about the comprehension strategies they are using as they listen.

Introduce the book by reading the information on the cover and providing any necessary background information. Read the book aloud, showing the illustrations. You might stop periodically to have partners discuss what they have heard so far.

Discuss the reading as a class. Use "Turn to Your Partner" as appropriate to encourage thinking and participation. Be ready to reread passages to help the students recall what they heard. Ask questions such as:

Q   *What is the story about?*

Q   *What do you want to add to the summary [Dani] just gave?*

Q   *Is this a book you would recommend to someone? Why or why not?*

Q   *What comprehension strategies did you use as you listened to this story? How did that help you?*

Day 2

Materials

- *Student Response Book* page 87

- Students' book reviews (from Unit 9, Week 4)

Guided Strategy Practice

In this lesson, the students:

- Recommend books for summer reading
- Make choices about books they want to read
- Read independently for up to 30 minutes
- Discuss opinions respectfully

▶ 1 Prepare to Share Book Recommendations

Remind the students that last week they wrote reviews for books they want to recommend to their classmates for summer reading. They also each chose a passage from the book to read aloud to the class.

Explain that today the students will begin sharing their book recommendations. They will take turns reading their reviews and passages aloud and answering questions about their books. As they hear recommendations for books they might want to read this summer, they will add these titles to the "Summer Reading List" on *Student Response Book* page 87. Ask:

Q *If you hear about a book you are interested in reading, how might you find that book this summer?*

Teacher Note

You might consider taking your students on a short field trip to a local library.

Students might say:

"I might find the book at the public library."

"If a friend has the book, I could borrow it."

"I might look for it at the bookstore or on the Internet."

If the students have difficulty answering this question, suggest some ideas like those in the "Students might say" note.

Facilitate a brief discussion about how the students will interact in a kind and respectful way during the sharing. Ask:

Q *How do you want your classmates to respond to your book recommendation, whether they would choose to read your book or not? Why?*

Q *How can you let your classmates know that you are interested in the book they are sharing and that you appreciate the work they've done to share it with you?*

 Share Book Recommendations

Call on a volunteer to share her book recommendation with the class. Remind the student to show the cover of the book and read the title and the names of the author and illustrator before reading the review and the selected passage to the class.

When the student has finished, facilitate a brief class discussion using questions such as:

Q *What questions do you want to ask [Joan] about the book [she] shared?*

Q *What did you hear in the book review or passage that intrigued you?*

Q *[Joan], what were you thinking when you chose that passage?*

Q *Do you have enough information to decide whether you want to add this book to your summer reading list? If not, what else do you want to know?*

Have the student who shared write the book's title and author on the board for interested students to copy onto their summer reading list. Have several more students share their book reviews, using the same procedure. Allow time for questions and discussion after each student shares and for interested students to copy the title and author information onto their reading list.

3 ▶ Discuss Working Together

Ask the students who recommended books today to talk briefly about how they felt their classmates treated them while they were sharing. Ask:

Q *What made you feel like your classmates were interested in what you were sharing?*

Q *If you weren't sure that your classmates were interested, what made you unsure?*

Open the discussion to the whole class, and ask:

Q *What should we do [the same way/differently] as a class when we continue to share our book recommendations?*

Remind the students of your expectation that they will do their part to help create a safe, caring community in the classroom. Tell them that more students will recommend books tomorrow.

INDIVIDUALIZED DAILY READING

4 ▶ Read Independently and Discuss Reading Comprehension Strategies

Have the students read independently for up to 30 minutes.

As the students read, circulate among them. Ask individual students questions such as:

Q *What is this passage about?*

Q *What comprehension strategies are you using to help you understand what you are reading? Tell me what you thought about when you used that strategy.*

You might need to stimulate the students' thinking with questions such as:

Q   *What are some questions that come to your mind about what you are reading?*

Q   *How did reading the [information in this chart] help you understand and make sense of the text? What other text features helped you make sense of your reading? How did that help you?*

Q   *What do you think is an important idea in this story?*

At the end of independent reading, have each student verbally summarize what he read for his partner and explain how he used a reading comprehension strategy. As the students share, circulate and listen, observing students' behaviors and responses.

Day 3

Materials

- Students' book reviews (from Unit 9, Week 4)
- *Student Response Book* pages 2 and 90

Guided Strategy Practice and Reflection

In this lesson, the students:

- Recommend books for summer reading
- Make choices about books they want to read
- Read independently for up to 30 minutes
- Discuss opinions respectfully

▶1 Discuss Sharing Ideas Respectfully

Remind the students that yesterday they began to recommend books for summer reading. They will hear several more book recommendations today and consider these books for their summer reading. Explain that they will also spend some time reflecting on their own reading lives.

Remind the students of yesterday's discussion about how they were interacting. Ask:

Q *What did we say we want to do the same way or differently as a class today as we listen to book recommendations? How will that help the people who are sharing?*

Encourage them to keep the things they talked about in mind as they participate today.

▶2 Continue to Share Book Recommendations

Use the same procedure you used yesterday to have several more students share their book reviews and passages. Remind them to begin by showing the cover of their book and reading the title and the names of the author and illustrator aloud.

Facilitate brief class discussions after each student shares, using questions such as:

Q   *What questions do you want to ask [Kenji] about the book [he] shared?*

Q   *What did you hear in the book review or passage that intrigued you?*

Q   *[Kenji], what were you thinking when you chose that passage?*

Q   *Do you have enough information to decide whether you want to add this book to your summer reading list? If not, what else do you want to know?*

Remind the students who shared books to write the title and author of their book on the board for interested students to copy onto their summer reading list.

After the remaining students have shared their book recommendations, ask:

Q   *How did we do at being a caring community during today's sharing? What do we want to do the same way or differently tomorrow?*

Teacher Note

If all the students are not able to share their book recommendations, make time later in the day or on another day for them to share before proceeding with the Day 4 lesson.

▶3 Write About Our Reading Lives

Explain that the students will now have a chance to think about how they have grown and changed as readers over the year. Remind them that they started the year thinking about their reading lives, and tell them that they will think about this again now that they are nearing the end of the year.

Ask the students to close their eyes and think quietly as you pose the following questions. Give the students time to think between the questions:

Q   *What are some of your favorite books now? Why?*

Q   *Where is your favorite place to read?*

Q   *What does the word* reading *mean to you?*

Q   *When you don't understand something you are reading, what do you do?*

Q   *What kinds of books did you read for the first time this year? What topics did you read about for the first time?*

After the students have had a chance to think, ask them to turn to *Student Response Book* page 90, "Thoughts About My Reading Life." Have them record their answers to these questions.

 Reflect on Growth as Readers

Have the students review page 90, "Thoughts About My Reading Life," and give them a few minutes to reflect on what they wrote.

Then have them turn to "Thoughts About My Reading Life" from the beginning of the year, on *Student Response Book* page 2. Ask them to reread what they wrote at the beginning of the year, and then spend a few quiet moments thinking about how they have changed and grown as readers this year.

 After a few moments, have the students use "Turn to Your Partner" to share how they have changed as readers.

Tell them that they will share some of their thoughts during a class meeting tomorrow.

INDIVIDUALIZED DAILY READING

 Revisit the Students' Reading Lives/Read Independently

Have the students read independently for up to 30 minutes.

As the students read, circulate among them and talk to individual students about their reading lives. To guide your discussion, refer to their written comments on *Student Response Book* page 90, "Thoughts About My Reading Life," or ask questions such as:

Q   *What kinds of books do you like to read? What other kinds of books do you think you might want to read?*

Q   *How do you think you have grown or changed as a reader this year?*

Q   *What do you still want to work on to become an even stronger reader?*

 At the end of independent reading, give partners time to verbally summarize for one another what they read. Remind the students to ask one another clarifying questions when necessary.

EXTENSIONS

Create a Class Collection of Book Recommendations

If you have had the students revise and edit their reviews to create final drafts, you might want to collect these in a class book entitled *Class Recommendations for Summer Reading*. Put the book together after all the students have shared their recommendations, and make a copy of the book for each student.

Review the Summer Reading Lists

Have the students review the books on their summer reading lists. Ask:

Q   *What kinds of books did you choose for summer reading? Does that surprise you? Why or why not?*

You might ask the students to put a star next to the books they want to read first. Encourage them to read as many of the books on their list as they can this summer. Also encourage them to talk with family members and friends about the books they are reading and to add any interesting books to their reading list.

Day 4

Materials

- *Student Response Book* page 91
- Space for the class to sit in a circle
- "Class Meeting Ground Rules" chart
- Self-stick notes for each student
- *Student Response Book,* IDR Journal section
- *Assessment Resource Book*
- Unit 10 Parent Letter (BLM19)

Reflection and Class Meeting

In this lesson, the students:

- Think and write about how they have grown as members of a community
- Have a class meeting to discuss how they have grown as readers and as members of a community
- Read independently for up to 30 minutes

1 Reflect on Our Classroom Community

Ask partners to sit together. Remind the students that yesterday they reflected on and wrote about their growth as readers. Explain that the students will now have a chance to think about how they did creating a safe and caring community this year and how they personally have changed as members of the community. Tell the students that they will have a chance to share their thoughts about how they have grown as readers and as members of a classroom community during a class meeting later.

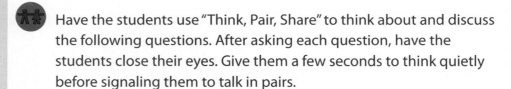 Have the students use "Think, Pair, Share" to think about and discuss the following questions. After asking each question, have the students close their eyes. Give them a few seconds to think quietly before signaling them to talk in pairs.

Q *Think about how you worked with your first partner this year. Think about how you are working with your partner now. How have you grown in your ability to work with a partner?*

Q *How have we done becoming a caring and safe community this year? What makes you think so?*

Q *How has being part of this community helped you this year?*

After the students have discussed the questions, ask them to turn to *Student Response Book* page 91, "Thoughts About Our Classroom Community." Have them record their answers for these questions.

▶ 2 Gather for a Class Meeting

Review the procedure for coming to a class meeting, and have the students move to the circle with their *Student Response Books* and with partners sitting together. Explain that during the first part of the class meeting they will discuss how they have grown as readers and during the second part of the class meeting they will talk about their classroom community and what they enjoyed about working with a partner.

Make sure the students can see each member of the class, and briefly review the "Class Meeting Ground Rules" chart.

▶ 3 Discuss Growth as Readers

Remind the students that one of the ways they built their reading community this year was to share their reading lives with one another. Tell the students that the purpose of the first part of this class meeting is to talk about how they have changed and grown as readers. Facilitate a discussion using questions such as:

Q *How do you think you have changed or grown as a reader? What makes you think that?*

Q *Do others think they have changed or grown in a similar way? Why do you think so?*

Q *In what ways are you the same kind of reader as you were before?*

Q *What questions do you want to ask [Tyra] about what [she] said?*

Use "Turn to Your Partner" as needed during this discussion to increase accountability and participation.

◀ **Teacher Note**

You may want to hold the class meeting later in the day or on the following day.

Class Meeting Ground Rules

- *one person talks at a time*
- *listen to one another*

Students might say:

"My favorite books used to be the books about Ramona. I still like those books, but my new favorite books are mysteries."

"At the beginning of the year, I wrote 'I don't know' for the question 'When you don't understand something you are reading, what do you do?' At the end of the year, I wrote, 'I ask myself questions, and then I read it again.'"

"In September, I wrote that I wanted to read about space this year, and I did. I read a bunch of books about the solar system."

"I used to think reading meant reading words. Now I think reading means thinking about a story."

You might want to share some of your general observations about ways your students have changed or grown as readers over the year. (For example, you might say, "I noticed that all of you have improved in your ability to choose books that are at the right reading level for you and that you are choosing books now that are at a higher reading level than the ones you chose at the beginning of the year.")

4 ▶ Discuss Our Community and Partner Work

Explain to the students that the second purpose of this class meeting is to talk about the classroom community and to share some of their favorite things about working with a partner this year. Facilitate a discussion using questions such as:

Q *How did we do at creating the kind of classroom we wanted this year? What makes you think so?*

Q *How has being part of this community helped you this year?*

Q *What are three things that you liked most about working with partners this year?*

Students might say:

"At first it was hard, but we got better and better at it."

"I think the more we got to know each other, the more we were a community."

"I agree with [Franklin]. Being in this community has helped me because I used to be too shy to say anything to the class. I don't feel that way anymore."

"In addition to what [Teresa] said, I liked working with a partner. I liked having someone to talk to, not having to be quiet all the time, and getting to work with different partners."

You might want to share some of your general observations about ways your students have changed or grown as members of the community over the year. (For example, you might say, "I remember how some students didn't want to work with an assigned partner at the beginning of the year. Now you are much better at working with any partner. I also noticed that you relied much more heavily on me at the beginning of the year to help you solve your problems. Now you are able to solve many problems by yourselves.") Ask:

Q *What is one thing you learned about working well with a partner that you want to take with you next year?*

▶5 Reflect and Adjourn the Class Meeting

Facilitate a brief discussion about how the students did following the ground rules during the class meeting, and adjourn the meeting.

INDIVIDUALIZED DAILY READING

▶6 Write About Reading Comprehension Strategies in Their IDR Journals

Have the students read independently for up to 30 minutes.

Have the students use self-stick notes to mark places where they notice they are using a reading comprehension strategy.

As the students read, circulate among them. Ask individual students questions such as:

Q *What is your reading about?*

Q *I notice that you placed a self-stick note in this part of your book. What comprehension strategy helped you understand this part?*

FACILITATION TIP

Reflect on your experience over the past year using the facilitation tips included in the *Making Meaning* program. Did using the facilitation techniques feel natural to you? Have you integrated them into your class discussions throughout the school day? What effect did using the facilitation techniques have on your students? We encourage you to continue to use the facilitation techniques and reflect on students' responses as you facilitate class discussions in the future.

At the end of independent reading, have each student summarize her reading and write about a comprehension strategy she used—the name of the strategy and where she used it—in her IDR Journal.

SOCIAL SKILLS ASSESSMENT

Take this opportunity to reflect on your students' social development over the year. Review the "Social Skills Assessment" record sheet on pages 2–3 of the *Assessment Resource Book* and note student growth. Use this information to help you plan for next year. Ask yourself questions such as:

Q *What was challenging for my students this year in terms of their social development?*

Q *How might I help next year's students grow socially?*

Q *What skills should I emphasize with the students next year to help them build a safe and caring reading community?*

EXTENSION

End-of-year "Summer Reading Fair"

Have the students invite fourth- or fifth-grade classes to a "Summer Reading Fair." Have the students present their book reviews to small groups of students. The invited students will have an opportunity to listen to reviews, preview the books, and get a glimpse of the reading life of the students. Students might also make posters to advertise their favorite books. If there is a school library or librarian available, you might want to involve the library in the activity.

Parent Letter

Send home with each student the Parent Letter for this unit (see "Do Ahead," page 603).

Appendices

Scan

Grade 5

	Lesson	Title	Author	Form	Genre/Type
Unit 1	▶ Week 1	*The Lotus Seed*	Sherry Garland	picture book	realistic fiction
		Something to Remember Me By	Susan V. Bosak	picture book	realistic fiction
	▶ Week 2	*Everybody Cooks Rice*	Norah Dooley	picture book	realistic fiction
Unit 2	▶ Week 1	*Life in the Rain Forests*	Lucy Baker	chapter book	expository nonfiction
	▶ Week 2	"Follow That Ball!"		article	expository nonfiction
		"All Work and No Play"		article	expository nonfiction
	▶ Week 3	*Chinese Americans*	Tristan Boyer Binns	chapter book	expository nonfiction
Unit 3	▶ Week 1	*Big Cats*	Seymour Simon	picture book	expository nonfiction
	▶ Week 2	*Big Cats*	Seymour Simon	picture book	expository nonfiction
Unit 4	▶ Week 1	*The Summer My Father Was Ten*	Pat Brisson	picture book	realistic fiction
		Uncle Jed's Barbershop	Margaree King Mitchell	picture book	historical fiction
	▶ Week 2	*Star of Fear, Star of Hope*	Jo Hoestlandt	picture book	historical fiction
Unit 5	▶ Week 1	*The Van Gogh Cafe*: "The Cafe" and "The Possum"	Cynthia Rylant	short stories	fiction
	▶ Week 2	"Circles"	Myra Cohn Livingston	poem	poetry
		"Speech Class"	Jim Daniels	poem	poetry
		"October Saturday"	Bobbi Katz	poem	poetry
	▶ Week 3	"Eraser and School Clock"	Gary Soto	poem	poetry
		"back yard"	Valerie Worth	poem	poetry
Unit 6	▶ Week 1	*Richard Wright and the Library Card*	William Miller	picture book	historical fiction
	▶ Week 2	*Wildfires*	Seymour Simon	picture book	expository nonfiction
	▶ Week 3	*Earthquakes*	Seymour Simon	picture book	expository nonfiction
		Life in the Rain Forests	Lucy Baker	chapter book	expository nonfiction
Unit 7	▶ Week 1	"Copycats: Why Clone?"		article	expository nonfiction
		"The Debate on Banning Junk Food Ads"		article	expository nonfiction
	▶ Week 2	"All-girls' and All-boys' Schools: Better for Kids"		article	expository nonfiction
		"Do Kids Really Need Cell Phones?"		article	expository nonfiction
	▶ Week 3	"How to Make an Origami Cup"		functional text	expository nonfiction
		"Ashton Hammerheads Schedule for July, 2008"		functional text	expository nonfiction
		"Frontier Fun Park" Ticket Prices		functional text	expository nonfiction
	▶ Week 4	*Survival and Loss: Native American Boarding Schools*		textbook	expository nonfiction
	▶ Week 5	*Survival and Loss: Native American Boarding Schools*		textbook	expository nonfiction
Unit 8	▶ Week 1	*Letting Swift River Go*	Jane Yolen	picture book	historical fiction
	▶ Week 2	*A River Ran Wild*	Lynne Cherry	picture book	narrative nonfiction
	▶ Week 3	*Harry Houdini: Master of Magic*	Robert Kraske	chapter book	narrative nonfiction
	▶ Week 4	*Hey World, Here I Am!* "Mrs. Buell"	Jean Little	chapter book	realistic fiction
	▶ Week 5	Student-selected text			
Unit 9	▶ Week 1	"Zoo"	Edward D. Hoch	short story	science fiction
		Hey World, Here I Am! "Mrs. Buell"	Jean Little	chapter book	realistic fiction
	▶ Week 2	*True Stories of Heroes*: "12 seconds from death"	Paul Dowswell	chapter book	expository nonfiction
	▶ Week 3	"Is Dodge Ball Too Dangerous?"	Dina Maasarani	article	expository nonfiction
		"Turn It Off!"	Kathryn R. Hoffman	article	expository nonfiction
	▶ Week 4	Review of *The Legend of Sleepy Hollow*	Jennifer B. (age 12)	book review	critical essay
Unit 10	▶ Week 1	Student-selected book			

Grade K

Brave Bear	Kathy Mallat
Building Beavers	Kathleen Martin-James
Cat's Colors	Jane Cabrera
"Charlie Needs a Cloak"	Tomie dePaola
Cookie's Week	Cindy Ward
A Day with a Doctor	Jan Kottke
A Day with a Mail Carrier	Jan Kottke
Flower Garden	Eve Bunting
Friends at School	Rochelle Bunnett
Getting Around By Plane	Cassie Mayer
Henry's Wrong Turn	Harriet M. Ziefert
I Want to Be a Vet	Dan Liebman
I Was So Mad	Mercer Mayer
If You Give a Mouse a Cookie	Laura Joffe Numeroff
Knowing about Noses	Allan Fowler
A Letter to Amy	Ezra Jack Keats
Maisy's Pool	Lucy Cousins
Moon	Melanie Mitchell
My Friends	Taro Gomi
Noisy Nora	Rosemary Wells
On the Go	Ann Morris
A Porcupine Named Fluffy	Helen Lester
Pumpkin Pumpkin	Jeanne Titherington
A Tiger Cub Grows Up	Joan Hewett
Tools	Ann Morris
When Sophie Gets Angry— Really, Really Angry…	Molly Bang
Whistle for Willie	Ezra Jack Keats

Grade 1

Caps for Sale	Esphyr Slobodkina
Chrysanthemum	Kevin Henkes
Curious George Goes to an Ice Cream Shop	Margret Rey and Alan J. Shalleck (editors)
A Day in the Life of a Garbage Collector	Nate LeBoutillier
Did You See What I Saw? Poems about School	Kay Winters
Dinosaur Babies	Lucille Recht Penner
Down the Road	Alice Schertle
An Elephant Grows Up	Anastasia Suen
An Extraordinary Egg	Leo Lionni
George Washington and the General's Dog	Frank Murphy
A Good Night's Sleep	Allan Fowler
A Harbor Seal Pup Grows Up	Joan Hewett
Hearing	Sharon Gordon
In the Tall, Tall Grass	Denise Fleming
It's Mine!	Leo Lionni
Julius	Angela Johnson
A Kangaroo Joey Grows Up	Joan Hewett
A Look at Teeth	Allan Fowler
Matthew and Tilly	Rebecca C. Jones
McDuff and the Baby	Rosemary Wells
Peter's Chair	Ezra Jack Keats
Quick as a Cricket	Audrey Wood
Raptors!	Lisa McCourt
Sheep Out to Eat	Nancy Shaw
The Snowy Day	Ezra Jack Keats
Throw Your Tooth on the Roof	Selby B. Beeler
When I Was Little	Jamie Lee Curtis
Where Do I Live?	Neil Chesanow

Read-aloud Books

Grade 2

Alexander and the Terrible, Horrible, No Good, Very Bad Day	Judith Viorst
The Art Lesson	Tomie dePaola
Beatrix Potter	Alexandra Wallner
Bend and Stretch	Pamela Hill Nettleton
Big Al	Andrew Clements
Chester's Way	Kevin Henkes
Eat My Dust! Henry Ford's First Race	Monica Kulling
Erandi's Braids	Antonio Hernández Madrigal
Fathers, Mothers, Sisters, Brothers: A Collection of Family Poems	Mary Ann Hoberman
Fishes (A True Book)	Melissa Stewart
Galimoto	Karen Lynn Williams
The Ghost-Eye Tree	Bill Martin Jr. and John Archambault
The Incredible Painting of Felix Clousseau	Jon Agee
It Could Still Be a Worm	Allan Fowler
Jamaica Tag-Along	Juanita Havill
little blue and little yellow	Leo Lionni
McDuff Moves In	Rosemary Wells
Me First	Helen Lester
The Paper Crane	Molly Bang
The Paperboy	Dav Pilkey
Plants that Eat Animals	Allan Fowler
POP! A Book About Bubbles	Kimberly Brubaker Bradley
Poppleton	Cynthia Rylant
Poppleton and Friends	Cynthia Rylant
Sheila Rae, the Brave	Kevin Henkes
Snails	Monica Hughes
The Tale of Peter Rabbit	Beatrix Potter
A Tree Is Nice	Janice May Udry
What Mary Jo Shared	Janice May Udry

Grade 3

Alexander, Who's Not (Do you hear me? I mean it!) Going to Move	Judith Viorst
Aunt Flossie's Hats (and Crab Cakes Later)	Elizabeth Fitzgerald Howard
Boundless Grace	Mary Hoffman
Brave Harriet	Marissa Moss
Brave Irene	William Steig
Cherries and Cherry Pits	Vera B. Williams
City Green	DyAnne DiSalvo-Ryan
A Day's Work	Eve Bunting
Fables	Arnold Lobel
Flashy Fantastic Rain Forest Frogs	Dorothy Hinshaw Patent
The Girl Who Loved Wild Horses	Paul Goble
Have You Seen Bugs?	Joanne Oppenheim
Julius, the Baby of the World	Kevin Henkes
Keepers	Jeri Hanel Watts
Knots on a Counting Rope	Bill Martin Jr. and John Archambault
Lifetimes	David L. Rice
Mailing May	Michael O. Tunnell
The Man Who Walked Between the Towers	Mordicai Gerstein
Miss Nelson Is Missing!	Harry Allard and James Marshall
Morning Meals Around the World	Maryellen Gregoire
Officer Buckle and Gloria	Peggy Rathmann
The Paper Bag Princess	Robert Munsch
Reptiles	Melissa Stewart
The Spooky Tail of Prewitt Peacock	Bill Peet
What Is a Bat?	Bobbie Kalman and Heather Levigne
Wilma Unlimited	Kathleen Krull

Grade 4

Amelia's Road	Linda Jacobs Altman
Animal Senses	Pamela Hickman
A Bad Case of Stripes	David Shannon
Basket Moon	Mary Lyn Ray
The Bat Boy & His Violin	Gavin Curtis
Chicken Sunday	Patricia Polacco
Coming to America	Betsy Maestro
Digging Up Tyrannosaurus Rex	John R. Horner and Don Lessem
Farm Workers Unite: The Great Grape Boycott	
Flight	Robert Burleigh
Hurricane	David Wiesner
In My Own Backyard	Judi Kurjian
Italian Americans	Carolyn P. Yoder
My Man Blue	Nikki Grimes
The Old Woman Who Named Things	Cynthia Rylant
Peppe the Lamplighter	Elisa Bartone
A Picture Book of Amelia Earhart	David A. Adler
A Picture Book of Harriet Tubman	David A. Adler
A Picture Book of Rosa Parks	David A. Adler
The Princess and the Pizza	Mary Jane and Herm Auch
Slinky Scaly Slithery Snakes	Dorothy Hinshaw Patent
Song and Dance Man	Karen Ackerman
Teammates	Peter Golenbock
Thunder Cake	Patricia Polacco

Grade 6

America Street: A Multicultural Anthology of Stories	Anne Mazer, ed.
And Still the Turtle Watched	Sheila MacGill-Callahan
Asian Indian Americans	Carolyn P. Yoder
Baseball Saved Us	Ken Mochizuki
Chato's Kitchen	Gary Soto
Dear Benjamin Banneker	Andrea Davis Pinkney
Encounter	Jane Yolen
Every Living Thing	Cynthia Rylant
Life in the Oceans	Lucy Baker
New Kids in Town: Oral Histories of Immigrant Teens	Janet Bode
Out of This World: Science Fiction Stories	Edward Blishen, ed.
Rosie the Riveter: Women in a Time of War	
The Strangest of Strange Unsolved Mysteries, Volume 2	Phyllis Raybin Emert
Train to Somewhere	Eve Bunting
Voices from the Fields	S. Beth Atkin
Volcano: The Eruption and Healing of Mount St. Helens	Patricia Lauber
Whales	Seymour Simon
Why Mosquitoes Buzz in People's Ears	Verna Aardema

Grade 7

Ancient Ones: The World of the Old-Growth Douglas Fir	Barbara Bash
Children of the Wild West	Russell Freedman
Death of the Iron Horse	Paul Goble
The Dream Keeper and Other Poems	Langston Hughes
Finding Our Way	René Saldaña, Jr.
the flag of childhood: poems from the middle east	Naomi Shahib Nye, ed.
The Friendship	Mildred D. Taylor
It's Our World, Too!	Phillip Hoose
The Land I Lost	Huynh Quang Nhuong
Life in the Woodlands	Roseanne Hooper
New and Selected Poems	Gary Soto
Only Passing Through: The Story of Sojourner Truth	Anne Rockwell
Roberto Clemente: Pride of the Pittsburgh Pirates	Jonah Winter
Shattered: Stories of Children and War	Jennifer Armstrong, ed.
Sports Stories	Alan Durant, ed.
Step Lightly: Poems for the Journey	Nancy Willard, ed.
The Village That Vanished	Ann Grifalconi
What If…? Amazing Stories	Monica Hughes, ed.
Wolves	Seymour Simon
The Wretched Stone	Chris Van Allsburg

Grade 8

the composition	Antonio Skármeta
The Giver	Lois Lowry
Immigrant Kids	Russell Freedman
In the Land of the Lawn Weenies	David Lubar
Life in the Polar Lands	Monica Byles
Nellie Bly: A Name to Be Reckoned With	Stephen Krensky
The People Could Fly	Virginia Hamilton
Satchel Paige	Lesa Cline-Ransome
Sharks	Seymour Simon
She Dared: True Stories of Heroines, Scoundrels, and Renegades	Ed Butts
When I Was Your Age: Original Stories About Growing Up, Volume One	Amy Ehrlich, ed.

Bibliography

Anderson, Richard C., Elfrieda H. Hiebert, Judith A. Scott, and Ian A. G. Wilkinson. *Becoming a Nation of Readers: The Report of the Commission on Reading*. Washington, DC: The National Institute of Education, 1985.

Anderson, Richard C., and P. David Pearson. "A Schema-Theoretic View of Basic Process in Reading Comprehension." In *Handbook of Reading Research*, P. David Pearson (ed.). New York: Longman, 1984.

Armbruster, Bonnie B., Fred Lehr, and Jean Osborn. *Put Reading First: The Research Building Blocks for Teaching Children to Read*. Jessup, MD: National Institute for Literacy, 2001.

Asher, James. "The Strategy of Total Physical Response: An Application to Learning Russian." *International Review of Applied Linguistics* 3 (1965): 291–300.

———. "Children's First Language as a Model for Second Language Learning." *Modern Language Journal* 56 (1972): 133–139.

Beck, Isabel L., and Margaret G. McKeown. "Text Talk: Capturing the Benefits of Read-Aloud Experiences for Young Children." *The Reading Teacher* 55:1 (2001): 10–19.

Beck, Isabel L., Margaret G. McKeown, and Linda Kucan. *Bringing Words to Life: Robust Vocabulary Instruction*. New York: Guilford Press (2002).

Block, C. C., and M. Pressley. *Comprehension Instruction: Research-Based Best Practices*. New York: Guilford Press, 2001.

Calkins, Lucy M. *The Art of Teaching Reading*. New York: Addison-Wesley Longman, 2001.

Contestable, Julie W., Shaila Regan, Susie Alldredge, Carol Westrich, and Laurel Robertson. *Number Power: A Cooperative Approach to Mathematics and Social Development Grades K–6*. Oakland, CA: Developmental Studies Center, 1999.

Cummins, James. "The Role of Primary Language Development in Promoting Educational Success for Language Minority Students." In *Schooling and Language Minority Students: A Theoretical Framework*. Los Angeles, CA: California State University, Evaluation, Dissemination, and Assessment Center, 1981.

Cunningham, Anne E., and Keith E. Stanovich. "What Reading Does for the Mind." *American Educator* Spring/Summer (1998): 8–15.

Developmental Studies Center. *Blueprints for a Collaborative Classroom*. Oakland, CA: Developmental Studies Center, 1997.

———. *Ways We Want Our Class to Be*. Oakland, CA: Developmental Studies Center, 1996.

DeVries, Rheta, and Betty Zan. *Moral Classrooms, Moral Children*. New York: Teachers' College Press, 1994.

Dewey, J. *Democracy and Education*. New York: Macmillan, 1916.

Farstrup, Alan E., and S. Jay Samuels. *What Research Has to Say About Reading Instruction*. 3rd Ed. Newark, DE: International Reading Association, 2002.

Fielding, Linda G., and P. David Pearson. "Reading Comprehension: What Works." *Educational Leadership* 51:5 (1994): 1–11.

Fountas, Irene C. and Gay Su Pinnell. *Leveled Books, K–8: Matching Texts to Readers for Effective Teaching*. Portsmouth, NH: Heinemann, 2006.

———. *Leveled Books for Readers Grade 3–6*. Portsmouth, NH: Heinemann, 2002.

———. *Matching Books to Readers: Using Leveled Books in Guided Reading, K–3*. Portsmouth, NH: Heinemann, 1999.

Gambrell, Linda B., Lesley Mandel Morrow, Susan B. Neuman, and Michael Pressley, eds. *Best Practices in Literacy Instruction*. New York: Guilford Press, 1999.

Hakuta, Kenji, Yoko Goto Butler, and Daria Witt. *How Long Does It Take English Learners to Attain Proficiency?* Santa Barbara, CA: University of California, Linguistic Minority Research Institute, 2000.

Harvey, Stephanie. *Nonfiction Matters: Reading, Writing, and Research in Grades 3–8*. York, ME: Stenhouse Publishers, 1998.

Harvey, Stephanie, and Anne Goudvis. *Strategies That Work: Teaching Comprehension to Enhance Understanding*. York, ME: Stenhouse Publishers, 2000.

Harvey, Stephanie, Sheila McAuliffe, Laura Benson, Wendy Cameron, Sue Kempton, Pat Lusche, Debbie Miller, Joan Schroeder, and Julie Weaver. "Teacher-Researchers Study the Process of Synthesizing in Six Primary Classrooms." *Language Arts* 73 (1996): 564–574.

Herrell, Adrienne L. and Michael L. Jordan. *Fifty Strategies for Teaching English Language Learners*. Upper Saddle River, NJ: Merrill, 2000.

International Reading Association. "What Is Evidence-Based Reading Instruction? A Position Statement of the International Reading Association." Newark, DE: International Reading Association, 2002.

Johnson, David W., Roger T. Johnson, and Edythe Johnson Holubec. *The New Circles of Learning: Cooperation in the Classroom*. Alexandria, VA: Association for Supervision and Curriculum Development, 1994.

Kagan, Spencer. *Cooperative Learning*. San Juan Capistrano, CA: Resources of Teachers, 1992.

Kamil, Michael L., Peter B. Mosenthal, P. David Pearson, and Rebecca Barr, eds. *Handbook of Reading Research, Volume III*. Mahwah, NJ: Lawrence Erlbaum Associates, 2000.

Keene, Ellin O., and Susan Zimmermann. *Mosaic of Thought: Teaching Comprehension in a Reader's Workshop*. Portsmouth, NH: Heinemann, 1997.

Kohlberg, Lawrence. *The Psychology of Moral Development*. New York: Harper and Row, 1984.

Kohn, Alfie. *Beyond Discipline: From Compliance to Community*. Association for Supervision and Curriculum Development, 1996.

————. *Punished by Rewards: The Trouble with Gold Stars, Incentive Plans, A's, Praise, and Other Bribes*. New York: Houghton Mifflin Company, 1999.

Krashen, Stephen D. *Principles and Practice in Second Language Acquisition*. New York: Prentice-Hall, 1982.

Moss, Barbara. "Making a Case and a Place for Effective Content Area Literacy Instruction in the Elementary Grades." *The Reading Teacher* 59:1 (2005): 46–55.

NEA Task Force on Reading. *Report of the NEA Task Force on Reading 2000.*

Neufeld, Paul. "Comprehension Instruction in Content Area Classes." *The Reading Teacher* 59:4 (2005): 302–312.

Nucci, Larry P., ed. *Moral Development and Character Education: A Dialogue*. Berkeley, CA: McCutchan Publishing Corporation, 1989.

Optiz, Michael F., ed. *Literacy Instruction for Culturally and Linguistically Diverse Students*. Newark, DE: International Reading Association, 1998.

Pearson, P. David, J. A. Dole, G. G. Duffy, and L. R. Roehler. "Developing Expertise in Reading Comprehension: What Should Be Taught and How Should It Be Taught?" In *What Research Has to Say to the Teacher of Reading*, J. Farstup and S. J. Samuels (eds.). Newark, DE: International Reading Association, 1992.

Piaget, Jean. *The Child's Conception of the World*. Trans. Joan and Andrew Tomlinson. Lanham, MD: Littlefield Adams, 1969.

————. *The Moral Judgment of the Child*. Trans. Marjorie Gabain. New York: The Free Press, 1965.

Pressley, Michael. *Effective Beginning Reading Instruction: The Rest of the Story from Research*. National Education Association, 2002.

————. *Reading Instruction That Works*. New York: Guilford Press, 1998.

Pressley, Michael, Janice Almasi, Ted Schuder, Janet Bergman, Sheri Hite, Pamela B. El-Dinary, and Rachel Brown. "Transactional Instruction of Comprehension Strategies: The Montgomery County, Maryland, SAIL Program." *Reading and Writing Quarterly: Overcoming Learning Difficulties* 10 (1994): 5–19.

Routman, Regie. *Reading Essentials: The Specifics You Need to Teach Reading Well*. Portsmouth, NH: Heinemann, 2003.

Serafini, Frank. *The Reading Workshop: Creating Space for Readers*. Portsmouth, NH: Heinemann, 2001.

Soalt, Jennifer. "Bringing Together Fictional and Informational Texts to Improve Comprehension." *The Reading Teacher* 58:7 (2005): 680–683.

Taylor, Barbara M., Michael Pressley, and P. David Pearson. *Research-Supported Characteristics of Teachers and Schools That Promote Reading Achievement*. National Education Association, 2002.

Bibliography

Trelease, Jim. *The Read-Aloud Handbook*. New York: Penguin Books, 1995.

Weaver, Brenda M. *Leveling Books K–6: Matching Readers to Text*. Newark, DE: International Reading Association, 2000.

Williams, Joan A. "Classroom Conversations: Opportunities to Learn for ESL Students in Mainstream Classrooms." *The Reading Teacher* 54:8 (2001): 750–757.

Blackline Masters

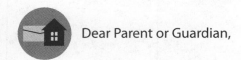

Dear Parent or Guardian,

Our class just finished the sixth unit of the *Making Meaning®* program. During this unit, the students continued to *make inferences* about fiction and nonfiction texts by using clues to figure out things that aren't stated directly in the text. They also practiced asking "why" questions during and after reading to explore causes and effects. Socially, the students practiced including one another and contributing to group work.

You can support your child at home by previewing books together before you read. Read the title and look at the cover illustration, read any information on the back cover, and leaf through the pages. Discuss questions such as:

- (Before reading nonfiction texts, ask:) What do you already know about this topic?

- (Before reading fiction stories, ask:) What do you think might happen in this story? Why do you think that?

- (Before reading fiction stories, ask:) What do you wonder about the story?

You can also help your child understand stories more deeply by stopping every so often while reading fiction aloud to discuss questions such as:

- What happens in this story (or what is the plot)?

- When and where does this story take place (or what is the setting)? Is the setting an important part of the story? Why do you think that?

- How is this character feeling? Why is the character feeling that way?

- What problem or conflict does the main character face? How do you think that problem will be solved?

- What happens at the end of the story? Why does that happen?

I hope you and your child continue to enjoy reading together!

Sincerely,

Apreciado padre de familia o guardián:

Nuestra clase acaba de finalizar la sexta unidad del programa "*Making Meaning.®*" Durante esta unidad los estudiantes continuaron *haciendo deducciones* de los textos de ficción y no ficción al utilizar pistas para poder darse cuenta de cosas que no están directamente descritas en el texto. Los estudiantes también practicaron el hacer la pregunta "por qué", durante y después de la lectura para explorar causas y efectos. Socialmente, los estudiantes practicaron el incluir a todos y el contribuir al trabajo de grupo.

En casa usted puede apoyar la lectura de su niño al ver juntos de antemano el libro que van a leer. Lea el título y mire la ilustración de la portada, si la hay lea la información en la contra portada y déle un vistazo a las páginas. Hablen acerca de preguntas como:

- (Antes de leer textos de no ficción haga preguntas como:) ¿Qué sabes del tema?

- (Antes de leer historias de ficción haga preguntas como:) ¿Qué crees que puede pasar en esta historia? ¿Qué te hace pensar eso?

- (Antes de leer historias de ficción pregúntele:) ¿Qué preguntas tienes acerca de la historia?

También, cuando estén leyendo ficción en voz alta, usted le puede ayudar a su niño a entender las historias más a fondo al parar de vez en cuando para hacer preguntas como:

- ¿Qué pasa en esta historia (o cuál es la trama)?

- ¿Cuándo y dónde se desarrolla la historia (o cuál es el medio ambiente)? ¿Es el medio ambiente una parte importante de la historia? ¿Por qué piensas eso?

- ¿Cómo se siente este personaje? ¿Por qué se está sintiendo así el personaje?

- ¿Cuál es el problema que enfrenta el personaje principal de la historia? ¿Cómo crees que ese problema se resolverá?

- ¿Qué pasa al final de la historia? ¿Por qué pasa eso?

¡Espero que continúen disfrutando el tiempo que comparten leyendo juntos!

Sinceramente,

Dear Parent or Guardian,

Our class just finished the seventh unit of the *Making Meaning*® program. During this unit, the students heard and read nonfiction books, articles, and functional texts such as instructions, charts, and maps.

One of the comprehension strategies the students have been learning this year is recognizing how texts are structured. When they read fiction, they discussed the plot and setting of the story. During Unit 7 they discussed how articles and nonfiction books are structured or organized. *Analyzing text structure* or understanding how texts are organized can help readers make sense of what they are reading.

Articles are often organized to inform from one point of view or by discussing the pros and cons of a subject. Nonfiction books often use structures such as compare and contrast or cause and effect to organize information. During Unit 7 the students were introduced to these concepts. They will learn more about how nonfiction is structured as they go through middle school and high school. Right now they are just recognizing that fiction and nonfiction are structured differently.

You can support your child's reading life at home by reading nonfiction articles and books aloud to your child, or by encouraging your child to read independently and then talk about what he or she read.

Before reading nonfiction texts ask your child questions such as:

* What do you think you know about [extreme sports in the Olympics]?

* What questions do you have about [life in the Arctic Circle]?

If your child is reading a nonfiction book, ask your child to look at the table of contents and think about what information readers might learn from the book. If your child is reading an article, discuss what the article might be about, by reading the section headings and skimming the text.

After reading ask your child questions such as:

* What information did you learn about [extreme sports in the Olympics]?

* What information surprised you?

* What do you notice about how the [article] was organized?

I hope you and your child continue to enjoy reading together. Happy reading!

Sincerely,

Apreciado padre de familia o guardián:

Nuestra clase acaba de finalizar la séptima unidad del programa "*Making Meaning.*®" Durante esta unidad los estudiantes escucharon y leyeron libros y artículos del género de no ficción y textos funcionales como mapas y cuadros.

Una de las destrezas de comprensión que los estudiantes han estado aprendiendo este año es el reconocer la estructura que tienen los textos. Cuando los estudiantes leen ficción, ellos hablan acerca de la trama y del ambiente en el que se desarrolla la historia. Durante la séptima unidad, ellos hablaron acerca de como los libros y artículos de no ficción están organizados o estructurados.

Muchas veces los artículos están organizados para informar desde un punto de vista o para discutir los puntos a favor o en contra de un tema. Los libros de no ficción muchas veces utilizan estructuras como la de comparación y contraste o la de causa y efecto para organizar la información. Durante la séptima unidad se le presentaron estos conceptos a los estudiantes. Ellos aprenderán más acerca de como el género de no ficción está estructurado cuando cursen los grados medios y de secundaria. Ahora ellos están solamente reconociendo que los géneros de ficción y de no ficción tienen distintas estructuras.

Usted puede apoyar la lectura que su niño hace en la casa al leerle en voz alta libros y artículos del género de no ficción, o al alentar a su niño a que lea por si solo y luego hable acerca de lo que leyó.

Antes de leer textos de no ficción, hágale preguntas a su niño como:

*   ¿Qué piensas acerca de (los deportes extremos en las olimpiadas)?
*   ¿Qué preguntas tienes acerca de (la vida en el círculo polar ártico)?

Si su niño está leyendo un libro de no ficción, haga que lea la lista del contenido y que haga conjeturas acerca de la información que el lector va a obtener del libro. Si su niño está leyendo un artículo, haga que lo lea por encima y que lea los encabezamientos de las secciones para que le deje saber de que puede tratarse el artículo.

Después de haber leído hágale a su niño preguntas como:

*   ¿Qué información obtuviste acerca de (los deportes extremos en las olimpiadas)?
*   ¿Qué información te sorprendió?
*   ¿Qué notaste acerca de la manera como (el articulo) estaba organizado?

Espero que continúen disfrutando de la lectura que comparten juntos. ¡Feliz lectura!

Sinceramente,

Dear Parent or Guardian,

Our class just finished the eighth unit of the *Making Meaning*® program. In this unit, the students explored important ideas in fiction and nonfiction. They identified what they felt were the important and supporting ideas in books and short stories and supported their opinions with evidence from the text. They also practiced putting important ideas together to write summaries. *Determining important ideas* and *summarizing* are both powerful strategies for helping readers understand and communicate what they read. Socially, the students developed the group skills of giving reasons for their opinions, discussing their opinions respectfully, giving feedback in a caring way, and reaching agreement.

You can support your child's reading life at home. While reading aloud, consider stopping to discuss questions with your child, such as:

- What is most important to understand or remember in the part I just read? Why do you think that?

After reading, you can help your child practice summarizing by asking questions such as:

- What are some important ideas that you remember from our reading today?

- If you were to tell someone in a couple of sentences what this book is about, what would you say?

I hope you and your child enjoy your reading conversations!

Sincerely,

Apreciado padre de familia o guardián:

Nuestra clase acaba de finalizar la octava unidad del programa "*Making Meaning.®*" Durante esta unidad los estudiantes exploraron ideas importantes en los géneros de ficción y no ficción. Ellos identificaron lo que creían que eran las ideas importantes de los cuentos cortos y libros. Y, así mismo apoyaron sus opiniones con muestras del texto. Ellos también practicaron el poner ideas importantes juntas para crear un resumen conciso. *El determinar ideas importantes* y *el resumir* son estrategias muy poderosa que ayudan al lector a entender y comunicar lo que leyó. Socialmente los estudiantes desarrollaron las destrezas de grupo de poder dar razones del porqué tuvieron una opinión y poder discutir y compartir sus opiniones en una manera respetuosa y llegar a un acuerdo.

Mientras le lee en voz alta a su niño, considere parar para hablar acerca de preguntas como:

- ¿Qué es lo más importante de entender o recordar en la parte que te acabo de leer? ¿Por qué crees eso?

Después de leer, usted le puede ayudar a su niño a que practique resumir, al hacer preguntas como:

- ¿Cuáles son algunas de las ideas importantes que recuerdas de la lectura que hicimos hoy?

- Si le fueras a decir a alguien de lo que se trata este libro en un par de frases, ¿qué le dirías?

¡Espero que usted y su niño disfruten de sus conversaciones acerca de la lectura!

Sinceramente,

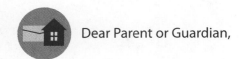 Dear Parent or Guardian,

Our class just finished the ninth unit of the Making Meaning® program. During this unit the students continued to verbally summarize fiction and nonfiction. They wrote reviews of books they read independently to share with the class during the next unit. They practiced *synthesizing* by making judgments and forming opinions about what they read. Synthesizing helps readers think more deeply and critically and communicate more meaningfully about what they are reading. The students used stories, articles, published book reviews, and their own written book reviews to analyze and practice synthesizing. Socially, they practiced the group skills of giving and receiving feedback, giving reasons for their opinions, and expressing their opinions respectfully.

You can support your child's reading at home by having him or her stop every so often to verbally summarize and give an opinion about the reading. During and after your reading together or your child's independent reading, discuss questions such as:

- What is this story about? What are the important events in this story?

- What do you think of this story? Why do you think that?

- Would you recommend this story to someone? What are the reasons for your opinion?

- Do you agree with the opinion expressed in this article? Why or why not?

- Did your opinion change during the reading? Why or why not?

There are many resources on the Internet for articles and editorials or reviews that you can explore with your child. Some websites you might visit are www.timeforkids.com and www.pbs.org/newshour/extra.

I hope you and your child continue to have fun reading, discussing your opinions, and giving one another recommendations about books and articles.

Sincerely,

Apreciado padre de familia o guardián:

Nuestra clase acaba de finalizar la novena unidad del programa "*Making Meaning.®*" Durante esta unidad los estudiantes continuaron resumiendo verbalmente el género de no ficción y ficción. Escribieron reseñas de los libros que leyeron independentemente para compartirlas con sus compañeros durante la próxima unidad. Ellos practicaron *el hacer síntesis* al formular opiniones y criterios acerca de lo que leyeron. El hacer síntesis ayuda a que el lector piense críticamente y más a fondo, también ayuda a que se comunique acerca de textos en una manera más significativa. Los estudiantes utilizaron historias, artículos, críticas de libros publicados y sus propias críticas escritas para practicar hacer análisis y síntesis. Socialmente ellos practicaron destrezas de grupo al dar y recibir sus reacciones, dar razones por sus opiniones y expresarlas respetuosamente.

Usted puede apoyar a la lectura que su niño hace en la casa al pedirle que pause periódicamente para que verbalmente le haga un resumen y le de sus opiniones de la lectura. Cuando su niño esté leyendo con usted o cuando esté leyendo independientemente, hágale preguntas como éstas:

- ¿De qué se trata esta historia? ¿Cuáles son los hechos importantes en la historia?

- ¿Qué piensas de la historia? ¿Por qué piensas eso?

- ¿Le recomendarías esta historia a otra persona? ¿Qué razones tienes para formular esa opinión?

- ¿Estás de acuerdo con la opinión que el artículo expresa? ¿Por qué?

- ¿Cambiaste de opinión a medida que ibas leyendo? ¿Por qué?

Hay muchos recursos en la red para conseguir artículos, editoriales o críticas de libros que puede explorar con su hijo. Algunas de las páginas de la red que puede visitar son www.timeforkids.com y www.pbs.prg/newshour/extra.

Espero que usted y su niño continúen divirtiéndose al leer, al intercambiar opiniones y al recomendarse libros y artículos para leer.

Sinceramente,

 Dear Parent or Guardian,

We have come to the end of our school year and the end of the *Making Meaning*® grade 5 reading comprehension program. The children have shown great enthusiasm for the variety of texts we read aloud and the conversations we had about reading. They eagerly explored a number of reading comprehension strategies, including: questioning, recognizing text features, making inferences, determining important ideas, summarizing, analyzing text structure, and synthesizing. The use of these comprehension strategies strengthened the children's reading comprehension skills and should continue to be a source of support for them for years to come.

In the last unit of the *Making Meaning* program, the students used book reviews they wrote in the previous unit to help them make summer reading recommendations to their classmates. They also reflected on their growth as readers and as members of a classroom community and continued to develop the group skills of giving reasons for their opinions and discussing their opinions respectfully.

Summer is a great time for trips to the library and quiet moments curled up with a good book. Your child made a list of books he or she would like to read this summer. Please help your child find the books on the list and encourage him or her to read the books and discuss them with friends. Of course, your child might want to add new books to the list as the summer progresses. Every so often, you might want to read some of the books aloud to your child and discuss their meaning together. Throughout the summer, encourage reading for enjoyment.

Thank you for helping to make the home-school connection successful. Your participation was essential. I hope along the way you and your child enjoyed the reading and the conversations about books.

Have a great summer!

Sincerely,

Apreciado padre de familia o guardián:

Hemos llegado al final del año escolar y al final del programa de comprensión de lectura para quinto grado de "*Making Meaning.*®" Los niños han mostrado mucho entusiasmo por la variedad de textos que leímos en voz alta y por las conversaciones que tuvimos acerca de la lectura. Ellos exploraron afanosamente un número de estrategias de comprensión de lectura, incluyendo: visualizar, el hacer preguntas, el explorar los aspectos del texto, el hacer deducciones, determinar ideas importantes, el resumir, analizar la estructura de un texto y sintetizar. El uso de estas estrategias de comprensión fortalece las destrezas de comprensión de lectura que los niños tienen y han de continuar siendo una fuente de apoyo para ellos por muchos años más.

En la última unidad del programa "*Making Meaning,*" los estudiantes utilizaron las críticas de libros que escribieron en la unidad anterior para hacer recomendaciones a sus compañeros para la lectura durante el verano. Ellos también se pusieron a reflexionar sobre el desarrollo que han tenido como lectores y como miembros de la comunidad de lectores, y continuaron desarollando destrezas de grupo al dar las razones por sus opiniones y al discutir estas opiniones en una manera respetuosa.

El verano es un gran momento para hacer viajes a la biblioteca y para pasar ratos sentados en silencio con un buen libro. Su niño hizo una lista de los libros que le gustaría leer este verano. Por favor ayúdelo a encontrar los libros que tiene en la lista y aliéntelo a que los lea y a que hable acerca de ellos con sus amigos. Claro, es posible que a medida que progrese el verano su niño quiera añadir otros libros a la lista. De vez en cuando, tal vez usted quiera leerle en voz alta algunos de los libros a su niño y hablar acerca del significado. Durante el verano, aliente a su niño a que lea para divertirse.

Le agradezco su ayuda en hacer que la conexión de la casa con la escuela fuera un éxito. Su participación fue esencial. Espero que durante el proceso usted y su niño hayan disfrutado de la lectura y las conversaciones acerca de los libros.

¡Espero que tengan un buen verano!

Sinceramente,

Excerpt
from *Richard Wright and the Library Card*
by William Miller (pages 14–16)

For the most part, they were like so many white men he had known before. They would never understand a black boy who wanted a library card, a black boy who wanted to read books even they didn't read.

Only one man seemed different from the others. Jim Falk kept to himself, and the other men ignored him, as they ignored Richard. Several times, Richard had been sent to the library to check out books for him.

One day, when the other men were out to lunch, and Jim was eating alone at his desk, Richard approached him.

"I need your help," Richard said.

"Are you in some kind of trouble?" Jim asked with a suspicious look.

"I want to read books. I want to use the library, but I can't get a card," Richard said, hoping Jim would not laugh in his face.

"What do you want to read?" Jim asked cautiously. "Novels, plays, history?"

continues

Richard felt confused. His mind was racing so fast, he couldn't think of a single book.

Jim said nothing, but reached into his desk and brought up a worn, white card. He handed it to Richard.

"How will you use it?" Jim asked.

"I'll write a note," Richard said, "like the ones you wrote when I got books for you."

"All right," Jim said nervously. "But don't tell anyone else. I don't want to get into trouble."

Excerpt from *Richard Wright and the Library Card*, by William Miller. Copyright © 1997 William Miller. Used by permission of Lee & Low Books.

Excerpt
from *Wildfires* by Seymour Simon
(page 24)

Just two years after the 1988 fires, burned areas had sprouted new plants of all kinds. The pink flowers of fireweed soon appeared. Asters, lupine, and dozens of other kinds of plants grew among the burned trees. Insects returned in great numbers and began to feast on the plants. In turn, the insects became food for birds and other insect eaters. Elk and bison grazed on the plants. Chipmunks gathered seeds, and small rodents built nests in the grasses.

The young lodgepole pines are now waist high, and many different kinds of plants surround them. Before the fire, the towering older trees blocked sunlight from the forest floor, allowing only a few other species of plants to flourish there. Without periodic fires, low-growing plants that have survived in the park for thousands of years would die off completely.

In fifty to one hundred years, the lodgepoles will again be tall enough to deprive other plant species of the light they need to grow. The forest will become mostly pines. Then the fires are likely to return, and the cycle of burning and rebirth will continue.

Most earthquakes take place in Earth's crust, a five-to thirty-mile-deep layer of rocks that covers our planet. Cracks in the rocks, called faults, run through the crust. In one type of fault, called a strike-slip fault, the rocks on one side of the fault try to move past the rocks on the other side, causing energy to build up. For years, friction will hold the rocks in place. But finally, like a stretched rubber band, the rocks suddenly snap past each other. The place where this happens is called the focus of an earthquake.

From the focus, the energy of the quake speeds outward through the surrounding rocks in all directions. The shocks may last for less than a second for a small earthquake to several minutes for a major one. Weaker shocks, called aftershocks, can follow an earthquake on and off for days or weeks.

— — — — — — — — —

Our planet's solid rocky crust floats on the mantle, a 1,800-mile-thick layer of very hot and dense rock that slowly churns around like a huge pot of boiling soup in a very slow

continues

motion. The slowly moving mantle carries along the solid crust, which is cracked like an eggshell into a number of huge pieces called plates.

The plates float slowly about on the mantle up to four inches a year. As the plates move, they run into or pull away from each other, producing enormous strains in the rocks along their edges. The United States and Canada are riding on the North American plate, which is slowly moving against the Pacific plate. The colliding plates cause most of the earthquakes along the West Coast. But earthquakes can occur anywhere there are stresses in underlying rocks.

Large areas of rain forest are sold to timber companies. They send bulldozers and chainsaw gangs into the forest to cut down the hardwood trees. The wildlife flees and, although only the oldest and largest trees are felled, over half of the forest may be damaged by the time all the work is finished.

— — — — — — — — — —

It can take less than 10 years for rain forest land to become as barren and lifeless as a desert. This is because most rain forests are found on poor clay soils. Only a thin layer of nutritious topsoil covers the forest floor, and this is anchored by giant tree trunks.

Slash-and-burn farmers clear rain forest land to grow their crops. But after only a few years, the tropical rains wash the topsoil away, and the land becomes too difficult to cultivate.

The wastelands left behind by farmers are baked by the sun and drenched by rain. The rain, which would have watered thirsty trees and plants, falls straight to the ground

continues

and runs downhill, carrying tons of soil with it. Valleys are flooded, and freshwater rivers become clogged with mud.

Tropical scientists believe that, at the present rate of destruction, there will be no rain forests left by the year 2050. If this paradise is lost, thousands of different plants and animals will disappear forever.

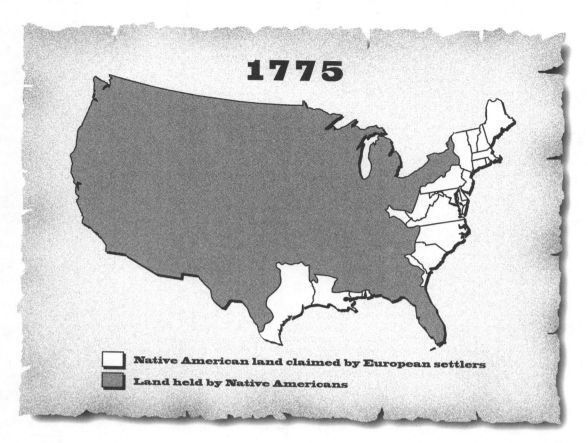

1775

Native American land claimed by European settlers
Land held by Native Americans

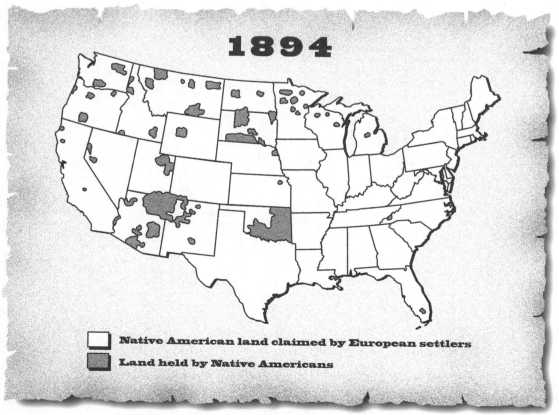

1894

Native American land claimed by European settlers
Land held by Native Americans

Double-entry Journal
About *Survival and Loss: Native American Boarding Schools*

Relationships		
Compare and Contrast	Cause and Effect	Chronological

Examples from the text

When I was six years old
the world seemed a very safe place.
The wind whispered comfortably
through the branches
of the willow by my bedroom window.
Mama let me walk to school all alone
along the winding blacktop,
past the Old Stone Mill,
past the Grange Hall,
past our church,
not even meeting up with
Georgie Warren or Nancy Vaughan
till the crossroads.

Excerpt 2
from *Letting Swift River Go* by Jane Yolen (page 14)

But then everything began to change.
The men went to the Grange Hall
time after time after time. The women, too.
Only nobody asked us kids.
They all listened to men from Boston
because the city of Boston, sixty miles away,
needed lots of water.
Boston had what Papa called
"a mighty long thirst,"
and no water to quench it.
We had water here in the valley:
good water, clear water,
clean water, cold water,
running between the low hills.
We could trade water for money,
or water for new houses,
or water for a better life.
So it was voted in Boston to drown our towns
that the people in the city might drink.

At the start of the new century, an industrial revolution came to the Nashua's banks and waters. Many new machines were invented. Some spun thread from wool and cotton. Others wove the thread into cloth. Some machines turned wood to pulp, and others made the pulp into paper. Leftover pulp and dye and fiber was dumped into the Nashua River, whose swiftly flowing current washed away the waste.

These were times of much excitement, times of "progress" and "invention." Factories along the Nashua River made new things of new materials. Telephones and radios and other things were made of plastics. Chemicals and plastic waste were also dumped into the river. Soon the Nashua's fish and wildlife grew sick from this pollution.

The paper mills continued to pollute the Nashua's waters. Every day for many decades pulp was dumped into the Nashua, and as the pulp clogged up the river, it began to run more slowly.

As the pulp decomposed, bad smells welled up from the river. People who lived near the river smelled its stench and stayed far from it. Each day as the mills dyed paper red,

continues

green, blue, and yellow, the Nashua ran whatever color the paper was dyed.

Soon no fish lived in the river. No birds stopped on their migration. No one could see pebbles shining up through murky water. The Nashua was dark and dirty. The Nashua was slowly dying.

This book tells the story of the Nashua River, a river that ran wild through forests filled with animals. A group of native people settled near the river and named it Nash-a-way, which means River with the Pebbled Bottom. These people lived in peace until white settlers arrived and began taking more of the land for themselves. The two groups fought and the native people were driven from the land.

Over the years, factories were built that polluted the river, killing the animals and turning the water murky and smelly. After years of neglect, two people decided to do something to save the Nashua River. Their efforts led to the passing of new laws that stopped factories from polluting the river. Slowly the Nashua's current cleaned the river, and once again, a river runs wild.

Story

"Mrs Buell" in *Hey World, Here I Am!* by Jean Little

(pages 42–47)

Section 1

For years and years, for what seems like forever, I've gone to BUELLS when I had a dime to spare. It's a run-down, not very clean corner store. Kids go there mostly, for licorice and bubble gum and jawbreakers and Popsicles and comic books and cones. She only has three flavors and the cones taste stale. Still, she'll sell you one scoop for fifteen cents. It's not a full scoop but it's cheaper than anywhere else. It's the only place I know where a kid can spend one penny.

Mrs. Buell is run-down too, and a grouch. She never smiles or asks you how you are. Little kids are scared to go in there alone. We laugh at them but really, we understand. We felt it too, when we were smaller and had to face her towering behind the counter.

Section 2

She was always the same except that once. I tripped going in, and fell and scraped my knee. It hurt so much that I couldn't move for a second. I was winded too, and I had to gasp for breath. I managed not to cry out but I couldn't keep back the tears.

Mrs. Buell is big but she moved like lightning. She hauled a battered wooden chair out from behind the curtain that hung across the back. Then, without a word, she picked me up and sat me down on it. We were alone in the store but I wasn't afraid. Her hands, scooping me up, had been work-roughened; hard but kind.

She still didn't speak. Instead, she took a bit of rag out of her sweater pocket, bent down and wiped the smear of blood off my knee. The rag looked grayish but her hands were gentle. I think she liked doing it. Then she fetched a Band-Aid and stuck it on.

"Does it still sting?" she asked, speaking at last, in a voice I'd never heard her use before.

Section 3

I shook my head. And she smiled. At least I think she did. It only lasted a fraction of a second. And I wasn't looking straight at her.

At that moment Johnny Tresano came in with one nickel clutched in his fist. He was so intent on the candies he hardly noticed me. He stood and stood, trying to decide.

"Make up your mind or take yourself off," she growled.

She had gone back behind the counter. I waited for her to look at me again so that I could thank her. But when he left she turned her back and began moving things around on the shelves. I had meant to buy some jujubes but I lost my nerve. After all, everybody knew she hated kids. She was probably sorry now that she'd fixed my knee. I slunk out without once opening my mouth.

Yet, whenever I looked down and saw the Band-Aid, I felt guilty. As soon as one corner came loose, I pulled it off and threw it away. I didn't go near the store for weeks.

Section 4

She was terribly fat. She got so hot in summer that her hair hung down in wet strings and her clothes looked limp. In winter she wore the same sweater every day, a man's gray one, too big, with the sleeves pushed up. They kept slipping down and she'd shove them back a million times a day. Yet she never rolled up the cuffs to make them shorter.

She never took days off. She was always there. We didn't like her or hate her. We sort of knew that selling stuff to kids for a trickle of small change wasn't a job anybody would choose—especially in that poky little place with flies in summer and the door being opened all winter, letting in blasts of cold air. Even after that day when she fixed my knee, I didn't once wonder about her life.

Then I stopped at BUELLS one afternoon and she wasn't there. Instead, a man and woman I'd never laid eyes on were behind the counter sorting through stacks of stuff. They were getting some boxes down off a high shelf right then so they didn't hear me come in. I was so amazed I just stood there gawking.

Section 5

"How Ma stood this cruddy hole I'll never know!" the woman said, backing away from a cloud of dust. "Didn't she ever clean?"

"Give the subject a rest, Glo," he answered. "She's dead. She won't bother you any longer."

"I tried, Harry. You know I tried. Over and over, I told her she could move in with us. God knows I could have used a bit of cash and her help looking after those kids."

I think I must have made a sound then. Anyway, she whirled around and saw me.

"This place is closed," she snapped. "Harry, I thought I told you to lock the door. What did you want?"

I didn't want anything from her. But I still could not believe Mrs. Buell wasn't there. I stared around.

"I said we're shut. If you don't want anything, beat it," she told me.

Section 6

The minute I got home I phoned Emily. She said her mother had just read it in the paper.

"She had a daughter!" Emily said, her voice echoing my own sense of shock. "She died of a heart attack. Kate, her whole name was Katharine Ann Buell."

"Katharine," I said slowly. My name is really Katharine although only Dad calls me by it. "I can't believe it somehow."

"No," Emily said. "She was always just Mrs. Buell."

I told her about Glo and Harry. After we hung up though, I tried to imagine Mrs. Buell as a child. Instead, I saw her bending down putting that Band-Aid on my knee. Her hair had been thin on top, I remembered, and she'd had dandruff. She had tried not to hurt me. Glo's voice, talking about her, had been so cold. Had she had anyone who loved her? It seemed unlikely. Why hadn't I smiled back?

But, to be honest, something else bothered me even more. Her going had left a hole in my life. Because of it I knew, for the first time, that nothing was safe—not even the everyday, taken-for-granted background of my being. Like Mrs. Buell, pushing up her sweater sleeves and giving me my change.

Review
"Mrs Buell" by Jean Little

In this story, a girl named Kate tells about Mrs. Buell, a grouchy old lady who owns a store in her neighborhood. One day Kate trips and falls in the store, and Mrs. Buell picks her up and puts a Band-Aid on her knee. Kate is surprised to find out that Mrs. Buell has a nice side. She doesn't think about Mrs. Buell much after that until she goes into the store one day and discovers that Mrs. Buell has died. Kate learns that the old woman had children and a whole other life that Kate knew nothing about. Kate realizes that she never tried to get to know Mrs. Buell. She also realizes that "nothing was safe" in her life. Even the everyday things that she takes for granted can suddenly disappear.

I would recommend this story because it made me think about my own life and how I sometimes overlook people. In the story, Kate didn't pay much attention to Mrs. Buell, and she was sorry about that when the lady died. That made me think about how I need to pay more attention to people in my life and show them that I care about them.

This science fiction story about a zoo of the future has a surprising ending. The story begins when a spaceship lands in Chicago. Inside is Professor Hugo's Interplanetary Zoo. Each year the professor brings creatures from faraway planets to Earth for people to see. Inside the barred cages this year are the horse-spider people of Kaan, strange and frightening horselike animals that climb their cage walls like spiders. Thousands of horrified and fascinated Earthlings file by to see the creatures. But when Professor Hugo returns the creatures to their own planet, you discover that the horse-spider people had some thoughts of their own about Earthlings.

Double-entry Journal

My Opinions About _____

Opinions	Evidence

Review
from spaghettibookclub.com
by Jennifer B. (age 12)

The Legend of Sleepy Hollow
by Washington Irving

Ichabod Crane has just arrived to Sleepy Hollow and has met a lot of people. Those people have told Ichabod the legend of Sleepy Hollow.

This legend is about a headless horseman who goes around cutting other people's heads in search of his own. This legend scared Ichabod every time it was told. Ichabod Crane had fallen in love with Katrina, a very rich girl, a couple of weeks after he arrived to Sleepy Hollow. One day Ichabod was invited to Katrina's party, and before the party was over a woman started to say the legend of Sleepy Hollow and at the end she said the only way you can escape the headless horseman is by crossing the bridge. That night Ichabod and his horse ran as fast as they could to reach their house. Finally he was up to the bridge that meant that he was near his house. Then something got in his way, it was the headless horseman. Did Ichabod ever escape?

continues

I think that this book was very interesting because it was a legend about a headless horseman that lost his head in a war and since then has been looking for it by cutting other people's heads off. I recommend this book to people who like scary legends that took place a long time ago.

This story reminds me of 'Bloody Mary' because they are both scary and they are both legends. What makes this story more scary is that it has been told for more than 100 years and it has been told by people who are already dead.

Things to Include in My Book Review

Book Title: _____

_____

_____

_____

_____

_____

_____

_____

_____

_____

_____

_____

_____

_____

_____

_____

_____

_____

_____

_____

Making Meaning® Reorder Information
SECOND EDITION

Kindergarten

Complete Classroom Package	MM2-CPK

Contents: Teacher's Manual, Orientation Handbook and DVDs, and 27 trade books

Available separately:

Classroom materials without trade books	MM2-TPK
Teacher's Manual	MM2-TMK
Trade book set (27 books)	MM2-TBSK

Grade 1

Complete Classroom Package	MM2-CP1

Contents: Teacher's Manual, Orientation Handbook and DVDs, Assessment Resource Book, and 28 trade books

Available separately:

Classroom materials without trade books	MM2-TP1
Teacher's Manual	MM2-TM1
Assessment Resource Book	MM2-AB1
Trade book set (28 books)	MM2-TBS1

Grade 2

Complete Classroom Package	MM2-CP2

Contents: Teacher's Manual, Orientation Handbook and DVDs, class set (25 Student Response Books, Assessment Resource Book), and 29 trade books

Available separately:

Classroom materials without trade books	MM2-TP2
Teacher's Manual	MM2-TM2
Replacement class set	MM2-RCS2
CD-ROM Grade 2 Reproducible Materials*	MM2-CDR2
Trade book set (29 books)	MM2-TBS2

Grade 3

Complete Classroom Package	MM2-CP3

Contents: Teacher's Manual (2 volumes), Orientation Handbook and DVDs, class set (25 Student Response Books, Assessment Resource Book), and 26 trade books

Available separately:

Classroom materials without trade books	MM2-TP3
Teacher's Manual, Vol. 1	MM2-TM3-V1
Teacher's Manual, Vol. 2	MM2-TM3-V2
Replacement class set	MM2-RCS3
CD-ROM Grade 3 Reproducible Materials*	MM2-CDR3
Trade book set (26 books)	MM2-TBS3

* CD-ROMs available Summer 2009

Grade 4

Complete Classroom Package	MM2-CP4

Contents: Teacher's Manual (2 volumes), Orientation Handbook and DVDs, class set (30 Student Response Books, Assessment Resource Book), and 24 trade books

Available separately:

Classroom materials without trade books	MM2-TP4
Teacher's Manual, Vol. 1	MM2-TM4-V1
Teacher's Manual, Vol. 2	MM2-TM4-V2
Replacement class set	MM2-RCS4
CD-ROM Grade 4 Reproducible Materials*	MM2-CDR4
Trade book set (24 books)	MM2-TBS4

Grade 5

Complete Classroom Package	MM2-CP5

Contents: Teacher's Manual (2 volumes), Orientation Handbook and DVDs, class set (30 Student Response Books, Assessment Resource Book), and 19 trade books

Available separately:

Classroom materials without trade books	MM2-TP5
Teacher's Manual, Vol. 1	MM2-TM5-V1
Teacher's Manual, Vol. 2	MM2-TM5-V2
Replacement class set	MM2-RCS5
CD-ROM Grade 5 Reproducible Materials*	MM2-CDR5
Trade book set (19 books)	MM2-TBS5

Grade 6

Complete Classroom Package	MM2-CP6

Contents: Teacher's Manual (2 volumes), Orientation Handbook and DVDs, class set (30 Student Response Books, Assessment Resource Book), and 19 trade books

Available separately:

Classroom materials without trade books	MM2-TP6
Teacher's Manual, Vol. 1	MM2-TM6-V1
Teacher's Manual, Vol. 2	MM2-TM6-V2
Replacement class set	MM2-RCS5
CD-ROM Grade 6 Reproducible Materials*	MM2-CDR6
Trade book set (19 books)	MM2-TBS6

Ordering Information:

To order call 800.666.7270 * fax 510.842.0348
log on to www.devstu.org * e-mail pubs@devstu.org

Or Mail Your Order to:

Developmental Studies Center * Publications Department
2000 Embarcadero, Suite 305 * Oakland, CA 94606-5300

DEVELOPMENTAL STUDIES CENTER™